THE KENNEDYS IN HOLLYWOOD

THE
KENNEDYS
IN
HOLLYWOOD

by
LAWRENCE J. QUIRK

TAYLOR PUBLISHING COMPANY
Dallas, Texas

BOOKS BY LAWRENCE J. QUIRK

Robert Francis Kennedy
The Films of Joan Crawford
The Films of Ingrid Bergman
The Films of Paul Newman
The Films of Fredric March
Photoplay Anthology
The Films of William Holden
The Great Romantic Films
The Films of Robert Taylor
The Films of Ronald Colman
The Films of Warren Beatty
The Films of Myrna Loy
The Films of Gloria Swanson
The Complete Films of Bette Davis (update from 1965)
The Complete Films of Katharine Hepburn (update from 1970)
Claudette Colbert: An Illustrated Biography
Lauren Bacall: Her Films and Career
Jane Wyman: The Actress and the Woman
The Complete Films of William Powell
Margaret Sullavan: Child of Fate
Norma: The Story of Norma Shearer
Some Lovely Image (a novel)
Fasten Your Seat Belts: The Passionate Life of Bette Davis
Totally Uninhibited: The Life and Wild Times of Cher
The Great War Films
The Kennedys in Hollywood

To the memory of my grandfather
William P. Connery
(1855–1928)
Mayor of Lynn, Massachusetts, when John F. Fitzgerald
was mayor of Boston
Delegate to the Democratic National Convention of 1904
An honest, forceful, loved, and respected Irish-Catholic politician
and father of two congressmen

Published by Taylor Publishing Company
            1550 West Mockingbird Lane
            Dallas, Texas 75235

Library of Congress Cataloging-in-Publication Data

Quirk, Lawrence J.
    The Kennedys in Hollywood / Lawrence J. Quirk.
        p.   cm.
    ISBN 0-87833-934-5
    1. Kennedy family.   2. Motion picture actors and actresses—
United States.   I. Title.
E843.Q57   1996
973.922'092'2—dc20   96-2890
                                                            CIP

Printed in the United States of America

10   9   8   7   6   5   4   3   2   1

Acknowledgments

With special thanks to my colleague, William Schoell, author and editor. And with deep appreciation to my editor, Michael Emmerich, Anita K. Edson, and Jim Green. Also warm thanks to my agent and lawyer, Dimitri Nikolakakos.

And with appreciation to the many who over the years provided interviews, anecdotes, and general information for this book, some of whom are now deceased, a number of whom did not wish to be named, and others who are quoted and mentioned throughout this book.

Thanks also to Howard Mandelbaum of *Photofest*; Ron Mandelbaum; Ed Maguire; Mary Atwood; Jerry Ohlinger's Movie Material Store; Gene Massimo; the James R. Quirk Memorial Film Symposium and Research Center, New York; the British Film Institute, London; the Margaret Herrick Library of the Academy of Motion Picture Arts and Sciences, Hollywood; the Billy Rose Theater and Film Collection, New York Public Library at Lincoln Center;

the Museum of Modern Art Library; the Kennedy Center, Boston.

Also thanks to James E. Runyan, Don Koll, John Cocchi, Romano Tozzi, Jim McGowan, Arthur Tower, Dr. Rod Bladel, Doug McClelland, Barbara Barondess MacLean, Gregory Speck, Robert Dahdah, Douglas Whitney, Lou Valentino, Ernest D. Burns, Joe Bly, Mike Snell, Frank Rowley, Albert B Manski, John A. Guzman, Stephen Jerome, and Mark Vieira. Special thanks to Jean Quirk Sullivan, the late Frances Quirk Wanek, and their families.

And with warmest thanks to my good friends in New York, Hollywood, London, and elsewhere, some living, some now deceased, who provided me with a wealth of reminiscences, variegated information, general comfort, and spiritual guidance as well as inside material on the Kennedys and many others during my writing and journalistic career, the fiftieth anniversary of which (1946-1996) I celebrate this year.

Contents

	Acknowledgments	*vii*
	Preface	*xi*
1	The Root Source	1
2	The Boston Beginnings	9
3	Mentor Jimmy Quirk and Hollywood	31
4	Enter Gloria	49
5	Nancy, Connie, Greta—and Joan	63
6	Fred Thomson: Joe Kennedy's Only Hero	75
7	Joe in the 1930s	103
8	Marlene	121
9	Lem the Adoring, Eddie the Faithful	133
10	Jack Goes Hollywood	145
11	The Poignant Gene Tierney	151
12	Peter Lawford: Friday's Child	163
13	Peter and Lana and Ava—and Bob	179
14	Chris Lawford's Lonely Journey	191
15	Frank and the Kennedys	199
16	Marilyn	207

17   Clowning Around with Jayne   259

18   The Kennedys on Camera   269

19   Jackie, the Fan Mags, and Me   285

20   More Kennedy Lovers, Friends, and Enemies   293

21   Maria and Her Body Boy   321

22   The Trials of John-John   337

     Epilogue   353

     Notes   357

     Bibliography   363

     Index   367

Preface

The Kennedys in Hollywood represents the cumulative results of fifty years' knowledge, acquaintance, research, insight, and intimate awareness of the Kennedys. On July 28, 1946, I joined the editorial staff of William Randolph Hearst's *Boston Record-American*, serving under the aegis of the great editor Walter Howey, close friend of Joseph P. Kennedy, and another unforgettable mentor, Myles McSweeney, who knew all there was to know about everyone and everything. As editor, McSweeney taught me much while I worked for Hearst, and he did me many good turns later in my career, as did such mentors as film critic Bosley Crowther of *The New York Times* and Henry Hart, editor of *Films in Review*. Allan Wilson, who edited many of my early books, also deserves special mention in any review of my early positive influences.

That summer and fall of 1946 when I was a twenty-two-year-old Hearst cub hot-to-trot, I worked from 5 P.M. to 1 A.M. at the *Boston Record-American*, worked my way through Boston's Suffolk University from 9 A.M. to 4 P.M., and after taking my B.A. degree at Suffolk, went on to Boston

University Graduate School. That fall of 1946 was a time I held down *three* jobs: the third was handing out leaflets and working any way I could in Jack Kennedy's first congressional campaign.

My association with the Kennedys goes back much further than fifty years, in fact, because my grandfather, William P. Connery, to whom this book is dedicated, was mayor of Lynn, Massachusetts, when John F. Fitzgerald, whom he knew well, was mayor of Boston, and my uncles, William P. Connery Jr. and Lawrence J. Connery, served in Congress and also knew the Kennedys and Fitzgeralds. My uncle, James R. Quirk, editor-publisher of *Photoplay* magazine in its great days, 1914–1932, knew the Kennedys and Fitzgeralds intimately, having served as John F. Fitzgerald's top aide when the latter was editing his publication, The *Republic*, in 1904. Later my uncle would be Joe Kennedy's guide and mentor when Joe entered the motion picture industry in the 1920s. He bears the—to some—dubious distinction of having facilitated the original 1927 meeting of Joe Kennedy and Gloria Swanson.

As a boy and adolescent, before I joined Hearst's *Boston Record-American*, I met many members of the Kennedy and Fitzgerald families. Jack was eighteen in 1935 when I was twelve; I met him that summer. I remember Bobby as a child of eight in 1933; Kick (Kathleen) as a vibrant presence when she was seventeen in 1938; Joe Jr., athletic, self-confident, cocky, and magnetic at nineteen in 1934, when he thought he had all the world before him, though he was to know but ten more years.

My uncles talked a lot about the Kennedys throughout my youth. They didn't agree with Joe on everything, just as my grandfather Billy Connery didn't agree with John "Honey Fitz" Fitzgerald on some crucial matters.

But there was a bond that held them all close despite themselves, despite differences in privilege, money, and status in its various forms. All of us had struggled over from Ireland—our ancestors coming in the 1840s, the Fitzgeralds and Quirks to the North End of Boston, the Kennedys to East Boston, the Connerys to nearby Lynn. All wended their way upward from those humble, cattle boat, famine beginnings.

The story of the Irish in America, the Irish who spawned the Kennedys, the Fitzgeralds, the Connerys, and the Quirks, is detailed in subsequent chapters in all its many aspects. Did my family know the Kennedys—on both sides? They did. And so, in a sense, this book comes from an insider viewpoint. I do not come to praise or affirmatively publicize the Kennedys in this story of their Hollywood adventures. I see them clearly and I see them whole, as the saying has it. No saints or angels were they. Profoundly, often tragically, human and fallible they were. But I think I have the key to what has made them so continually and so enduringly potent in their hold on the minds and hearts of the American public. Wonderful old Honey Fitz, so lively and vital even at eighty-three, the year I met him, so anxious that summer and fall of 1946 to see his grandson-namesake go to Congress, would have understood it—in fact he did, always.

Honey Fitz in 1946 was living in the Hotel Bellevue, one short block from the corner of Park and Beacon Streets where, as a teenage boy in the 1870s, he had intrepidly sold newspapers at his little stand, fighting off rival newsboy gangs, learning the hard way, the realistic way, the truth of the old saw—it is a mistake to be *too* good when surrounded by those who are *not* good. From his window he could see that spot where once he had labored and suffered—and survived—seventy-odd years before, and he pointed it out to me. "Larry Quirk," he said, "you can do *anything* you want, if you persist; if you *want* it with a *passionate* wanting!"

Fitzie's son-in-law Joe Kennedy had his passionate wants—and he brought them to fruition. He wanted money, power, intimacy with many women, glamor, excitement, travel, maneuvering room—and a sensible, shrewd, and forbearing (if not always happy) wife who would give him children to make him, in the course of time, immortal. Joe achieved all his aims; he cut many corners, did things that were not admirable, was an unfaithful husband, and exploited many people, but in the face of all this, he forged ahead so valiantly and unflinchingly that he commands a reluctant respect. Worldly and self-indulgent, he was also vital, upwardly mobile with a vengeance, and ruthlessly determined to have as much money and power—and eventually top-drawer acceptance—as the Yankee aristocrats who had snubbed him in his youth. Joe had a mesmeric effect on all about him. If his sons absorbed and imitated the bad as well as the good in him, it was doubtless because for them it all spelled vitality, success, the full acceptance and absorption of life in all its aspects, good or ill.

Just what is this hold the Kennedys have kept all these seventy-plus years on the minds, hearts, sensibilities, loyalties—and less admirable, often imitative and destructive traits—of the American public?

After all these years of inside knowledge the answer to me now is obvious: the Kennedys represent one vast, all-encompassing, passionate *soap opera* to the people of America. Traits that in other families would be regarded as vulgar, common, gross, unforgivable, or outside the pale are accepted in the Kennedys as reflections of the universal human condition. And with this acceptance has gone a startling humility, a realization that when the Kennedys go blatantly awry—as at Chappaquiddick, as at the rape trials, as with drug misadventures—it is consummate hypocrisy to label them "a vulgar family" as some more straight-laced characters have. For they have done nothing in the garish brutal public eye that many of the less-known, nonpublicized, left-in-peace denizens of our good old USA have not done over and over—and gotten away with. For the average, unknown, unobserved citizen uncared-about by either press or public is *free*—as the fishbowl-inhabiting Kennedys are not—to do his mischief, pay whatever penalty that boomerangs on him (or doesn't), and get on with his life. But if Dr. William Kennedy Smith gets himself into a rape scandal, he is expected to serve as cluck-cluck-tut-tut fodder for tabloids forevermore. If an unknown young doctor had gone to trial and been acquitted, or served his sentence, the public wouldn't have given a damn and he could have gotten on with his life, rather than pay the public penance expected of Dr. William Kennedy Smith. Which excuses neither public nor private, neither the famous and privileged nor the unknown and deprived—but there is a price, a karmic return, for everything one does in life. For the famous and to the obscure alike, the price has to be paid.

The Kennedys, in their adventuring in both Hollywood and politics, have been accused of *enjoying* all the media attention, no matter how they deny it. If they do, and undoubtedly some of them do, they have long since come to terms with the price to be paid—a price ruthless, inevitable, and tragic. Assassination, drug problems, rape trials, marital infidelities, all the other negative manifestations of the imperfect human condition have made them the country's favorite ongoing soap opera.

This book zeroes in on one aspect of the Kennedy adventures through life: their involvement with the Hollywood scene over roughly a seventy-year period, from the early 1920s to the present.

The Kennedy Hollywood saga began when Jimmy Quirk helped banker-financier Joe Kennedy get his bearings in the movie industry. Even more significant, Jimmy facilitated in 1927, through his friend and go-between Bob Kane, Joe Kennedy's introduction to glamorous film star Gloria Swanson, triggering not only what is unquestionably the most notorious and harped-on "back street" romance of the century, but also inaugurating the recurring obsession of Joe's children and grandchildren with Hollywood. The tragicomic Kennedy divertissements in La-La Land included the endless dalliances of Jack Kennedy with such Hollywood ladies as Gene Tierney, Marilyn Monroe, Angie Dickinson, June Allyson, and you-name-her-he-probably-had-her. The most scandalous and dissected of these, of course, was the Marilyn Monroe liaison. Marilyn was the gaudiest and brassiest of 'em all. She also attracted Bobby Kennedy and made a pimp *par excellence* of Peter Lawford. Her death on August 4, 1962, precipitated some of the most sensational news copy of the century.

Then there was Peter's marriage to Joe's daughter Patricia. Peter Lawford was in his and my youth a personal friend; I have always found in his inexorably downward course and tragic destruction—marrying a Kennedy was the worst mistake Peter ever made—one of the more regrettably lurid chapters in the Kennedy's Hollywood hegira.

There is also the attraction of the Kennedys' third generation to Hollywood, culminating in the tragic also-ran status of Peter's hapless and unfortunate actor-son Christopher and the eyebrow-raising marriage of Joe Kennedy's granddaughter Maria Shriver to the superbody-boy, action-film entrepreneur Arnold Schwarzenegger. The alliance has stumbled through ten years now, but will it hit twenty—or even fifteen?

The old patriarch and naughty-example-setter Joe Kennedy's involvements with a host of Hollywood lovelies, Gloria followed by Connie Bennett followed by Nancy Carroll followed by—well, *you* name her—are set forth with telling new details and insights, as is his attempted seduction of movie star Joan Fontaine in the early 1950s (he was sixty-five, she was thirty-six).

And persistent and tabloid-teasy questions are posed—and answered—such as: Is John Kennedy Jr. inexorably drifting toward Hollywood and its charms and distractions now that Jackie is gone from his life? Has Chris Lawford, his drug-ridden early life a thing of the past, given up on his father Peter's "heritage"—and is that a bad or a good thing for married, forty-one-year-old father and ex-soap-opera actor Chris?

And is news anchor and reporter Maria Shriver, who has striven for her own form of public limelight, demonstrating in her fascination for Schwarzenegger only the latest in a persistent series of inevitably trouble-brewing attachments? And is it possible that all these attachments have as their unconscious source the intertwined shame and irresistible seduction that the collective family memory retains of the original, scandalous involvement of the old patriarch Joe and the glorious Gloria?

ONE

The Root Source

T wo dates—three years apart—marked occasions that would eventually set off the tragic chain of multigenerational Kennedy family involvements with Hollywood.

The first was November 15, 1926, when Joe Kennedy, heavy into film-business finance and production, learned of the marriage of his friend, Jimmy Quirk, the powerful and prestigious editor-publisher of the screen's most respected magazine, *Photoplay*, to May Allison, the beautiful silent-screen star. Jimmy at forty-two had dared to do what Joe at thirty-eight dared not risk: he had divorced his first wife, Elizabeth North, mother of his two daughters, Frances and Jean, after an eighteen-year-marriage and, after two years of womanizing bachelor life in New York and Hollywood, had married May. Joe, married for twelve years and the father of (at that time) seven children, had wanted it both ways: in spite of his private transgressions, he sought to remain, in the public eye, a Catholic in good standing, playing to the hilt the husband-and-daddy role for popular consumption.

Jimmy Quirk, for his part, didn't give a damn about public or church approval. Though every bit as well-known as Joe Kennedy in 1926, if not as wealthy, he had defied his Boston Irish Catholic conventions as far back as 1908, when he had wed his first wife in a Protestant ceremony. Between his 1924 divorce and 1926 marriage, Jimmy had led an existence of wine, women, and song, complete with Manhattan bachelor apartment on West Fifty-Fifth Street and Japanese valet. During this time he had bedded down such Hollywood lovelies (during his frequent visits to the Coast) as the up-and-coming Lucille LeSueur (whom Louis B. Mayer, after getting Jimmy's input, renamed Joan Crawford), Renee Adoree, and Phyllis Haver.

In New York, Jimmy and his hell-raising close pal, Ray Long, famed editor of Hearst's successful *Cosmopolitan* magazine, were silent partners in a high-style establishment on West Fifty-Eighth Street where the most beautiful, intelligent, and well-mannered ladies of the evening, some showgirls and models, all carefully culled from Jim's and Ray's numerous nights on the town, all ambitious for male attachments and hopefully marriages, sought only to please and to physically fulfill New York's most successful and prominent men. Visitors from Los Angeles, London, and Paris sang the praises of the establishment. Joe Kennedy frequented it and was duly impressed.

Jimmy, arbiter of film trends, often consulted by producers and movie power men, and Ray, who had started many a writer on the road to fame, worked hard—and played hard. They drank too much, wenched too much, and burned out before their time.

Joe Kennedy envied both men in 1926. Jimmy Quirk had bagged himself a beautiful, top-drawer movie star, had he? Well, Joe vowed to himself, he would bag one, too—an even bigger star. Within a year he would make it happen.

And then there was that other date, August 17, 1929. The screen's top female star, Gloria Swanson, for two years Joe Kennedy's secret mistress (though both of them were married), had come to visit the Kennedy family at their summer place on the Cape, to the accompaniment of great fanfare and excitement on the part of the press and public.

Gloria and Joe had sought some needed privacy by taking—just the two of them—a ride in his sailboat, the *Rose Elizabeth* (ironically, the first names of Jimmy Quirk's discarded and Joe's retained but neglected wives, respectively). What they didn't know was that twelve-year-old Jack Kennedy was hiding below deck. Insecure and frail, Jack, bullied and kept down by his all-American older brother, Joe Jr., was hungry for the love and attention of the father he saw so rarely. Fully aware that Joe Sr. was no great sailor, hoping to shore up his almost obliterated self-esteem, Jack was set to emerge, if needed, to back up his father in the event of a possible storm or other emergency.

Then the male and female voices wafted down to him— voices that at first purred casually, then turned more personal, cajoling, sensuous. Curious and strangely alarmed, young Jack sneaked up the stairs and to his horror saw his father and Gloria entwined in an unmistakably sexual embrace.

Devastated, confused, and trembling, Jack ran to the edge of the sloping deck, jumped off, and began swimming frantically toward the distant shore.

Gloria froze in horror. Joe dropped her abruptly, and after a quick dive pushed swiftly through the waves, caught his frail, already tiring boy, and somehow got him back to the boat. Embarrassed and devastated, the guilty lovers, more alarmed over the scandal that might ensue than by the stricken boy's obvious emotional reaction, dried him, calmed him down, gave him a fruit drink, and coached him intensively on what—and what not—to say when they reached land. Sad, sullen, fearful of paternal ostracism and other unforeseen possible consequences, Jack held his peace and obeyed orders.

But young Jack Kennedy had learned some things that August day—and they were to affect his destiny permanently and profoundly. A family man could cheat and get away with it—often. Women were sources of fun and pleasure and didn't belong on their old-fashioned, artificial pedestals. Sex was all-important. Feelings were to be held suspect—they spelled vulnerability, responsibility. Getting away with something was what counted. His father had imparted that day, by his behavior, a new attitude, a new outlook for this boy trembling on the verge of pubescence. The experience seared into Jack's spirit. He would never forget, nor in his heart forgive. For though he still cared for his father as an authority figure, a role model to be respected and, alas, emulated, for his strengths so fully employed and exploited in life's battle, he was deeply hurt, too, and as time proved, disillusioned to the point of inner detachment—and contempt.

In 1946, seventeen years after the event that had traumatized Jack's life forever, I found myself, at twenty-three, working in twenty-nine-year-old Jack's first campaign for Congress. Eighty-three-year-old Honey Fitz was busy that fall generating as much input as his grandson and namesake would allow into the steadily accelerating campaign effort, which in time would enlist the help of Jack's family and friends. I had met Honey Fitz and some of the Kennedys in childhood years, but that year I would really zero in on them. Honey Fitz seemed to like me—I was the descendant of some of his most rabid North End political supporters. My uncle Jimmy Quirk, at nineteen, had worked for Honey Fitz when he owned and operated the Republic. Honey Fitz was the first to ask me to help out with Jack's campaign, and I was doing what I could, albeit in a lowly, highly peripheral, and part-time capacity. While our paths had crossed early in life, Jack and I formed our first adult connection on Boston Common, just below the state house lawn, while I was walking and chatting with Honey Fitz on one of those constitutionals that his doctor had advised to keep what Jack called "those four-score pegs" in shape.

Jack had made a speech in the auditorium of Suffolk University two days before, and when he stopped to greet his grandfather, I congratulated him on it. Honey Fitz refreshed Jack's memory of me as the grandson of William P. Connery, my mother's father who had been mayor of nearby Lynn when Honey Fitz was mayor of Boston. He also reminded Jack about my two late uncles, Billy and Larry Connery, who had been congressmen from the Seventh Massachusetts District. Jack's face brightened. "Oh yes, Billy Connery was chairman of the House Labor Committee in the 1930s, sponsored a lot of labor legislation," he remarked.

Honey Fitz added that my uncle on my father's side was Jimmy Quirk. Jack gave a sharp, ironic smile. "Oh sure, Jimmy Quirk—a great pal of Dad's. I met him as a kid, read *Photoplay* all the time. He once had an article about my family in it—pictures of all of us—and he married that beautiful movie star, May Allison!" Jack's expression then took on an enigmatic, quizzical expression. "Jimmy Quirk," he said, "helped my father when he got into movies. He was a real influence—in more ways than one!" He and Honey Fitz winked slyly at one another.

But he registered as pleased and receptive when Honey Fitz told him I was helping, in an admittedly minor way, on the campaign: "The kid goes to college days and then over to the *Record-American* nights and he's *still* willing to pitch in for you, carry fliers, whatever!"

Jack Kennedy shook my hand. "The more on the team the better!" he smiled.

Even Jack's most rabid supporters considered him a playboy and fun seeker. The jokes proliferated around the Kennedy-for-Congress headquarters concerning Jack's forays earlier in 1946 among the young Hollywood actresses when he was visiting California. Nor had it been his first visit over the years. Gene Tierney, then at the peak of her screen career, twenty-six to Jack's twenty-nine, was the name most frequently mentioned. The fact that Gene was a married woman, her projected divorce from Oleg Cassini not having been finalized, did not seem to upset anyone—least of all Jack. They thought Jack's adventures among the ladies, married and unmarried, cool—a word not in fashion in 1946, but the phrase they *did* use conveyed the same cavalier approach by Jack's campaign staff to what was technically an adulterous Hollywood alliance. That 1946 term was a pungent "sharp shit!"

My top boss on the Boston Hearst paper in those years was the famous Walter Howey, the devil-may-care, get-that-story-anyway-you-can newspaperman on whom Charlie MacArthur had based his *Front Page* protagonist. Howey was close to the Kennedys—and he knew his Hollywood. He had foisted his young niece on a producer many years before, demanding he employ her in exchange for a favor, and the silent star Colleen Moore was born. Myles McSweeney, another Hearst editor, enjoyed telling me stories about Jack Kennedy's "frantic feminine fans," as he called them, adding "those gals alone will ensure that boy's election!" Myles asked me to keep my Hearstling eye open around Kennedy headquarters and relished whatever tidbits I could bring back to the office.

Jack Kennedy at twenty-nine in 1946 did not seem to me, at close range, at all suited to a political career. His always frail health and slightly dislocated back muscles had been exacerbated by a back injury he had sustained in the grossly overpublicized (by his father) PT-109 Pacific war incident of 1943. As a naval commander of the boat, Jack had saved the lives of crewmen (one report had him saving one; others had him saving several) in an accident that, Myles McSweeney laughed, seemed "more stupid than heroic!" But Walter Howey always insisted that this as well as other aspects of Jack Kennedy's life be played up with maximum affirmativeness in Hearst's Boston papers. Meanwhile old Joe's well-oiled publicity machine had turned the event into one of Jack's prime campaign cards. Jack always seemed embarrassed by any attention brought to it.

Intelligent and adaptable, and affable enough when he wanted to be, Jack ran around with a crowd of tough Irish ward heelers and politicos, some dating from the Honey Fitz mayoral era, and managed to pick up the backslapping, superficially affable traits of the standard candidate. When I observed him in one of his quiet, reflective moods, I wondered if Jack's heart were in any of it. Walter Howey claimed Jack wanted to be a writer, but after the death of his father's favorite, golden-boy Joe, in a combat plane bombing accident over the English Channel in August 1944, Joe Sr. elected Jack as the man to carry on the family power game, this time in the world of politics. Even then the story went the rounds that Jack had never really liked Joe Jr., remembered him primarily as a bully and a braggart, and knew perfectly well that Joe Jr. had taken on that dangerous mission ferrying high explosives over the Channel hoping to outdo the PT-109 incident, which he knew was specious yet made him bitterly jealous.

After smiling here and smiling there for several hours, Jack's face often took on a bored, to-hell-with-it look. His skin did not look right—it was colorless, peculiar in shading and texture—it would in time indicate a far more serious physical condition (kept a state secret) than the "fatigue" and "bad back" and "recent VA hospital convalescence" (the popular 1946 explanations for his frail look) indicated at the time.

It has now been fifty years since that campaign. There was so much enthusiasm and hope for Jack in that watershed year of 1946. No one could have dreamed then that the boy they were pushing and promoting into a freshman congressional term would have but seventeen years of life left to him. We were young, hot-to-trot, full of life and hope. The terrible tragedies of the future—tragedies that had their root sources in traumas of the 1920 past—were *far* in the future. Endings and beginnings—in the Kennedy fates, they were to be inextricably intertwined. The preamble to those 1946 beginnings happened back in the 1920s—in Los Angeles, in Palm Beach, in Jimmy Quirk's wild, jazzy, free-loving New York. There and then we can trace the roots that grew into the hegira of the Kennedys in Hollywood.

TWO

The Boston Beginnings

J oe Kennedy in his later years liked to give the impression at times that he was a totally self-made man. That was far from the truth. It was true that his grandfather, Patrick Kennedy, had come from Ireland in 1849 poor as dirt and had died at a relatively early age in 1858, worn down by poverty and physical debility fed by the many plagues and unsanitary conditions that existed in the Irish enclave of East Boston at the time.

But Joe's father, the second Patrick Kennedy, known as "PJ" to his cronies, was a fiercely ambitious man who in his twenties owned a popular East Boston bar, after which he branched out into other fields including banking. Joe's mother, Mary Augusta Hickey, who doted on Joe, noted early his high order of intelligence and energy, and determined to take him out of the East Boston Catholic schools and send him to a prep school where he would hobnob with the sons of the Protestant aristocracy. One of Mary's brothers had gone to Harvard, and she was determined that was where Joe would land.

An ornery kid, Joe Kennedy was an adept alley fighter and, in his teens, so ambitious, despite his family's comfortable circumstances, that he did whatever odd jobs would bring him in spending money. Mary Hickey Kennedy liked that Joe, far from being weakened by a prosperous upbringing, seemed to use it as a base to move on to bigger and better things.

After branching out into coal and banking pursuits that resulted in his Columbia Trust Company, the only bank controlled by Irish in the entire Boston area, tough old PJ developed political ambitions.

As a saloon keeper, PJ became intimately acquaintanced with the struggle of his fellow Irish for acceptance and equality in a Boston of the 1880s and 1890s dominated by the wealthy Yankee families, most of whom traced their pedigree to the seventeenth century.

The Irish had a deeply entrenched hatred of the English-descended first families of Boston who, in the decade after the Irish had arrived, had put out "No Irish Need Apply" signs and when forced to employ these immigrants had humiliated them as ill-paid servants and laborers in their commercial establishments and on the wharves. The banks and other commercial institutions might be closed to the Irish, but politics—dependent on voting numbers—was not, and Joe Kennedy's father was one of the first ward bosses to corral new Irish immigrants from the dock and help them with food, lodging, and job references—in return for those votes that would elect Irishmen to ever more prominent offices.

As the number of immigrant Irish voters grew between the 1840s and the 1880s, their votes began to speak with an ever louder voice. Boston elected its first Irish mayor, Hugh O'Brien, in the year Joe Kennedy was born, 1888, and soon

Pat Kennedy and other ward bosses were calling the shots in the Democratic party.

The first Patrick Kennedy and the woman he was later to marry, Bridget Murphy, had come over on a ship called the *Washington Irving* in 1849 and had married in Boston soon after. A few ships earlier, escaping stricken Ireland and its misery and the potato famine that had decimated the population drastically, forcing immigration as an only out, had come my own great-grandfathers, William Quirk and Patrick Connery. Patrick settled in Lynn and married another recent immigrant, Bridget Clancy. Their son, William P. Connery, born in 1855 in Lynn, would find his prosperity as a coal merchant after spending his youth as an actor named Billy Barlow. His wife, my grandmother, was the former Mary Haven, who came at age sixteen from Thurles, Ireland.

Martin Quirk, the son of William Quirk and his wife Joanna Carr, would marry Mary Reddy, and they would become North Enders and fervent supporters of the rising Irish politician John F. Fitzgerald, who would dominate Boston's North End from the 1890s on, as Patrick Kennedy would rule East Boston.

John F. Fitzgerald in all his political speeches, which got him into Congress and later into the mayoralty of Boston, referred lavishly and affectionately to his "Dear Old North End"—and Martin and Mary Quirk and their neighbors came to be referred to as "dearos." Loyal—even fanatic—dearos they were. Mary Quirk in particular helped rally the votes for Fitzie, Honey Fitz, or "the North End's Little Napoleon" (as he was variously termed)—and this some thirty years before women were given suffrage in 1920.

Many years later John F. Fitzgerald was to sing the praises of my grandmother Mary Quirk: "Oh was she a lively one, and oh how she believed in me and worked for me!"

Honey Fitz believed that friendship was a two-way street, and he paid back a number of his supporters with generous concern. When Mary Quirk died unexpectedly at forty-two in 1904, Honey Fitz took a special interest in her nineteen-year-old son, Jimmy. When Fitzie took over an almost defunct Boston paper called the *Republic*, he took Jimmy Quirk on as his aide. The paper made money, and Jimmy helped not only on the editorial end, as John F. recalled to me, but was instrumental in picking up so many well-paying ads that he helped his boss obtain a financial prosperity of a kind he had not known before.

Jimmy Quirk always spoke of his debt to Honey Fitz, telling my father (his younger brother Andrew), "I learned about advertising, circulation, editorial approaches and nuances at the feet of Honey Fitz."

PJ, who used his saloon as a political strategy headquarters and extended his influence over the years, worked his way in time into such posts as election and fire commissioner.

Honey Fitz and PJ both had their problems with Martin Lomasney, Boston's top political boss in the 1890s: "It was probably the one thing on which we agreed," John F. Fitzgerald later told me. "PJ and I didn't like each other—he didn't like my methods and I didn't like his." Both were agreed that Lomasney was too centrifugally dictatorial; they also didn't like any trickle-down association with Lomasney's notorious corner cutting, grafting, and influence peddling.

"Yes, they all were corner-cutting crooks and opportunists," Jimmy Quirk later said of the Irish bosses of his youth in Boston. "But what choice did they have, when you come down to it? The Yanks had the money, the banks, the influence, the connections. If it is true that no one ever made a millions bucks honestly, then no one ever succeeded in politics honestly—not ninety percent of them anyway!"

Jimmy Quirk continued: "There were always too many guys feeling for the soft spots, ferreting-out weaknesses in the competition. If a guy wanted to be a rinso-white, Fitzie used to say, then let him go for the priesthood!"

Jimmy, at twenty-one, and his pal Fred Enwright, later a Lynn newspaper publisher, were active in 1905 in Honey Fitz's first successful campaign for mayor. In 1905 Jimmy and Fred, according to the city directory of that year, were rooming together in an old 1847 converted townhouse at 70 Pinckney Street on Beacon Hill where I was later to live.

Honey Fitz and PJ, during their endless early office-seeking and office-holding, served in the 1890s in the state senate. Their off-and-on feuding and rivalry cooled down after Fitzgerald was elected mayor in 1905. After that they were allies—of a sort—though they never really liked each other.

The two families enjoyed vacationing at Old Orchard Beach, and it was there that PJ's son Joe and Honey Fitz's daughter Rose met as children. During his several (separated) terms as mayor, John F. Fitzgerald was often under attack for alleged dishonesty, graft, and manipulations of one kind or another. He always had a cavalier attitude toward his bad reputation, and to the end maintained that he had to cut corners and rule "flexibly" in order to accommodate the various interests and "get things done." That he managed to pick up some private funding along the way is indisputable, and he was able to raise Rose and her siblings in comfortable surroundings. His approach to problems of politics—and problems of life in general—mirrored the famed axiom of the Italian philosopher Machiavelli's: "It is a mistake to be *too* good when surrounded by others who are *not* good."

In the 1905–1906 period, Honey Fitz began escorting fifteen-year-old Rose to various affairs, his wife being a retiring type who scorned the political rat race. Jimmy Quirk was to recall that he was one of Rose's first youthful "dates." For a while Martin Quirk theorized that Honey Fitz saw in Jimmy a potential son-in-law of "the right kind" for the daughter he doted on and adored. "But the spark was never there—for either of us," Jimmy recalled. Martin Quirk felt that Honey Fitz was a little disappointed in this development. Jimmy, meanwhile, matriculated at Boston University Law School while working as a reporter for the *Boston Advertiser* and other publications, having moved on from the *Republic* after Honey Fitz became mayor. Jimmy recalled later that the new mayor had offered him a post in his administration, but he felt journalism was his true calling.

Rose Kennedy, attractive, intelligent, alert, and enterprising, probably gained her first awareness of the wandering male from observing her father's infidelities. The name of a certain "Toodles" Ryan began to figure in Honey Fitz's opponents' diatribes against him at election time. Toodles, his critics alleged, was his mistress, and she later cost him a mayoral election. There were other women in Honey Fitz's life along the way. When confronted with this, he would turn the matter at hand into a joke, along such lines as: "If, as they say, drinking is a 'good man's fault' then womanizing is 'a needy man's consolation.'" This was his indirect way of referring to his wife's frigidity and stiff approach to sex (as a *non*pleasurable means of procreation only). Honey Fitz obviously didn't share this view.

Joe Kennedy's mother looked down on politics. She wanted a better future for her boy Joe, who was idolized by her and his younger sisters. In 1901 Joe was sent to the

Boston Latin School, saturated as it was with the sons of the Yankee elitists she wanted Joe to cultivate. Joe Kennedy, however, was far from a mama's boy; his self-esteem profited from the worship the women in his family accorded him, but he was a fiercely enterprising, monumentally self-confident youngster from the beginning. "Those fierce blue eyes," Jimmy Quirk remembered, "told whomever looked into them that this guy was forging ahead and nobody better block him—*nobody!*"

Next on the agenda was Harvard; though never an outstanding student, Joe made up for this lack in other ways, socializing, politicizing, making the right sports teams. But the seeds of his anger toward the entrenched Boston Yankee aristocracy were really sown at Harvard, where he found himself the recipient of snubs, both subtle and unsubtle, and was blackballed from "in" clubs like Porcellian.

By 1907 Rose, then seventeen, and Joe, then nineteen, were dating; their friendship, fostered in childhood at both families' beach gatherings, was slowly developing. Rose wrote in later years that during those teenage beginnings, that mutual spark was always there. Not that Fitzie approved. He felt that the Fitzgeralds were "higher-class Irish" than the Kennedys and that coming from Boston proper (the old North End), they made the East Boston Kennedys seem provincial. He just didn't care for the idea of a Kennedy-Fitzgerald alliance, he told his wife, and let Rose know it.

Rose recalled as one of the great disappointments of her life her father's refusal to send her to Wellesley College; instead he sent her to a Catholic school abroad. She always blamed Archbishop (after 1911 Cardinal) William O'Connell for this. Like the rest of the Roman Catholic clergy in Boston, O'Connell felt Catholic children should be educated in Catholic schools "among their own," as he put it. Rose's father—his political fortunes in mind—went along with the clergy on this. But not Joe's mother. Joe remembered his mother telling him that in the world of banking, to which he shortly would aspire after graduating from Harvard, one needed only one's financial shrewdness and ability to swing deals; one did *not* depend on the approval of various factions later manifested by votes at the polls.

The Fitzgeralds in the 1910-1911 period were moving up. John F. had taken his daughter on European tours; at school in Holland, Rose had met daughters of wealthy and influential families, and in her travels had rubbed shoulders with people calculated, as Honey Fitz hoped, to give her polish and social facility of a high order.

Joe also made sure to make the "right' connections at Harvard; though some of the top family scions avoided and scorned him, he made friends with the later influential Yankee lawyer Guy Currier; Robert Benchley, the future humorist; and others in a position to help later. He soon decided that banking was what he found most engrossing. Thanks to his father's influence, Joe received an appointment after graduation as a bank examiner for the state. In his travels around Massachusetts he learned about moneymaking, balancing ledgers, investments, and what stocks and bonds could—and could not—do. His earlier courses in economics at Harvard were put to good use.

Joe felt money "was the key to everything," as Guy Currier later put it. Money meant power, flexibility, gracious living, maneuvering room; money gave one mobility, put one in flight above the common herd. Money was to be respected. Money, Joe concluded at twenty-five, would buy everything—or anyway, anything that counted in *his* priority scheme.

Soon he invested in Old Colony Realty, to the tune of one-third of the stock. John H. Davis, in his book *The Kennedys: Dynasty and Disaster*, would give *his* retrospective analysis of Old Colony Realty: "[It] capitalized on the misfortunes of others, particularly poor people. It took over defaulted mortgages on modest two-and-three-family tenements, repaired and maintained the houses, then quickly resold them."

Joe Kennedy once told Guy Currier that "God helps those who help themselves," and that a large percentage of the poor and underprivileged were in that unenviable state because they were too lazy or too stupid or too defective in character or too path-of-least-resistance oriented to do anything about their circumstances. "And what are you to do with or about people like *that!*" Joe posited. "There'll *always* be underdogs because that's what they *want* to be!" Joe added that such folk had no right to pull the more intelligent and enterprising down with them.

By 1913, after touring Europe and acquainting himself with financial practices there, Joe came back ready to run a bank of his own; that turned out to be the Columbia Trust, founded by his father and other East Boston merchants. Thanks to parental influence and boostings from former Harvard classmates, Joe went after the stock, put $45,000 of his father's money into the failing institution, then informed its board of directors that he wanted to be Columbia Trust's president. PJ's clout, and the board's awareness of the brash twenty-five-year-old's obvious promise in the world of finance, transformed him that 1913 into one of the youngest bank presidents in the country.

Joe had continued to steadily court Rose, who was by then twenty-two and knew her own mind, which said, despite her father's objection, she wanted to marry Joe

Kennedy. Honey Fitz by 1914 was more minded to take Joe seriously. "Certainly he has a sound head for finance—maybe a winner after all," he told an associate. He was further mollified by the reversals he had suffered as of 1914. The ambitious politician James Michael Curley, whose disreputable grafting practices were to give him, in time, a reputation far worse than the far-from-rinso-white Fitzgerald, threatened to revive the gossip about Toodles Ryan during the 1914 mayoral campaign he was busily fighting. Wife Josie and daughter Rose were embarrassed by the revival of Toodles stories and were anxious for Fitzie to withdraw from the race. Still, for a time, he held on. Then Curley announced that he would give a series of lectures, the first being "Graft in Ancient and Modern Times," the second "Great Lovers from Cleopatra to Toodles." That did it. Elizabeth "Toodles" Ryan, who had been a secretary at the Ferncroft Inn when Honey Fitz first beheld her, was paid to take a long vacation as far from Boston as possible, and Fitzie withdrew from the mayoral race.

In October 1914 Joseph P. Kennedy and Rose Fitzgerald were married by Cardinal William O'Connell; a fateful dynasty was inaugurated. Fitzie took it well: his daughter was happy with the man she loved, Joe Kennedy was obviously a man on the way up in finance, a future millionaire by his own cocky predictions, and—well, she could have done worse, as he philosophically put it to his wife.

The young president of Columbia Trust ensconced his bride in a modest but roomy and well-structured house on Beale Street in Brookline. Most of their neighbors were upwardly mobile Protestants. For Joe this was only the beginning. Joe Jr. was born in 1915, Jack in 1917, Rosemary in 1918, and Eunice and Kathleen in the early 1920s. Patricia, Robert, Jean, and Edward followed.

When World War I broke out, Joe, though only twenty-nine, pleaded family-man status (no seeker after battlefield heroics was he). He used his connections with Guy Currier to get the ear of Charles Schwab, Bethlehem Steel Yard's potentate-in-chief, and persuaded him to make him manager of Fore River Shipyard, which in 1917 and 1918 launched a number of quickly but soundly constructed battleships. He turned over the Columbia Trust to his father and went to work for a reported $20,000 a year. Schwab offered generous bonuses to Joe if he came up with inventive methods for increasing the output, and Joe delivered in fine style. During this stint, Joe met Franklin D. Roosevelt, another gentleman who had avoided direct involvement in war by using his own (in this case New York) connections to win him the post of assistant secretary of the navy. Joe saw FDR on several occasions, "doing our battleship chess-game," as he put it years later. "I don't think they *liked* each other that first item around but they sure *understood* each other!" Ed Derr, who joined Joe at this time and later became one of his chief aides, pronounced.

Next on Joe's onward-and-upward chessboard came Galen Stone, the Boston investment banker. He was head of a steamship line and partner in the prestigious Boston investment firm, Hayden Stone and Company. Stone was impressed by Joe's energy and consummate financial shrewdness and hired him in his stock department after the war had ended. Here Joe Kennedy learned the basics of the big-time finance that would take him on to untold millions. "Galen Stone accelerated my career as few men had," he later said. Meanwhile his father-in-law had sustained a Senate defeat in 1916 and realized his political career was virtually over.

With Prohibition becoming the law in 1920, Joe became the most brazen—if secretive—of bootleggers. He spruced up aspects of his father's liquor trade and without hesitation allied himself with the Mafia figures who were heavy into bootlegging themselves and had established a worldwide network of imports. Just as often, they created their own product—as did Joe. The terms "rotgut liquor" and "bathtub gin" originated in those 1920s in which an anything-goes attitude pervaded all aspects of life—women's skirts went up a mile and free love became the chic indulgence. Frank Costello, boss of the Luciano crime syndicate, told several Kennedy authors that he had worked closely with Joe Kennedy. Sam Giancana, head Mafia man in the Chicago syndicate, had a lot to say about Joe and his liquor dealings in his ironically titled 1983 autobiography, *A Man of Honor*. Meyer Lansky, another prominent bootlegger, attempting to counter assertions in Congress and elsewhere that Italians were the most heavily involved in crime, including bootlegging, told of Joe Kennedy's Irish Protection Squad, which took good care of the liquor shipments and could more than hold their own with any other nationality.

Around 1920 Joe began playing around with stocks in earnest, kiting then depressing them then kiting them again. Inside tips from Galen Stone and others helped make him a millionaire. He played the suckers for all they were worth, spreading news of "hot" stocks to attract buying runs, then unhesitantly selling at a profit, leaving many people holding the bag when the stocks in question reverted to their true (usually minimal) value. "It's a tricky art," Joe said later. "It calls for timing, a sense of how far you can push people's gullibilities, a sharp eye for trends. I learned it all the hard way, lost a few thousands 'experimenting' at the beginning, then got it to go my way, all the way."

Joe could also help people—if it were in his interest. Walter Howey, the Hearst executive, enjoyed telling how Joe had come to his rescue when the stock of the Yellow Cab

Company, in which Walter had made some heavy investments, proved erratic. John Hertz, president of Yellow Cab (his son was later to be, briefly, the husband of screen star Myrna Loy) was charged five million dollars by Joe to work up anonymous orders for Yellow Cab stock from all over the country. When the word got around, Yellow Cab was hot again, and the five million Hertz gave to Joe to implement the turnaround didn't even have to be used. "The man was a genius when it came to the financial market," Walter told me. "He had an uncanny sense of what was coming in and what was going out, what was hot and what was going cold, and he saved my fortune and I will always be grateful to him!" (Walter told me this in 1948.)

After Galen Stone decided to retire, Joe struck out on his own. His office on Boston's Milk Street had a simple sign on the door: Joseph P. Kennedy, Banker.

Joe began to take a serious interest in movies in 1924, but he had been considering its financial potential as far back as his Columbia Trust days. With partners he had bought a chain of New England picture houses in 1924, then had obtained the territorial franchise for Universal Pictures. After he bought the American rights to some second and third rate British films, he went to London to strengthen his contacts in England. Soon he was cultivating the acquaintance of such bigwigs as Jesse Lasky and Will Hays, who in 1922 had been set up as a censor supreme to control an industry racked by such scandals as film idol Wally Reid's drug addiction and comedian Fatty Arbuckle's alleged murder of a girl in a San Francisco hotel room.

The movies of the early 1920s were wild, woolly, and to many, out of bounds sexually. The more sedate film heroines like Mary Pickford had given way to wilder fillies like Gloria Swanson, Bebe Daniels, and May Allison. The public went to films in droves.

There was one man, known since boyhood and soon a close friend, that Joe Kennedy turned to for his principal advice on movie moneymaking. That man was James R. Quirk.

When I first interviewed Joe Kennedy in 1949 in connection with research on a book about my uncle, Jimmy Quirk, Joe spoke of him glowingly, his first words being: "Your uncle Jim was a great friend of mine and a real pioneer in a business that needed his forthrightness and his vision." As far back as 1914, in his Columbia Trust days, Joe had been getting feedback about movies from Jimmy Quirk, who that year, at age thirty, had taken over a pathetic little rag called *Photoplay*, which had little advertising and no respect in the fast-expanding new industry, but in short order metamorphosed into the most prestigious magazine on films, with a wide national readership and close connections to industry bigwigs and the stars who would shine from its pages in compelling photographs and percipient, penetrating articles highlighting their assets. Jimmy Quirk also spotlighted many film trends and initiated more than a few of them.

Over the years Jimmy and Joe had kept in touch, as Jimmy had moved from the Boston newspaper field to the managing editorship of the *Washington Times*, then on to *Popular Mechanics* in Chicago, which he had rescued from circulation doldrums and put resoundingly and profitably in the black by 1912.

Jimmy's fame preceded him, and many shrewd investors in Chicago and New York began wondering when he was going to get involved in his own publication. It was known that he was chafing at *Popular Mechanics* because he edited it but did not own it, the publisher being determined to put his son in charge in due time.

Two mainline executives of the W. F. Hall Printing Company of Chicago, Robert M. Eastman and Edwin Colvin, had acquired the languishing *Photoplay* (by then three years old, in 1914) and offered to let Jimmy Quirk run it. By 1926 Jimmy had the controlling interest in the magazine.

In 1914 he got two solid assistants: on the editorial end, Julian Johnson, and on the business end, Kathryn Dougherty, who was to be his loyal aide to the end and, after his death in 1932, editor and publisher herself.

"Kay Dee," as Kathryn Dougherty was known throughout the business, was one of my earliest guides and mentors in the 1940s. Kay Dee recalled the days of 1914–1915 in Chicago when Jimmy was welding his organization together, worrying about costs, pushing on ads. Whenever he felt she was doubtful or negative, he would say: "Look here, this job is pretty nearly as new to me as it is to you, but you're Irish and I'm Irish, and the Irish are never licked!"

"Jimmy Quirk believed all was well with life if we but had the courage to face life unafraid." She remembered one of his favorite stories, about a guy who fell off the top of a skyscraper and during his downward passage commented: "I have just passed the sixteenth story and everything is safe so far."

Chicago in the 1915–1919 period was a popular meeting place for the film crowd passing between New York and Los Angeles, and several major film companies had their bases there. Martin Quigley, another Irishman, was editor of *Exhibitors Herald* and an early friend of Jim's. He said of him: "What he set down on paper was but a small part of what he knew of the living, loving, striving communities that we call Hollywood and Broadway." He was a moving spirit in the famed White Paper Club, a group of writers on film that included such luminaries as James Oliver Curwood, Emerson Hough, Bob Munsey, Ray Long, Terry Ramsaye, and Watterson Rothacker, owner of the Rothacker Film Laboratories.

Mickey Neilan, who knew both Charlie Chaplin and Jimmy Quirk intimately, said that had Jimmy lived, his friend Chaplin would not have run into the long period of public opprobrium that he knew from the 1940s on.

Among the many writers Jimmy Quirk fostered were Adela Rogers St. Johns and Louella Parsons, who began writing for him in 1918. Burns Mantle, the Broadway critic, began writing pieces for *Photoplay* and was amazed that Jimmy gave him carte blanche to write as he pleased about movies. "He retained an independence of the studios when it came to ad interests that made his word and work highly respected," Hearst executive Daniel Henderson told me in 1952.

Terry Ramsaye was commissioned to write a "truthful, accurate, honest" history of the movies for Jimmy in 1922, which ran in *Photoplay* for three years (1922–1925) and in 1926 was published as *A Million and One Nights*. H. L. Mencken was later to make a visit to Hollywood and wrote about it in an article for *Photoplay*. Jimmy Quirk in turn wrote an article "Wowsers Tackle the Movies" for Mencken's prestigious *American Mercury* in 1927 in which he tackled the censors cross-country for overdoing the "virtue" and downplaying "artistic truth." Nonetheless he was a strong supporter of Will Hays, who was trying to keep bluenoses and censors from totally throttling the film industry in the 1920s while at the same time keeping artistic quality steady and high.

In 1920 Jimmy Quirk instituted the Photoplay Gold Medal, until the Oscars the most prestigious award in the industry, that went to the best film of the year. Dubbed "the Mencken of the Morons" by a literary and cultural elite that still looked down on movies as a potential art form in the 1920s, Jimmy fought for artistic betterment in films. His sayings became famous: "Anyone who tries to get a dollar and a half for a fifty-cent move is trying to pick your pocket." "A publication that doesn't make its readers mad has no vitality." "Advertisers, are you promoting this particular film because it will sell or because it *deserves* to sell?"

Jimmy won Joe's envy when he divorced his first wife to marry May Allison, the beautiful film star. Their wedding in 1926, as Lillian Gish told me in 1952, was one of the Hollywood events of the time.

May was one of the loveliest blond beauties of the era, with eyes extolled by H. L. Mencken as "unforgettably eloquent and expressive." May had been born in Georgia on June 14, 1890 (she gave the year as 1895 for years, but it *was* 1890). She had been on the stage in her teens, then debuted in films in 1914 in support of siren Theda Bara in *A Fool There Was*. Soon May was co-starring with handsome Harold Lockwood in a series of delightful and popular comedy-romances that transformed both of them into popular luminaries of the 1915–1918 screen.

After Lockwood's death in the 1918 flu epidemic, May went on to top stardom on her own, numbering Rudolph Valentino among her leading men. Offscreen, she cut a wide swathe, linking herself with the handsomest and sexiest male personalities in Hollywood. The fan magazines and newspapers from 1919 to 1924 were full of her romantic involvements and professional activities.

But by 1924 her unhappy marriage to the alcoholic, wife-beating, emotionally disturbed actor Robert Ellis had adversely affected her career, and by 1925 they were pinning the has-been tag on thirty-five-year-old May. Ellis had been her second husband.

Then Jimmy Quirk came to May's rescue. He spoke to his influential friends in Hollywood on her behalf, played her up in *Photoplay* constantly with flattering pictures and sympathetic articles, with the result that from 1925 until 1927, when she permanently retired from the screen, she landed some creditable leading roles.

Jimmy Quirk later recalled that he'd had a man-sized crush on May since her co-starring stints with Harold Lockwood. When they met yet again at a banquet in 1925, forty-one-year-old Jimmy, recently divorced and on the town with such lovelies as Renee Adoree, Phyllis Haver, and the very young Joan Crawford, fell for May hook, line, and sinker. Adela St. Johns, May's good friend and Jimmy's chief writer, helped the courtship along, and when Jimmy and May wed in Santa Barbara November 15, 1926, Adela and her then-husband Ike St. Johns, also of the *Photoplay* staff, were in attendance.

Early 1927 issues of *Photoplay* found Jimmy referring to May as "the beautiful blonde whose hand I hold in picture shows," and for a time they were regarded as the most in-love pair in Hollywood or New York. Jimmy was in love with May's beauty and charm, and *she* was in love with his charisma, power, and masculine authority. May's friends and associates of the time felt that she had climbed higher in the Hollywood hierarchy as wife of the lord of *Photoplay* than she ever would have in an acting comeback, however splashy. May couldn't have agreed more.

So there was Jimmy, freed of wife, kids, and family obligations, married to a beautiful star, living a glamorous, carefree life, while Joe was stuck with Rose and their kids. Joe had moved them all first to Riverdale, then to Bronxville, where he kept them in high style in fancy mansions from which he was often absent. His little affairs in the 1924–1927 era seemed to him tawdry compared to Jimmy's flings with Adoree, Crawford, Haver—and now marriage to May Allison! Yes, he'd had that little fling with Evelyn Brent, but she was third string as actresses went. Joe knew he could never divorce Rose and felt in many ways trapped—trapped, two-faced, hypocritical—and not a little depressed. All this aggravated his ulcers and other internal conditions, and his absences from home grew even more frequent.

Rose, in the Bronxville and Riverdale houses, and later at the compound he purchased for them at the Cape and the estate he added in Palm Beach, devoted herself to her religion, her prayers, her friendships, her motherly duties (which largely bored and drained her)—and the nagging realization that she and Joe were miles apart in many ways. As for the affairs she had always suspected (Joe had begun playing around as early as the late teens, especially during the pregnancies), the daughter of Honey Fitz shrugged and closed her eyes. Men were like that, she rationalized, rovers, curiosity seekers, sexually driven. Her church had taught her that sex (which she never enjoyed) was for procreation. She endured Joe's sudden attentions, but privately felt that there were too many children and agreed with her mother that "men get all the pleasure and women get all the pain." But she also knew that she had what the mistresses and brief affair mates did *not* have—the name and the money and the security. This was how Rose Kennedy was to feel straight up through—and after—the Gloria Swanson involvement.

At times Rose enjoyed twitting Joe, watching him blush and stutter, as when she said in 1931, "I saw Nancy Carroll in a movie, Joe; she's a pretty little thing, isn't she?" Since Joe at the time had it going hot and heavy with Nancy (albeit briefly), Rose had her inner laugh—a laugh more sardonic and bitter than gleeful. Looking back over many years, Rose realized that when she had learned of Honey Fitz's mistress Toodles Ryan, she had become disillusioned by men and was never thrown by whatever negatives they projected toward her—even when, as in her husband's case, it was the ultimate sin and insult, adultery.

Rose had known Jimmy Quirk, of course, from the early days in Boston, when he had worked for her father on the *Republic* and had dated her (innocently, with parental approval). She had been happy for his rise in the publishing field, took pleasure in his major success with *Photoplay*, a magazine she enjoyed reading for its wonderful fashion layouts, intimate stories, and scintillating movie coverage. In 1946, during Jack's first campaign, when Rose had been making many appearances for her son, I spent an enjoyable hour talking with her, and she had been lavish in praise of my uncle. When she asked about May Allison and I told her that May had remarried, she surprised me by saying that she had always felt that Jimmy Quirk went through a great disillusionment with May, certainly with their marriage. It was as if she were saying that Joe, whom she knew envied that glamorous marriage, had really nothing at all to envy. Rose also commented sadly and wistfully that "Jimmy should have stayed with his first wife and his kids." I commented that my grandfather, Martin Quirk, one of Fitzie's dearos whom Rose had known, would never receive May Allison in Boston; she snapped, "He was right. Marriage ties should be for life!"

Predictably, by 1928, two years into the marriage, Jimmy Quirk was straying, and with a vengeance. His close crony Ray Long, a compulsive womanizer himself (Kay Dee later recalled the virulent syphilitic infection Ray had acquired along the line), played pimp for Jimmy, steering a bewilderingly varied assortment of floozies, actresses, and "respectable" types his way. Mickey Neilan, Eddie

Sutherland, and on occasion Joe Kennedy, joined Jimmy and Ray on their romantic hegiras, though the Swanson involvement kept Joe relatively under leash—but only relatively—between 1928 and 1931.

Confronted with Jimmy's drinking, his infidelities, and his tendency to belittle and humiliate her at parties, May, consoled by her women friends, especially Miriam Hopkins, sat brooding and seething in their sumptuous apartment that took up almost the entire sixth floor of New York's posh Buckingham Hotel, two blocks away from *Photoplay*'s West Fifty-Seventh Street offices.

The gradual deterioration of their relationship puzzled and troubled Joe Kennedy. Certainly he lost any envy he might have felt toward Jimmy. Meanwhile he got his share of cuts and bruises. The sharp-tongued and mercurial Miriam Hopkins once told him: "You've got a nice wife, Joe, and all those kids. Why don't you leave Gloria and these other women alone and concentrate on *them!*" Ray Long, when inebriated, repeated to Joe—with consummate lack of tact—Miriam's put-downs. Kay Dee recalled these as variations of "Joe's not good-looking, he's putting on weight, his breath is lousy and he dresses like a clerk!"

The Quirk-Allison marriage deteriorated during 1930 through 1932. May Allison certainly had *her* side of the story. She had retired in 1927 so had no career to occupy her (she tried writing, halfheartedly, not successfully) and found herself married to a mercurial, tormented, hard-drinking, fast-living genius who alternately ignored her, hugged her, yelled at her, kissed her. By 1932 matters were reaching a crucial phase. Kay Dee remembered Jimmy telling her: "I've got to get rid of that dame! If we could only get a quarter of a million dollars together, I'd buy May off, divorce her and go back to Betty and the kids!" Unfortunately, Jimmy, who had not a smidgen of pal Joe Kennedy's money sense, had lost his shirt in the 1929 stock market crash. He had taken over some magazines from Hearst, *Smart Set* and *McClure's*, in addition to *Photoplay*, but when that arrangement (1928–1930) had collapsed in the wake of internecine quarrels and what writer Margaret Ettinger called "titanic displays of temperament," Jimmy had thrown the Hearst magazines back to the lord of San Simeon.

Joe Kennedy had visited San Simeon in company with Jimmy and Ray Long, and felt that Jimmy and "WR"—as Hearst was known to his intimates—had a love-hate relationship. Both had left their wives for other women, but Hearst had never divorced nor legalized his actress-mistress Marion Davies. Marion often cried on Jimmy's shoulder about her problems, and Hearst got the idea Jimmy sided with Marion; he was also annoyed over the way the magazine deals had turned out. Soon there was no love lost between them.

In reminiscing about that time, Joe Kennedy told me: "Your uncle didn't handle Hearst right. I thought a lot of the tension generated was unnecessary and unwarranted. But Jimmy lived and worked by his own rules."

THREE

Mentor Jimmy Quirk and Hollywood

I t was Jimmy Quirk who first got Joe Kennedy fired up over the potential of the motion picture industry. On his trips to New York, Joe was a frequent visitor to Jimmy's offices on the top floor of a slim white sandstone building at 221 West Fifty-Seventh Street. Evenings, Jimmy, Ray Long, and Joe would tour the night spots and go to show-business parties, winding up often at the high-class establishment Jimmy and Ray had set up on West Fifty-Eighth Street. Here Joe met the "actresses," "halfway girls," and "show dames," as Jimmy called them, and wild nights ensued. Jimmy at this time was between marriages and ensconced in a bachelor apartment at 45 West Fifty-Fifth Street. Jimmy, Ray, and Joe would often repair to what Jimmy called his "hideaway spot" to drink and compare notes on the girls they had bedded, and in conversations going far into the night, Jimmy would explain the lures and excitements of the film business to an eager and receptive Joe.

Though their match at womanizing, Joe kept the booze at bay; though Jimmy and Ray would kid him about it, Joe reiterated that a man needed a clear head to get ahead in business, and addictive stuff often detoured him to a destructive degree. "I am sure your uncle Jimmy would be alive today if he hadn't overdone the booze," Joe told me in 1949. "As for Ray, he had caught VD several times over; I liked my fun as much as any man but I *governed* things!"

Jimmy convinced Joe during their many talks that a wise business head like his was needed in the film business. The "pants-pressers," as Joe characterized titans like Schenck, Zukor, Mayer, and Thalberg, seemed to have no money sense; Jimmy was convinced that with most of their product they spent more than they earned, and if a blockbuster like *The Big Parade* came along, it was more a matter of lucking out than planning and foresight regarding the kind of product people wanted to see.

Jimmy shared with Joe his conviction that the movies were a great new art that would win over the mass public and in time cross all class and cultural lines; silent as of 1925, movies crossed ethnic and language barriers as well. As Jimmy pointed out, the expressive faces and pictorial situations so characteristic of the silent screen won universal response. Joe rapidly picked up Jimmy's enthusiasm. He later sniffed that the snobbish Boston aristocrats wouldn't go to pictures or let their children go, but the movie-going servants knew more about what was going on in the world than their employers. He believed the working class was getting smarter every day due to what they picked up culturally from pictures, which reflected so many ways of life, and that "snobs and snoots" were increasingly out of touch with real life. When Joe asked Jimmy about the rising radio threat to movies, Jimmy replied that radio would constitute no long-range threat of any kind because "people like to *look* at what's going on—they want their eyes as well as their ears to take things in."

Joe, while still at Hayden Stone and Company, had already bought, on Jimmy's advice, the small chain of New England theaters. Now he was thinking also of distribution and production.

He focused on a movie company, Film Booking Office of America, that seemed to be sinking due to bad management policies. He sailed to London to consult with the British owners about selling it to him, offering a million dollars. Outraged, the Britishers replied that it was worth at least ten million. Later he joked to Jimmy and others that he had "bargained those damned jickies down with some business gobbledygook. I got them feeling that they were better off unloading the firm for a reasonable amount." But at first the company had put up resistance. Enterprising Joe soon had no less a personage than Edward, Prince of Wales, on his side. Learning that the prince, whom he had once met at a Boston event, was in Paris, he hopped over to France and got himself seated near the prince at a restaurant His Highness favored. After saying a quick hello and recalling their prior (highly superficial) encounter as if it had been a buddy-buddy kaffeeklatsch, Joe wheedled a letter of introduction from the prince with which he hoped to impress the recalcitrant banker-owners of FBO. The angle didn't work at first, but later the FBO people contacted him (after he had retreated home following an attack of his chronic ulcers). The upshot was that FBO was his.

Since there were no flies on Honey Fitz, the old man leaked the news and wangled the Boston press into portraying *him* as the prime catalyst in the negotiations. Result: the *Boston Post* ran a headline: "John F. Fitzgerald Latest Movie Magnate." Joe was not amused by his father-in-law's latest crass and tasteless spate of self-adoration, but he laughed it off with his friends. "He'll do anything to shore himself up—like any sinking ship" was the least scornful of his utterances on Honey Fitz's didoes.

Joe had no MGM, Paramount, or United Artists setup with the humble FBO. And though he scorned the "furriers, pants-pressers, and other merchants of drivel," as he called them, he was soon stooping to their level with his own product. Keeping his budgets under $30,000, he was soon grinding out cowboy second-runners and other forgettable films with titles like *The Gorilla Hunt*, *Red Hot Hooves*, and *The Dude Cowboys*. He went for stars who came cheap, like Tom Mix, Fred Thomson (cowboy star husband of Frances Marion, the screenwriter), and Red Grange. Though in actuality he was better educated, more cultured and intelligent than some of his top-drawer movie competitors, Joe was drawn to what would make the fastest buck. No *Ten Commandments* or *Ben-Hur* for Joe. He was much more interested in getting his cowboy and action movies into midwest and southern movie houses where the overhead would be low and the aggregate profits high. Following these methods over the next two years, Joe acquired a reputation in Hollywood as a shrewd businessman but a conscienceless dispenser of trash.

At first Jimmy Quirk had advised Joe to start with surefire programmers: Westerns, pictures that emphasized physical agility and breathtaking stunts. Sensing that Joe was more interested at the time in moneymaking than art, he tried to steer his film tastes into areas that would bring the profits he knew Joe craved. "Joe will back out of anything where he has to endure, or foresee, a financial loss," Jimmy told Mickey Neilan. Later Jimmy tried to get Joe to invest in more prestigious, carefully crafted product, but Joe said he didn't want to take the chance with bigger budgets and more creative talents that would come high, salary-wise. Jimmy cited to him one of his apothegms: "Do you want this picture just to sell, or *deserve* to sell?" Joe replied that that was all very well, but Jimmy was a journalist and commentator on the sidelines while Joe was the guy who had to sign the checks and guard the bottom line. Accused by Jimmy of being afraid to take a chance on a more expensive product, Joe merely replied, "It's not cowardice, it's just a shrewd appraisal of the odds."

Joe in his way resented Jimmy's urging him to try for quality in films. Though still heavy into stocks and other Wall Street maneuverings, Joe wanted a greater voice in film industry councils, having as he did a respect for the powerful film producers whose methods he scorned but whom he recognized as top industry figures nonetheless. Jimmy was conspicuously absent from the top industry movers-and-shakers whom Joe had invited to a Harvard Business School seminar on the movies. When he asked later why he, the editor and publisher of the most conspicuous and prestigious film journal of the time, and someone with a better overall knowledge of the film industry than any other journalistic commentator, had been overlooked on the speaker list, Joe cavalierly and offhandedly ducked the issue by saying he had concentrated on inviting top *producers* like Walter Wanger, Jesse Lasky, Adolph Zukor, and Marcus Loew. An even dozen movie bigwigs showed up, with Harvard footing the bill. Their egos were flattered at taking part in a seminar at America's most prestigious university, since most of them had had sparse formal educations.

Kennedy saw to it that the Harvard Business School affair got top coverage, and it was outstandingly successful. Then he worked up a volume called *The Story of the Films*, to which he contributed an article, and saw that each mogul received a copy. Flattered and disarmed, they began to speak more positively of their Irish-Catholic "colleague" from

Boston, even though several of them sensed Joe's latent anti-Semitism and knew of his "pants-presser" and "furrier" sallies about them. But the attitude of these gentlemen of humble European backgrounds and scant schooling was essentially: "This well-heeled mick got us to Harvard!"

Meanwhile Jimmy Quirk was giving Joe fine publicity in *Photoplay*, and when Terry Ramsaye began writing regularly for the magazine, Jimmy assigned him a series called An Intimate Visit to the Homes of Film Magnates. Joe Kennedy and his seven (as of 1927) kids were highlighted. In the pages of *Photoplay* were childhood vignettes of Joe Jr., JFK, Bobby, and the "Girls." Joe was so proud of the issue that he had a thousand copies distributed around the Harvard Club and other haunts. Jimmy joked that Joe had *not* left it hanging around the West Fifty-Eighth Street haunt he, Jimmy, Mickey Neilan, Ray Long, and others frequented.

In his speech at the 1927 Harvard seminar, Joe made some telling points about the inevitability of sound (Jolson's *The Jazz Singer* was to highlight its possibilities that year) and the necessity of correlating the production, distribution, and exhibition ends into a centralized unit. He also attacked movie wildcatting and emphasized the necessity of a few great studios calling the production shots. Some in the film industry were amused that Joe was coming on as the elder statesman and touting quality and production upgrading when his FBO continued to turn out the trashiest product of all. Joe blindly ignored the inconsistencies implicit in all this. His films were making money, money was the source of all good, and he was being—well, practical, shrewd, realistic. But many behind the scenes sneered at that "Boston mick's" essential hypocrisy and two-faced methods.

While not neglecting his Wall Street wheeler-dealings and his stock manipulations, which he still considered to be the lifeblood of his efforts to become, in as short an order as possible, a multimillionaire, Joe began to commute regularly between his FBO offices in Hollywood, where he bought a fancy house in Beverly Hills, and New York.

Also at this time, Joe had added to his West Fifty-Eighth Street activities an ever more intensive pursuit of young Hollywood starlets and upcoming actresses, one of whom was Evelyn Brent, a sullen-faced, sloe-eyed sexpot who was beginning to win fame in such pictures as *Underworld*. Evelyn, a cynical, bitter type who had been used by men ever since she hit Hollywood as a teenager, found her career diminished by the early 1930s, but for a time she had a vogue of a sort and made the most of it.

Mickey Neilan later said of Evelyn that she didn't really like Joe Kennedy but was realistic about his attraction to her—and also a little afraid of him. "Better to go along to get along," she told Mickey, who had also had a fling with her. "And maybe he'll help my career. And why get on the bad side of him? He has a mean streak, and he might blackball me!" Realistic Evelyn added, "Hell, I need *that* like a hole in the head!" But Joe's involvement with Evelyn followed the usual pattern. He courted her (but never in public, always at his Rodeo Drive house, where Eddie Moore delivered her on order), bedded her, for a while was sexed up by her, and then (to Evelyn's relief) dropped her. Evelyn told Mickey: "It's always better when the guy decides *he* wants to get rid of you—*you* get off the hook and no one's feelings get hurt!"

Joe, a little contrite because he had tired of Evelyn Brent rather abruptly after a few weeks, helped her to get better parts; he also gave her jewelry (which Evelyn, according to Mickey, sold after hard times hit her in the 1930s).

Phyllis Haver, who had bedded with Jimmy Quirk years earlier, was introduced to Joe by Jimmy, and it was off to the races with Phyllis for a while. Phyllis complained that Joe wasn't so hot at sex—it was too much the slam-bam-thank-you-ma'am kind for her. Adela St. Johns, a good friend of Phyllis, told her that he was probably more tender when he was in love. "I don't think he's in love with me, and thank goodness he isn't!" Phyllis told Adela. "*I'm* certainly not in love with *him!*"

Phyllis soon went the way of the other Hollywood women Joe consorted with in the 1925–1927 period, during which he also managed to conceive, with Rose, Bobby and Jean.

Joe's ulcers continued to plague him during this period—ulcers born of the constant intracoastal activity and also his subconscious guilts over his sex drive and his craving for variety in sexual partners. Adolph Zukor thought him a hypocrite, both personally and professionally, and told Jimmy Quirk that once at a Beverly Hills dinner party, Joe had expounded on the necessity of a strong family and parents' sound influences on their children, and even forced Zukor into a suppressed laugh with his variation on the saw, "Bring up a child in the way he should go and he shall not depart from it when grown"—a great favorite with the Catholic clergy for whom Joe would always have a secret contempt. (Jackie Kennedy later admitted that she had picked up from her father-in-law her tart observation about priests being "silly little men running around in black suits.") Zukor, who knew of Joe's womanizing and his cheap-jack practices at FBO, was not fooled as to his essential character.

Jack Warner heard from Tom Mix about Joe's mean financial practices. "I asked him for what I felt was an honest raise—he had me going from picture to picture—and he said, 'Don't jew me that way!' And who was more 'jewy' as he put it, than that money-mad mick!" Joe also waxed miserly about camera setups and back lots and sets and cafeteria equipment and anything and everything that came up. Fred Thomson, his cowboy star, confronted with a lecture from Joe on his "expensive" outfits, sharply rejoined, "Joe, don't worry—*you* don't have to pay for them!"

Many authors have tackled Joe Kennedy's wheeler-dealing in Hollywood from 1925 to 1931; some readers find his endless advances and withdrawals, manipulations and going-along-for-the-ride periods enthralling; others find it boring. But here is a—bear with me, folks—hopefully succinct account of Hollywood's Joe-come-lately.

From the beginning, Joe was in the business for the money. He had no altruistic attitudes about art and class, allowing for his brief detour with Erich Von Stroheim's disastrous *Queen Kelly* during his enthrallment with—and later desertion of—Gloria Swanson.

Joe considered the reigning Hollywood potentates—the likes of Goldwyn, Loew, Mayer, Zukor—"a bunch of pants-pressers," a reference to their early years in various areas of the garment industry. He claimed that they had no money sense, that they wasted extravagant sums on chancy movies—ignoring the fact that these men and their advisers had a very canny and shrewd awareness of what people in the 1920s wanted in film fare and film personalities. "Pants-pressers" they might have been in the long-gone past, but they had distinctly risen above their early environments and were now living on lavish estates, making frequent trips to Europe—in short they were Hollywood's aristocracy. The stars might have the publicity and prestige, but real power lay with the producers and their New York offices and financial backers.

Joe hightailed it to Hollywood in early 1926, took a fancy Beverly Hills house as an operating headquarters, and kept his cadre of "Horsemen" (as he called them) busy serving his various needs. These high-class flunkies included his assistant Eddie Moore. Eddie was entirely devoted to his boss, swore often and to all comers that he would give his life for him. Joe returned his affection. "I think Eddie Moore was the only man Joe Kennedy really loved," Mickey Neilan told me years later.

Joe called his flunkies the Four Horsemen after the Valentino film. Far from being famine, war, pestilence, and death, however, they embodied the superloyal service that Joe absolutely required. Along with Eddie Moore, there was E. B. Derr, one of the great financial calculators, prognosticators, and sly dogs of his time on whose money judgments Joe placed great store. Then there was Charlie Sullivan, who "looked like a typical Irish cop," Gloria Swanson later remembered, and who was dog and slave to Joe night and day. The fourth Horseman was Ted O'Leary, who looked and acted as dirt common as any East Boston street cleaner but who had the canny business sense, underworld connections, and beat-them-to-the-draw methods that Joe needed in a surrogate running his underground (due to Prohibition) liquor interests in America and abroad.

Joe's movies were in many ways the laughing stock of Hollywood. There were "gorilla goes wild" monster pictures and lots of superficial adventure movies and horse operas galore. Only Fred Thomson gave his pictures any semblance of class, but good guy that Fred was, no one claimed any cerebral or artistic quality of any kind existed in his movies. Joe often hired other stars on a whim. When told that Red Grange, the football hero, would make a lousy movie star (who would want to see him in a movie when anyone could get at him in person on a playing field, went the prevailing logic), Joe asked his sons Joe Jr. and Jack what *they* thought of Red as a possible movie star, and their enthusiastic thumbs up sold Joe into signing Red, whose trashy movies proceeded to make Joe Kennedy oodles of money.

In the late 1920s, realizing that consolidations were the name of the coming game, Joe persuaded the RCA mogul, David Sarnoff, to buy into his Film Booking Offices for a half million, after which he went to the grumpy, widely disliked mogul Edward Albee of KAO (Keith-Albee-Orpheum) and offered to buy 200,000 shares of Albee's company stock for $4.2 million. Albee didn't like Kennedy and at first wanted nothing to do with his propositions. The future adopted father of the famous playwright was something of a sharpie and shellacker himself, and he sensed danger. Then adverse business conditions forced Albee to do an about-face, and he sold out to Joe, who then appointed himself chief executive officer of the new amalgamated whatever-it-was. (Joe once jokingly remarked that with all the amalgamations and consolidations, he hadn't taken time out to find a name for whatever behemoth-hybrid he was presiding over at a given time.)

Not satisfied with being boss of Keith-Albee-Orpheum, Joe refused to abdicate as big boss of his parent outfit FBO and instead went on to become Pathé's "special advisor." Pathé was another of those lesser film companies dependent on the box-office clout of a few stars but shaky on its corporate-finance end. Mid 1928 found the ever money-conscious Joe making good salaries from all three of his firms—estimates at the time had him making $2,000 a week at Pathé, $2,000 a week at FBO, and $2,000 a week at KAO (Joe always liked his figures round and clear and accessible). This assured him (as per his canny thinking on such matters) more that $300,000 a year in takeout salaries alone.

In addition to his work for the three firms, Joe was also in charge of Gloria Productions from 1928 to late 1930. A disillusioned Gloria Swanson, doubling at this time as both paramour and partner, would later estimate that Joe had left her to foot the bills, stashing away the fancy profits for himself. When Gloria finally left Hollywood for keeps around 1938 and figured out all her assets, she was to find herself with a total of $250,000 (which she managed shrewdly, $250,000 buying a lot more in 1938 than in 1996, to be sure). Joe Kennedy, on the other hand, had walked away from her and his other Hollywood associates and ventures with millions.

Joe went on milking Pathé for all it was worth and demanded a new title: chairman of the board. Next, in the early 1930s, he went on to First National, demanding an annual salary of $150,000. When it came to Hollywood, Joe knew his wheeler-dealing. But by the time he made his final Hollywood exit in 1931, Joe Kennedy left Hollywood no more artistically richer than he had found it.

Meanwhile the "pants-pressers" (who returned the compliment by calling him a pushy, dishonest "mick") managed, along their moneymaking way, to turn out some films of genuine artistic quality. In 1931 the running Hollywood joke was that the only man in town who had ever made a fool of Joseph P. Kennedy was the redoubtable Erich Von Stroheim, who cost Joe more than $700,000 for the truncated *Queen Kelly*. (Joe, typically, had passed that loss on to Gloria Swanson, as she later found out to her chagrin. "In that three-person card game, *I* was the long-term loser," Gloria later sneered to Mickey Neilan.)

As of October 1928, Joe was far from through with his amalgamations and monkey business. Seeing the inevitability of the talkie boom (talkies came in full force in 1929 and any leave-over silents were dead as doornails), Joe merged KAO and FBO with RCA Photophone. The result was the new

company, Radio-Keith-Orpheum. The new RKO boasted
assets of some $100 million. Joe got a "mere courtesy"
$150,000 fee for arranging it all. When David Sarnoff took
over as chief executive officer of the new RKO, Kennedy
decided he wanted out (Derr had advised him it was always
good to know when it was time to move on). He exchanged
his 75,000 shares of KAO stock for an equal stock share in
RKO. The stock at sale time was twenty-one dollars a share.
Kennedy got cronies among the Wall Street trader crew to
bull the stock to fifty dollars a share. Kennedy then went on
a selling spree, unloading both FBO and RKO stock and
affiliated holdings for a whopping total of $7 million.

Next Joe unloaded Gloria Productions—*and* Gloria. He
affected to be peeved because Gloria thought he should
have paid for the car Sidney Howard received for thinking
up the title for their last movie together, *What a Widow!* but
Joe got out of the whole relationship because his instinct,
and E.B. Derr's, told him that Gloria was getting too inquisi-
tive about the money ins and outs. One excuse served as well
as another, and by pulling the hurt, high-dudgeon act, Joe
rid himself of her. The reasons, of course, were many: he was
bored with her, wanted to move on with Nancy Carroll,
Connie Bennett, and other cinema cuties, and certain folks
back home in Massachusetts, tolerant (barely) of his more
fleeting and frivolous romantic episodes, felt the Swanson
thing to be too heavy a proposition.

Joe got out of Hollywood in 1931 far richer than he had
come in, but the continuous tension and outright fears for
his own and his family's financial future, especially during
the uncertain 1929 stock market crash period (which he had
shrewdly weathered by selling the right stocks short at the
right time, to put it simply and with a minimum of financial
jargon), had made serious inroads on his physical health.

When he went east for the last time (with several of his Horsemen defecting to major studios as tokens of their ultimate disgust and disillusionment with him), he was fifty pounds underweight (and he had never been a pudgy man) and neuritis and painful ulcers were, he claimed to the still and eternally faithful Eddie Moore, "killing me." In this period Joe, safe with his estimated ten million bucks, set up trust funds for his kids. He said in future years that he had given them each a million bucks with more to come "so they could tell me to go to hell anytime they wanted to," but Jack Kennedy in his usual cool manner later put that legend to rest by claiming that it was just another of his father's methods of "spreading the family patrimony shrewdly."

By early 1932, in acute physical pain and confined at times to hospitals for weeks with his ulcers, Joe was to demonstrate his rare, "loving" side by informing the masochistically loyal Eddie Moore that the Kennedys' new son would be named after him.

There is a story that Ed Gargan enjoyed repeating about his aunt Rose. When informed in Joe's usual peremptory, paterfamilias style that the new baby boy born February 22, 1932, would be named after Eddie Moore, Rose said, "Fine and dandy—god knows he deserves it after the way you have treated him for years—but where *I'm* concerned, there will be *no more babies*! I'm forty-one and I want a permanent rest. I want travel, good clothes, lots of help for the kids, and *you* are to *get out of my bed and stay out!*" Rose had put up with his infidelities, his month-long absences in Hollywood, the Gloria thing, "and all the rest of the nonsense," as she put it, long enough, and from 1932 on she would be her own woman.

After spending part of 1931 dallying with Nancy Carroll and Connie Bennett, both of whom shortly got the heaveho, Joe began availing himself of the 1931 equivalent of call girls. There were some excellent services in New York, and through his friend Jimmy Quirk, who continued secretly financing one on West Fifty-Eighth Street, Joe met up with some acquiescent lovelies who helped relieve his ulcers and other tensions.

By 1932 his cronies and companions on the woman prowl, Jimmy Quirk and Ray Long, had both fallen on relatively hard times. Too much smoking and drinking, and catastrophic losses sustained in the crash, along with a chronically tricky heart, had taken a toll on Jimmy Quirk. Ray Long had lost his job at the magazine he had made famous, *Cosmopolitan*, and was floundering around doing "self-employed" stints and contemplating what turned out to be a disastrous hegira in the South Seas. Joe had tried to advise Jimmy to be careful with his stock market dealings but Jimmy did not have the business head Joe had (neither did Ray), and he found things tight, though he still owned (on paper) the controlling interest in *Photoplay* that he had obtained in 1926 and still drew a high salary from the corporation.

Jimmy and May Allison went to Hollywood in late May 1932, where Jimmy was to fight (to a hung-jury conclusion) a frivolous lawsuit brought by the mother of actress Alma Rubens, who had died of drug addiction the year before; the mother claimed *Photoplay* had downgraded the guest list at Alma's funeral. Jimmy had reacted with more inner tensions than the lawsuit was worth, went to the Bohemian Grove revels outside San Francisco, came back to Hollywood with a heavy cold, had a sudden heart attack, and within three days was dead (August 1, 1932).

Jimmy had two wakes and funerals, in Hollywood and New York, and Joe Kennedy was on hand to comfort May Allison and the family during the New York services. My mother and father remembered him as solicitous, concerned, and singing Jimmy's praises. He also seemed, along with Roy Howard, quite solicitous of May's welfare, and soon there were stories that Joe Kennedy was showing up at the Buckingham Hotel with roses and affectionate messages for May.

"Widows are a new speed for Joe, especially forty-two-year-old ones!" Ray Long observed. Joe was to get nowhere—but nowhere—with May.

After Jimmy's New York wake and funeral, May decided that, at forty-two, a face lift was in order, and she holed up for several months in her Buckingham Hotel apartment until she was "fit to be seen in public." It was the perfect time for a face lift, she told Miriam Hopkins, her close friend, because no one expected to see her out and about so soon after Jimmy's death.

"Joe was constantly on the telephone with May," Adela St. Johns remembered. And when she began to get around again in December, he invited her up for family gatherings with Rose and the kids. "The Nancy Carroll thing was over by then, and after wading through a few floozies, Joe decided he would find out firsthand what Jimmy had seen in May years before," Mickey Neilan remembered. "Of course May was in her forties by then and Joe's taste went to younger women, but she kept herself up so well, looked so youthful and vivacious, that he decided she would make a good addition to his conquests."

But May Allison, shrewd and practical, had other ideas as of late 1932. Jimmy had left the control of *Photoplay's* stock to his first wife and Kay Dee. May, to her chagrin, had been cut off with a $50,000 insurance policy that she soon used up. She had always enjoyed a lavish style of living and had long since spent up her earnings as a film star. A consummate survivor, she was determined to bag herself a rich man.

But no "back street" lady was May. She wanted marriage, and all the security that went with it. "I told her there was nothing for her from the estate," Kay Dee remembered, "and threw her some article assignments to get her a little money, though editors had to fix up the articles to make them professional-looking!"

Humiliated and angered, May, according to Adela St. Johns, cried on the shoulder of the enterprising and tough Miriam Hopkins, who had achieved Hollywood talkie stardom after a rewarding stage career in the 1920s. Miriam knew everyone in Hollywood *and* New York, was forever between husbands, and was particularly notorious for the wild parties she had thrown in her apartment in Greenwich Village's one and only stone house, at 105 Waverly Place— parties that attracted the famous and notorious in the twenties, where Jim and May had frequently been guests.

Miriam went through her address book and, according to Adela, did a thorough analysis of the situation. She agreed that May was unsuited temperamentally for a role in the latest Joe Kennedy affair and finally persuaded Joe to leave May alone by stressing that May wanted marriage and security and could conceivably shoot off her mouth to Rose if Joe didn't leave her alone. Joe made one more try, though. He knew May was desperately in need of money and offered her a generous series of loans, but as Adela remembered it, May "didn't want to be beholden to him, fearing he would take advantage." Finally Joe gave up on May.

Miriam Hopkins came up with the solution—and the man—for May. He was Carl Norton Osborne, a wealthy Cleveland industrialist who, at the time (inconveniently), happened to be married. Gossip had it, though, that the marriage was in its final death throes, so Miriam introduced Carl to May. The occasion was one of Miriam's more sedate

1933 New York parties. Miriam was always good at setting and timing, and she knew May was after the main event. Deeply smitten with May, Carl Osborne sped up the divorce he had long been intent upon, and in March 1934, he and May were married in an Elkton, Maryland, elopement. "It couldn't have come at a better time," Adela St. Johns remembered. "May was too old by then for leading lady status on stage or in films [she was pushing forty-four] and she didn't really want to go back to acting. The writing assignments paid her peanuts and she was almost broke. Osborne, the new hubby, was the knight to the rescue."

Osborne insisted that his wife forget all about Hollywood and her previous life as Mrs. Jimmy Quirk. He forbade mention of the past. May took up her position in Cleveland society as the new Mrs. Carl Norton Osborne, and while some of his prior wife's friends snubbed her at first, she managed in time to solidify her position—and her new identity. She died at age ninety-eight in 1989.

FOUR

Enter Gloria

When Gloria Swanson arranged to meet Joe Kennedy at New York's Savoy Plaza hotel in November 1927, she had no idea what she was getting into—a three-year affair-cum business partnership that would begin promisingly and end disastrously.

Jimmy Quirk had been worried about Gloria for more than a year and a half, from the time she walked out of her highly lucrative Paramount deal, refusing to sign a new contract that would have paid her a fortune each year. Instead, Gloria had elected to make films on her own, along the lines of "to the box-office magnet should accrue the profits." But Gloria had no business head, and after struggling through her first independent for United Artists, *The Loves of Sunya*, which had done relatively disappointing business, and then going arty with a film version of Somerset Maugham's play, *Rain*, retitled *Sadie Thompson*, Gloria was baffled by her financial situation. In 1926 the idea of being an independent star along with Mary Pickford, Douglas Fairbanks, and other

United Artists personalities had seemed mighty enticing; the financial fallout, the numerous charges and distribution costs had proved a letdown and, by late 1927, a threat to the affluent life she had achieved. Extravagant and high-living with luxurious tastes, Gloria found that the prestige of independence was offset by the financial complications implicit in producing her own films.

Gloria had fought her way up from small roles in 1915 to leading lady status and finally stardom in the early and middle 1920s; among her mentors along the way had been Cecil B. De Mille, in whose lavish romantic conceptions she had shone.

Millions of American women adored Gloria in the twenties; she had often led the lists of women's—and not a few men's—cinematic favorites. In 1915 Jimmy Quirk had predicted: "There's a big potential in that tiny girl!" A reigning clotheshorse deluxe, she starred in films that enthralled the feminine contingent with their girl-loves-boy, loses-boy, gets-boy-back-again plot motifs interspersed with glamor tales of girls of humble origin rising in the world to clothes, mansions, foreign cars, and handsome, ostensibly unattainable men. Gloria was the leading feminine sensation of 1920s films.

She was less lucky in her marriages, however. Her first, at seventeen, was to Wallace Beery, later a famed character star who in 1916 was a comedian; Beery tricked her into a painful abortion, behaved, as she put it later "with absolute boorishness," and found himself booted out within two years of the marriage. Then had come restaurateur Herbert Somborn, twice her age, whom she didn't really love. Their marriage lasted but a few years, and she said later that she recalled his devotion to their only child, Gloria, as his one redeeming quality.

By 1925, Paramount's top star, she returned in triumph from Paris to a tumultuous Hollywood reception as the Marquise de la Falaise. Her nobleman husband had no money and no particular ambition, but he boasted one talent: the ability to marry himself off to wealthy American film stars (he later married Constance Bennett when she was at the height of her stardom in the early 1930s). Gloria reveled in her new title (she soon had fellow stars Mae Murray and Pola Negri title hunting too), telling her mother and others that she was twenty-six years old, had it all, and where was there to go?

By 1928 she had gone in two directions: to independent production of her films and to the arms of Joe Kennedy.

Jimmy Quirk had a friend, Bob Kane, arrange the Swanson-Kennedy meeting, after discussing with Joe Kennedy Swanson's financial plight, the uncertain future she faced after bluenose censorship of the soon-to-be-released *Sadie Thompson*, and her indecisiveness over future plans and projects.

Joe Kennedy amused Swanson when they first met: his Boston accent, his habit of slapping his knee and laughing heartily—sometimes too heartily—at her humorous sallies. For a man of thirty-nine, he seemed to her boyishly crude and foolishly star-struck. But soon she realized how she had underestimated this ostensibly jovial but actually tough and realistic Boston Irishman. She outlined her business problems, and he promised to look over her books and recommend business changes, including the suggestion that he set her up in a new corporation run by his methods and with his staff. She left him that night relieved and hopeful.

A few months later, when Gloria and the marquis went to Florida, Joe Kennedy got rid of the marquis, entered her bedroom uninvited, and initiated spontaneous, hasty but (as she later admitted) enjoyable lovemaking. She realized that this ruthless, determined man had taken her over personally as well as professionally—and that her life would not be the same henceforth.

Swanson later speculated on this turning point: "Why?" she asked herself. Joe had a wife and (at the time) seven children. She was a veteran of three marriages, had a daughter and an adopted son. "We were both happily married with children. We were ten years apart in age. He was a staunch [she thought] Roman Catholic, and I was married to a thoroughly unexceptionable man I had no wish [as of 1928] to divorce. Furthermore, we had no domestic feelings for each other. In fact, at that instant [of their first lovemaking session in the Florida hotel bedroom] we would both probably have liked to have an extra life to live so we wouldn't have to forfeit the one we were already living!"

As she remembered, "All arguments were useless, however. I knew perfectly well that whatever adjustments or deceits must inevitably follow, the strange man beside me, more than my husband, owned me."

Hollywood chronicler Adela Rogers St. John said to me many years later concerning the Swanson-Kennedy affair: "She thought he would be her protector, that he would free her from all financial worries, that he would be always there for her. What she perceived at the time to be his strength of personality sealed her to him—for a time. She wanted to be safe; he represented just that, safety."

Incorrigible womanizer that he was, Joe Kennedy was delighted with his prestigious new conquest. This was not just another of his cheap floozies, not another of his little waiflike, also-ran actresses, but a world-famous star, a powerhouse celebrity. No, he could never marry her, but he had bagged himself a bigger movie star than his friend Jimmy Quirk. Yes, May Allison had been a catch, and Jimmy had even married her, but Swanson—she was (in the 1920s) bigger than any of them, and she was his, all his.

Gloria soon discovered that Joe Kennedy was a consummate egomaniac who lived by his own rules. He insisted that she visit him and his wife Rose and their kids at the Cape. He took her out on a family yacht and made love to her—while his twelve-year-old son John looked on from below deck, then made his wild swim toward shore.

Meanwhile their business association flourished, but creatively it took an uncertain turn. Gloria nailed Joe down decisively when she wrote of him: "Much as I cared for [Joe] he was a classic example of that person in the arts with lots of brains and drive but little taste or talent."

Sadie Thompson, which had come out under her auspices, was a critical success. Joe had had mixed feelings about it; not only had it been completed before they were associated, but also he had been one of those producers who signed a hypocritical, moralistic petition condemning it before its release. Gloria had playfully twitted him on this and had disconcerted him by her blasé, condescending attitude toward the speechmaking-by-movie-bigs project he had sponsored at Harvard, making him wince by commenting, "Adolph Zukor and Marcus Loew at Harvard? Well, that sure must have been something to see!"

Smarting under her none-too-subtle allusion that his film-producing career had hardly been prestigious, Joe was only too happy to take on arty director Erich Von Stroheim, who had proposed to Swanson an exciting new story. Jimmy Quirk, whom Joe had consulted about Stroheim and the project, warned him that Von was a difficult artist who wasted much film, did endless reshoots, and insisted on injecting sensational aspects into such films as *The Merry Widow*, a 1925 Mae Murray success in which foot fetishism figured largely. His *Greed* had been ruthlessly cut by Metro-Goldwyn-Mayer:

though a masterpiece, it had run four or five times as long as the longest films then extant. As of 1928, Von Stroheim was considered too difficult, and there was hesitancy to employ him on the part of many film moguls, who summed up their opinion of Von with "he's just too much!"

Jimmy Quirk understood Von Stroheim thoroughly. "He is a genius," Jimmy said of him, "but he has the virtues of his defects and the defects of his virtues." Jimmy's verdict on the celebrated *Greed*, shared with his *Photoplay* readers, was: "It reeks of good acting and wonderful direction." Jimmy added, "If [Von] could only get rid of that little mental twist that inspires him to show dead cats instead of morning glories open to the sun, there wouldn't be a director who could surpass him!"

Gloria wanted a critically exceptional picture, a genuine prestige success, and after hearing from Von the plot of *Queen Kelly* (at the time "graced" by a tentative title, *The Swamp*, no less), she persuaded Joe to produce it. Needled by Gloria about his lowlife approach to films, Joe was all for it. "It will be just great to be producer of an *art* work!" he told Jimmy enthusiastically.

The plot dealt with a convent girl seduced by a prince. His jealous queen evicts her from the palace, and she throws herself into a river and drowns. Later the plot would get Swanson's character to an African bordello and married to an ugly old cripple. And so on and so on. Gloria knew that trouble was afoot when in one scene she threw her panties at her leading man and he gently wafted them across his face. This was just a mild example of the "perverse" stuff Von was insinuating into the film. In wild hysteria Gloria called Joe in New York and begged him to close down the film. (It was later rescued and revamped by Swanson and shown in Europe in the early 1930s.) Gloria and Joe found that by shutting down the film they had lost hundreds of thousands of dollars, and Gloria later recalled that this had sent Joe into a long-standing fit of profound depression. He hated to fail, and here he had failed resoundingly.

Seeking to take up the slack, Gloria selected a smart, modern film, *The Trespasser*, to take advantage of the 1929 talkie boom and put herself on top again. With director Edmund Goulding and Laura Hope Crews, she wrote the screenplay, and under Goulding's direction she had herself a scintillating hit as a woman who—yes—loves, loses, and gets back again the father of her son after the man's crippled wife, to whom he is unhappily married, conveniently dies.

Joe Kennedy's nose was out of joint. Though nominally *The Trespasser*'s producer, he knew it had been Gloria's conception. The film he had hoped so much for (*Queen Kelly*) had been a disaster. Thinking to regain his lost ground—and his pride—he forced Gloria to agree to a weak comedy, *What a Widow!*—one of the less distinguished film offerings of 1930, which featured Joe Kennedy's name as producer in some fancy artwork that drew more laughter than praise when the credits rolled.

Meanwhile, on the personal front, Joe had insisted that Gloria and the marquis accompany him and Rose to Europe, a trip that would include the London premiere of *The Trespasser*. The idea of combining wife and mistress on a European trip seemed to Gloria the most blatant example yet of Joe's disregard for convention; he had further shocked her by suggesting that they have a child out of wedlock.

Swanson found Rose, on that trip as on other occasions, motherly, family-oriented, wrapped up in domestic concerns, her kids, and Paris fashions. She gave no hint that she knew what was going on between Gloria and her husband. Gloria later wondered: "Was [Rose] a fool? A Saint? Or just a better actress than I was?"

The truth was that Rose knew, was deeply hurt, but determined to maintain her position and tolerate the situation. Jimmy Quirk felt sorry for her and warned Joe that he was going too far, but Joe would not be dissuaded from doing things *his* way.

Swanson years later would tell of the strange encounter she had with Boston's Cardinal William O'Connell, who summoned her to a New York hotel suite and informed her that Joe had asked church authorities if it were possible to terminate his marriage—but without a divorce—and maintain separate living quarters with Swanson. The cardinal waxed very moralistically, but she cuttingly informed him that Joe was the Catholic, not she, and the cardinal should be taking the matter up with Joe. Whereupon she walked out.

By 1930, matters, in any event, were winding down for Gloria and Joe. The failure of the film he had so enthusiastically urged upon her, *What a Widow!*, dealt yet another blow to Joe's elephantine pride, and the silences in the Hollywood mansion where they met for their trysts grew starker and more frequent.

Swanson then began to discover that Joe was charging to her account presents he had allegedly given her, and when she had the temerity (as he saw it) to ask him why a car he had given writer Sidney Howard for naming *What a Widow!* had been charged to *her* account, he walked out and refused to see her again. Shortly thereafter he returned papers relating to their professional association and terminated it officially.

Years later it was revealed that John F. Fitzgerald had been growing increasingly irritated with the extended Joe-Gloria dalliance, felt it more than usually insulting to Rose, and demanded Joe end it or he would publicly expose him. Jimmy Quirk also advised Joe to end it, feeling that it had run its course and was harming all concerned. Joe had been planning to get out of the movie business anyway, with his profits of millions. Jimmy Quirk told Joe that he didn't really have a talent or feel for films of better quality, however clever he might be in the profits department, and Joe, humiliated and chagrined, felt he should take the money and run. By 1931 he had done just that.

Gloria recalled that she had sensed the beginning of the end even before the Sidney Howard car incident. She had brought up the subject of Joe's retarded eleven-year-old child Rosemary, recommending some special treatments of which she had heard, and Joe's whole personality changed. He became brutal and cutting and told her she was never again to bring up the subject. "He thought of Rosemary as another of his failures—to be the father of a *retard*—that was humiliating," Gloria's friend, actress Lois Wilson, said years later. "Gloria should have sensed right at that point what kind of man she had taken up with!"

Jimmy Quirk remained kind and understanding toward Gloria. "I have always admired Gloria Swanson," he wrote in his "Closeups and Long Shots" *Photoplay* column in January 1932. "She is courageous in a business where courage is as necessary as beauty and artistry. She has had to fight every inch of her way to her present high place in pictures. But there always seemed to be something pathetic about courageous, little five-foot half-inch Gloria."

In her autobiography, *Swanson on Swanson* written fifty years later in 1980, Gloria gave a telling rendition of her feelings early in 1931:

> When Joseph Kennedy left California, he claimed to have cleared millions in motion pictures and to have made me financially independent. [My accountant], however, soon made it clear that the second part of the claim, the

part about me, was not true. . . . He informed me that I was anything but rich, or even financially independent. I had been living a life of royalty but I had been paying for it out of my own earnings. . . . As the auditing proceeded, the figures began to tell the oldest story in the world. Moreover, the accounts were in an impossible tangle. It would take a year to sort them out, and it soon became clear that the Kennedy offices would provide no help in the matter.

She remembered:

It was imperative that I go back to work immediately and start recouping some of my recent losses. . . . Once again I had misjudged people and been deceived by someone I totally trusted, and I was stunned and in pain. In spite of my reputation for will and stamina and pluck and durability, all I wanted was to call for my mother, to hold my babies in my arms while I sobbed for a month, or a year for that matter, and claimed, for once, my natural right as a woman to feel nothing but vulnerable.

Meanwhile the Marquis de la Falaise, who had been dispatched to a movie executive job in Paris by Joe Kennedy to get rid of him during the height of the now-history affair and who—like Rose Kennedy—had stood by patiently while the Gloria-Joe affair ran its course, let Gloria know that their marriage was over. Soon he was squiring the hot new star Constance Bennett and later married her. Swanson's reaction to this: "It was as if the two men—my ex-husband and ex-paramour—had in some mysterious way, through me, cancelled each other out and moved on. I was completely on my own again, without love and without security."

Swanson grieved and mooned for only a short time. Determined to obey the law of self-preservation, especially with young children dependent on her, she talked herself into a contract with Joseph Schenck of United Artists and in 1931 was seen on the screen in a comedy, *Indiscreet*, and in *Tonight or Never*, a film about a temperamental opera diva, which was made under Sam Goldwyn's auspices and with the popular new leading man, Melvyn Douglas, who had appeared in the theatrical version with his wife Helen Gahagan.

Abroad for a good time in mid 1931, Swanson fell in love with a handsome Irish playboy, Michael Farmer, and married him. Unfortunately a premarriage pregnancy had occurred, and when she asked for time off (her daughter Michele was born in April 1932), Schenck canceled her contract. Farmer, she found, was an overgrown child, and the marriage didn't last long. She later wrote of him: "I had four children, not three, and the grown-up one was like the little girl with the curl. When he was bad, I almost couldn't bear him."

While nursing her new baby, Gloria, during the Democratic convention in the summer of 1932, got a surprise call from Joe Kennedy, who—full of gall and insensitive as ever given the circumstances of their last encounter— wanted her to meet the new Democratic candidate Franklin D. Roosevelt. When she told Joe she was busy with the care of Michele, he countered that he had a new baby, too, Edward Moore, who had debuted two months before Michele, in February. Appalled and disgusted by his insensitivity and obvious name dropping with FDR, she cut short the international phone call.

The Swanson-Kennedy encounters were to be few and far between as the years went on. She had occasion to ask his permission to sell *The Trespasser* to Warners around 1937—it became a Bette Davis vehicle with a new title, *That Certain Woman*—and he officiously and elaborately granted that permission from abroad with a pompous, condescending communication.

Her son Joseph—adopted in 1922 long before her meeting with Kennedy and named for her father, *not* Joe—later received help when he was in the service after Gloria asked Joe Kennedy to use his connections. Other than this, she and Joe kept their respective distances.

Gloria's career was on the downgrade in the 1932–1934 period. She had sold her United Artists stock to finish her production, *Perfect Understanding*, in England (her leading man was the twenty-five-year-old Laurence Olivier), and it did not do well in America when released in early 1933. She signed a contract with MGM but nothing came of it, especially after her mentor Irving Thalberg's death in 1936. There was but one loan-out from MGM, to Fox in 1934, for *Music in the Air*, a musical that did not do well. Later Gloria went to New York, where she did television work. She was called back for one picture, *Father Takes a Wife*, for RKO in 1941. "I got only $35,000 for it," she said later, "and that was $35,000 more than anyone else in Hollywood had offered me for years!"

At this time, she had heard that "the long arm of Joe Kennedy had been reaching out to prevent me getting any picture breaks," but Schenck, Louis B. Mayer, and other executives had only contempt for Kennedy and concern for the woman he had deserted, and disregarded his meddling. After the 1934 *Music in the Air*, it was obvious that Kennedy had relegated her to the past. "He thought I was through," she later said bitterly. "Had I gone on being successful it would have been like a reproach to him; it would have affronted his ego. And did that man have an ego!"

No one was more surprised—and chagrined—than Joe Kennedy when Gloria, at fifty, made her smash comeback in

Sunset Boulevard. "I thought she was out of the picture for good!" was his half-annoyed, half-dumbfounded observation. "Now here she is again! . . ."

I knew Gloria well beginning in 1949 when I as a Boston reporter interviewed her while she was making a tour for another Paramount picture (*The Heiress*). She had finished *Sunset Boulevard* that year, and its advent in 1950 made her a star to reckon with yet again. I was struck by her humor, resiliency, and philosophical approach to life. "I've been to Boston only a few times," she said reflectively. "But it has its associations . . ." (Joe Kennedy?) In that first 1949 interview and over the next thirty years, I found Gloria an understanding and mellow friend. Her memories of my uncle were always loving—and sad. "He died so young," she commented in 1952, "and with so much more to offer." In 1980, at the time her autobiography appeared, she told me that if she hadn't done it, too much distortion of her life would have ensued after she had passed on, and "I want it *right* and *true!*" One bit of advice she gave me I will always treasure: "There's always a fresh start! Remember that— always a fresh start! Never ruminate on negative things: age, sickness, death, money trouble. No matter how old you are, act *as if you are going to live forever.* Then life will never cease to be a beautiful, challenging adventure!" For Gloria, that indeed was what life was, from beginning to end.

FIVE

Nancy, Connie, Greta—and Joan

S wanson's immediate successor in Joe Kennedy's affections was the actress Nancy Carroll. There are differing versions of the Carroll-Kennedy meeting, but most of the evidence suggest it occurred in Palm Beach early in 1931. Nancy had been on the boat of Sport Ward, Gloria's friend, when Eddie Moore spotted her and introduced her to Joe, who for some time had been badgering Eddie to find him a new woman, preferably a movie star as big or bigger than Swanson.

Since the break with Swanson, Joe, with Eddie as pimp, had enjoyed the favors of an assortment of women, some of them prostitutes, some merely qualifying as "loose women" (a popular designation in 1931). But Joe was tired of slumming sexually and wanted bigger, classier game. Nancy found herself elected. Nancy, who was to marry three times, once to playwright Jack Kirkland, was temporarily up for grabs. Bored and restless, Nancy, then twenty-six, tried to come on sophisticated and soigné but was at heart rather vulnerable and at times self-destructively romantic.

Joe fed her the usual "my wife doesn't understand me" routine, and when Nancy asked about Swanson, Joe told her they'd had a "productive business friendship" but had come to a "friendly" parting of the ways, which certainly would have been news to Gloria.

In *Swanson on Swanson*, Gloria, who heard of Joe's new liaison from Sport Ward, commented on the irony that she and Nancy had both appeared on the Oscar-nomination list in 1930. Norma Shearer had eventually won out over a field that included (in the actress category) Greta Garbo and Ruth Chatterton. "If ever there was an example of oranges and apples in the short [then] history of the Academy, that was it!" Gloria snorted. She let Sport Ward know that Nancy was welcome to Joe and that she was glad to be out of it but wished Joe would stop bad-mouthing her to power brokers on the film front.

Nancy had been born Ann Veronica La Hiff in 1904 in New York, the daughter of restaurant and night-spot entrepreneur Billy La Hiff. Her dad's connections had fostered her stagestruck ambitions, and she was in musicals by 1920, age fifteen, and at eighteen was a chorine on Broadway. At twenty-two, in 1927, she went to Hollywood, armed with the best of contacts, and appeared in a number of silents, but when talkies came in in 1929, she really hit the big time, winning plaudits and gaining fans in both singing and acting roles. Described by one pundit as "a vivacious star with flaming red hair and a cupid's-bow mouth," she had a wide following well into the 1930s and got an Oscar nomination in 1930 for *The Devil's Holiday*. In 1931 she was just the type of up-and-coming Hollywood luminary that Joe Kennedy needed to enhance his "glamorous ladies' man" image, and he kept her romantically busy for some months. Then she found herself dropped as precipitously as she had been picked up.

Eddie Moore broke the news to her in April 1931. "Joe likes you, Nancy, and it's been fun, he said to tell you, but it is better that you both move on" was his concise and to the point message. Nancy, who had been carried away by Joe's charm and authority and felt (being a born romantic by nature) that it would be exciting and "naughty" to be Joe's "back street" woman, was more than a little disappointed. *Back Street*, the Fannie Hurst novel, had made a big public splash in 1930 and by 1932 was a film starring Irene Dunne and John Boles. It dealt with a famous and successful man's loyal mistress, who languished in the "back street" while her lover held the wife and kiddies aloft for public consumption. Reportedly, Nancy wanted the role Dunne later played in *Back Street*, feeling her liaison with randy Joe was giving her the needed emotional identification with the role. But all came to naught. Nancy went into a cycle of depression, but pouted her way through such hits as *The Night Angel* and *Stolen Heaven* (both 1931), *Scarlet Dawn* (1932), and *The Kiss Before the Mirror* (1933). There were to be many men and several more marriages for Nancy the Romantic. By the late 1930s her screen career had completely fizzled for reasons largely unknown. She claimed in later years that she had lost interest in her career and was more interested in her personal life, but there were stories that she had offended folk in high places and that her indiscreet personal life was making the Hays people nervous.

I met Nancy in 1951, having sought her out for material on my uncle Jimmy Quirk, who had been one of her *sub rosa* amours along the way. Her several-times-repeated injunction to me was "don't *canonize* him in print!" This had been her rejoinder when I took exception to a comment of Nancy's that "Jimmy Quirk liked to build up [stars] then tear them down in *Photoplay*."

"Sure, he did that to *maintain interest* in the star," Nancy insisted. "Didn't he increase Garbo's fan mail and public controversy about her when he said one time in *Photoplay* that the real reason Garbo was silent was simply that she had nothing the hell to say!" I liked Nancy and found her outgoing and outspoken. She was philosophical about her career ups and downs, and when I met her, she was prominently on display in the television series *The Aldrich Family*. "My personal life always kept me more absorbed than my career," she said. "When I realized that my big-time Hollywood career was over, I took it in stride. There are other satisfactions in life besides the constant glare of publicity and constant pryings into your personal life in that game called fame."

She was frank about her sojourn with Joe Kennedy. "Joe Kennedy was a real son of a bitch. He was dictatorial and demanding and mean and wanted his fun when he wanted it, even if I were having a damn period or were otherwise indisposed. He was very much disliked in Hollywood, and knowing him as I did, it was obvious why. I didn't like his bad-mouthing Gloria and told him so. But I think the real reason he dumped me when he did was he wanted to have another kid with Rose." Senator Edward Moore Kennedy was conceived in May 1931 and debuted on Washington's Birthday, 1932. "I thought Rose was smart to stand up to him and tell him 'no more kids' after that," Nancy said. "She had given him *nine*, and hell, that was *enough*! Rose wanted to dress up, travel and party—she had had her fill of the wife-and-mommy bit, and with a gallivanting philanderer like Joe, nobody could blame her if she wanted to kick up her heels a bit." For Rose, of course, "kicking up her heels" meant the aforementioned travel, expensive clothes, and nightlife, but being the best little Catholic girl in the world, there were no men in her life, then, before, or ever after.

Nancy laughed that after nine pregnancies Rose probably didn't want to get within a mile of a man, even if he possessed finely tuned muscles and a handsome face. "Men were not her thing—no sir!" Nancy laughed, adding that she had often wished through the years that she had gone the same route. "I don't know which is more hell for a woman," Nancy snickered. "No men at all or too many of them!"

Nancy died in 1965 at age sixty. I always found her a lot of fun; she never took herself too seriously, and she had an unaffected, refreshing liking for gamy language and racy anecdotes. I remember her laughing about a 1928 silent she had done called *Chicken a la King*. "When I ran up against Joe Kennedy, I guess he was the king and I was the chicken—a helpless one. Soon enough he had chopped my head off, stripped off my feathers, and put me in the pot to boil!"

If I hadn't gotten Nancy started on Jimmy Quirk's personal didoes, the name of Joe Kennedy might not have figured so heavily in her anecdotes, but once he came into the conversation, she didn't let up. It was obvious that, two years before her death, she still harbored, even at fifty-eight, considerable bitterness toward him. "Eddie Moore was a saint," she said. "He was devoted to Joe, and I still can't figure out why that bastard could command such unswerving loyalty. But then a lot of no-goods get love and friendship and loyalty and devotion they don't deserve, damn them!"

Nancy was a great gal; though gone for more than thirty years now, she is still missed by many.

There was always to be bad blood between Gloria Swanson and Constance Bennett. Oddly, at the height of her affair with Joe Kennedy, when Joe asked Gloria's advice on potential actresses to round out his Pathé starring list, Gloria suggested he sign on Connie Bennett. She always looked back on it as one of her crucial mistakes in Amour-land because she later suspected Connie of having an affair with Joe while she and Joe were still technically an item. Later, Connie made off with and married Gloria's husband, the marquis.

Gloria recalled that she brought Connie and the marquis into each other's awareness also, back in 1925, at the Colony in New York. Awkwardly pouring some sneaked-in illegal champagne, Henri had inadvertently squirted it on Connie's bare back (she was at the next table). He and Gloria were never to forget the prime example of Connie's characteristic sharp wit when, responding to Henri's embarrassed apologies, she rejoindered: "Think nothing of it, Marquis! I never complain about bathing in champagne!"

Connie was the eldest of the three Bennett daughters, the other two being Joan, who was to become an equally celebrated actress, and Barbara, who married the singer Morton Downey. Daughter of matinee idol Richard Bennett, Connie hit the movies at seventeen in 1922 and went on to success in the silents; after three years off the screen, during her marriage to steamship heir Phil Plant, she came back to conquer the talkies in 1929 and by the early 1930s was one of the highest-paid actresses on the screen.

Connie had a husky, languorous voice and a pert, often sardonic manner. Equally good in comedy and drama, she was also one of the queens of the early 1930s movie soaps, often figuring in stories where guys did her wrong but she survived anyway.

After leaving films for the stage in 1951, she later operated a cosmetics company under her name, and after a final "comeback" supporting role in Lana Turner's *Madame X*, she died suddenly of a cerebral hemorrhage in 1965. I once told her sister Joan Bennett (I was tendering her a James R. Quirk Award for Lifetime Achievement at Roosevelt House in 1990) that Connie was a tough interview, interjecting wisecracks and turning the interview around to ask *me* personal questions, and she said, "That was Connie—always out for the laugh and the put-down!" (Joan and Connie, rival stars, had their sisterly ups and downs over the years.)

Obviously Joe Kennedy followed up quickly on Gloria Swanson's original suggestion that he sign up Connie, for Gloria was to recall "tripping over" Connie in the foyer of Joe's Rodeo Drive house when she came for dinner with Joe and Vincent Youmans. The meeting was a tense one, and gabby, effervescent Connie was unusually laconic. When Connie beat a quick exit, Gloria asked Joe what Connie was doing there. "Going out with one of the boys," he winked, as she recalled. "She couldn't hook the boss so she settled for one of the boys!" But according to Eddie Moon and others (this was mid 1930 and Joe and Gloria's affair was in its latter stages), Connie was one of Joe's girls—for a brief while. But her keen put-down wit turned Joe off later. Gloria was to learn of the Connie involvement later from Edmund Goulding (no secret was ever safe around Eddie).

By 1931, with Gloria and the marquis divorcing, news came from Paris that Connie Bennett had snagged him. They were later married. The marriage dragged on for some years, then Henri wanted out. Gloria had the satisfaction of helping Henri finalize the divorce in America, because the French laws regarding divorce were complex. It later turned out that his marriage to Connie was never legal, since his divorce from Gloria had not been final, so his third wife, Emmita, as Gloria related gleefully in her memoirs, was actually the *second* Marquise de la Falaise de la Coudraye, not the *third*. Thus Gloria had a belated revenge on Connie for fiddling with Joe behind her back in 1930.

Greta Garbo came next on Joe's list of conquest-obsessions. When Jimmy Quirk told him that he and May had persuaded the Withdrawn One to attend one of their parties in late 1931, Joe was on tenterhooks. Garbo canceled out, then changed her mind, and when she finally arrived, she looked about nervously and tentatively. Having made the usual hellos and how-are-yous, she retired to a corner of the drawing room.

Joe was soon at her side. He kept up a line of hectic small talk, recounting his more platonic and businesslike experiences on the Hollywood scene. Jimmy remembered that Joe looked more and more deflated as he realized that he was boring Garbo. Soon May, sparkling and scintillating as ever, was over making amusing small talk to defuse the situation and help Garbo to relax.

Suddenly Garbo excused herself to go to the bathroom. The apartment had only two bathrooms, one in May's quarters and one in Jim's, used respectively by the female and male guests. Garbo remained in May's bathroom. An hour went by and the door was still locked while silence reigned within. "Greta!" May called every ten minutes or so, but still there was no reply.

Soon the women and men at the party were using the same bathroom off Jim's bedroom suite. Still Garbo did not emerge. Nor did she emerge until the last guest had gone, hours later. Then she came out quickly, as May recalled, gathered up her wrap and made a quick exit.

"Joe, you pushed too hard," May told the abashed and for once deflated Mr. Kennedy on the phone the next day. "You can't come on to *her* the usual way."

"I guess not," he replied in a tone that (for him) was muted, adding "you should have rehearsed me, May."

Determined to add Garbo to his list of conquests, Joe was not a man to give up. The next time he was in Hollywood he tried to get on the set of *Grand Hotel*, but Garbo heard of it and made herself thoroughly incommunicado. An irritated Mayer told his minions to "get that mick the hell out of the studio." Joe saw Garbo several more times at various gatherings, but even "the man who gets what he wants" had to eventually concede that *this* lady would be forever beyond his reach. .

Later, when the depression deepened, Joe heard that Garbo had lost some of her carefully saved MGM earnings at a defaulting bank. He let her business manager know that he was always good for any "tide-over" loan Garbo might conceivably need. Soon the answer came back, and it was not what he had hoped. It was to the effect that "Miss Garbo appreciates Mr. Kennedy's concern but she has ample funds at hand."

"What the fuck is it going to take to get that damned mick to leave Greta alone!" Mayer raged.

When Jimmy and May made their annual trip to Hollywood late in the spring of 1932, Joe asked Jimmy to try again to "put in a good word for me," and again May Allison was enlisted. But Garbo would have none of it, and soon she was off to Sweden, having completed *As You Desire Me*. Many reasons were given for her withdrawal to her native land, where she stayed for a full year, and Eddie Mannix joked that "she did it to get the hell away from Joe Kennedy!"

When Garbo returned in mid 1933, it was to make a favorite project of hers, *Queen Christina*, based on the legendary seventeenth-century Swedish monarch who wore men's clothes, converted later to Catholicism in Rome after abdicating, and won herself a historical reputation as a garish eccentric—all of which appealed to Garbo. The film's screenwriters left out the trek to Rome and the conversion to Catholicism and instead worked in a romantic hefty role for John Gilbert as the Spanish ambassador with whom Garbo falls in love; after a duel with Ian Keith, his rival for the queen's favors, he dies on the ship taking the lovers away, after which Garbo goes to the prow. In a famous fadeout close-up, the camera holds the face of the century closely and attentively as she stares into the mist. Rouben Mamoulian, the director, reportedly told Garbo to "think of nothing—just nothing" while the lens made love to her. Howard Strickling later laughed that the serenity and composure on the famous features just might have been occasioned by the happy thought that she had gotten away, for keeps, from the unwanted attentions of Joe Kennedy. Joe had maintained an uncharacteristically discouraged silence a few weeks earlier when the candy, flowers, and jewelry he sent her were summarily returned. It was one of the very few times Joe Kennedy admitted to being thoroughly licked.

Joan Crawford told me that Joe Kennedy had tried to put the make on her, too, in late 1931, at a time when she was cuckolding hubby Doug Fairbanks Jr. by her secluded assignations with Clark Gable, her on-again, off-again co-star with whom she was madly in love.

"Joe got my phone number and kept calling me and calling me," Joan laughed, "but I always had some excuse to duck him."

"If she can cheat on Doug with Gable why not cheat on him with me?" Joe asked Eddie Mannix, who dared to shoot back that she probably found Gable more attractive. But on this Joe managed to get in the last word. "At least I have my own teeth—that's more than can be said for *him*!" Joe snorted. (Gable's teeth had gone rotten a year or so before, and Mayer had ordered that he get them extracted in favor of false teeth.)

Years later, when Joan Crawford got to know other members of the Kennedy clan, including young Jack Kennedy, she was tempted to tell Jack, who was womanizing up a storm in Hollywood of the 1940s, that (like son, like father) his dad had once "come on" to her. "But I thought better of it," she said. "I had heard that Joe could be very nasty when he heard gossip about him—*that* kind of gossip."

"What do you think was the chief ingredient in Joe's appeal to a number of women?" I once asked Joan Crawford. She was succinct but pointed in her answer: "It was that take-charge vitality!" she said.

SIX

Fred Thomson: Joe Kennedy's Only Hero

One of the few people who had good words to say about Joe Kennedy was the screenwriter Frances Marion, whom I first met in 1949 and whom I was to treasure as a friend until her death in 1973.

"There was a lot more to Joe than people realized; he was really complex," she told me. "He did a lot of kind things for people he liked and respected—things no one ever heard about. He was like Frank Sinatra that way—and Joan Crawford, for that matter. Everyone demonizes Frank and Joe, and everyone thinks Joan Crawford is the acme of ruthless self-centeredness—but they could be great to people down on their luck. And there was a vein of strong sentimentalism in them." Frances told me this back in the 1960s, a full decade before Joan's daughter Christina exposed her mother's darker side in the notorious *Mommie Dearest*, which portrayed Joan as a rampant child abuser. I had heard since the 1940s how ruthless Joan could be when her vital interests were at stake. Louella Parsons had written in her first autobiography, the 1944 *Gay Illiterate*, that while Joan could be kind and generous and do wonderful things for those down on their luck (William Haines and Marie Prevost come to mind), to Louella's mind, Joan's best creation of all was— Joan Crawford.

Sinatra too had come in for his share of knocks in the 1960s, his alleged Mafia connections, his public insults to people who crossed him, his and Peter Lawford's and the Rat Pack's pimping for—and pandering to—Jack Kennedy's notorious womanizing proclivities. Frances thought people should be reminded of the hospital bills Frank paid for indigent friends, of a thousand little personal charities he had perpetrated incognito and without publicity.

Frances was particularly sad about Joe Kennedy, who had died (November 18, 1969) only a few weeks before we talked about him. He had finally reached what Frances called "a merciful and kind oblivion" after living helpless and speechless for eight years from a stroke.

"There were only two men in all his lifetime that I feel Joe Kennedy loved all the way, with all his heart, with pure, unselfish, idealistic, friendship-love," she told me. "One was Eddie Moore, the loyal aide he had inherited from John F. Fitzgerald's entourage. The other was my husband, Fred Thomson."

Mickey Neilan agreed: "I heard that the only time anyone saw Joe cry was when Fred died. . . . It was his personal character that moved and disturbed Joe; Fred didn't drink or smoke, was faithful to his wife, screenwriter Frances Marion, had begun life as an ordained minister, and was an all-round antiseptic, rinso-white good guy. Joe didn't believe in 'good' people, thought them all phonies and hypocrites. Fred was the only one who mollified him, gave him pause."

Why had Joe loved Eddie and Fred so deeply? I asked Marion. "One, Eddie was a completely loyal friend and supporter, an aide who was with him through thick and thin. Eddie and his wife Mary were friends both he and Rose treasured above all others," she said. And Fred? "Because Joe once said to me that Fred was the only thoroughly good and decent human being he had ever known."

"Fred makes me feel humble," Frances remembered Joe saying. "I can't think of a single fault in the guy."

Frances Marion had been, of course, a famous screenwriter who had won several Oscars (for the screenplays of *The Big House* (1930) and *The Champ* (1931), both Wally Beery films). She had begun as a reporter for Hearst's *San Francisco Examiner* after acting, modeling, and ad illustration assignments. Born in 1887, she had been one of the first female war correspondents, in 1918, and had written what were later estimated to be nearly two hundred adaptations and screen treatments for noted industry stars including her close friend Mary Pickford. In the talkie era, her writing credits included *Dinner at Eight*, *Camille*, *Anna Christie*, and (as in the silents) a number of Marion Davies films. Davies's "protector," William Randolph Hearst, held Frances in the highest regard, and she evolved in time into one of Hollywood's great personages, as well as a close and valued friend of many top stars.

In 1918, still recovering from two abortive marriages that had left her, as she recalled, somewhat disillusioned with the male sex, she had followed her friend Elsie Janis's injunction to "get out of that fake Hollywood atmosphere and into life that is real, ghastly, forbidding and magnificent."

One day in that year, pal Mary Pickford asked Frances to drive her out to Santa Ana, California, where the 143rd Army Field Artillery was encamped. There she met Fred Thomson, a Presbyterian minister and regiment's chaplain. A champion field and track athlete at the time, Fred was twenty-eight to her thirty-one. As she recalled, "No one had ever written more satirically about 'love at first sight' than I, but when I unpacked that evening I began to think lyrically instead of satirically about 'love at first sight.'" Within ten days the disillusioned twice-divorcee and the chaplain determined they'd be married when the war was over. "When his regiment was ready to leave," she recalled, "we clung to the fugitive hope that we might meet somewhere in France." There was later a reunion in Paris when Fred's regiment was preparing to go to the front. She remembered their last night together, wandering the romantic Montmartre and kneeling beside her soldier in Notre Dame, within her the prayer, "Please, God, bring my Fred back to me, safe and sound."

Fred did come back, and in 1919 they were married. "Fred sacrificed a great deal because of his love for me," she remembered. "He left the ministry because there was too much ingrained prejudice about his marrying a divorced woman. But he took into our life together all the accumulated cleanness, decency and goodness that had made him an ideal clergyman and a beloved artillery chaplain."

Fred wanted to help his fellow man. He was particularly interested in bettering children's lives, mentally, spiritually, and physically. His dream was to make Westerns for youngsters. He had been a Boy Scout leader, and he wanted to create Western figures (he scorned the word "heroes") who would set the kids a good example. He wanted the violence kept within restrained limits, he wanted excitement and adventure, but Good would triumph over Evil, always. Such was Fred's ideal.

But it didn't happen at once. The year 1920 found Fred and Frances living temporarily on a farm in New York. There he found "the dapple gray hunter, seventeen

James R. Quirk, powerful and prestigious editor of *Photoplay* magazine (in 1929, left), was Joe Kennedy's film industry mentor.
COLLECTION OF LAWRENCE J. QUIRK

The 1926 marriage of Jimmy Quirk and beautiful screen star May Allison (above in Hollywood in 1932) made Joe Kennedy envious and imitative.
COLLECTION OF LAWRENCE J. QUIRK

Joe Kennedy and Jesse Lasky at Harvard, 1927. Jesse, with Jimmy Quirk, was an early Kennedy mentor in Hollywood.
COLLECTION OF LAWRENCE J. QUIRK

Jimmy Quirk and wife May Allison (in 1926 above, at right) moved with the top literati of Hollywood. In photo: producer John Emerson, left; Walter Wanger, top left; H.L. Mencken, top middle; screen star Aileen Pringle (to Allison's right); Anita Loos, in baby crib.
COLLECTION OF LAWRENCE J. QUIRK

Glamorous actress Gloria Swanson began her affair with Joe Kennedy in 1928.
ARCHIVE PHOTOS/AMERICAN STOCK

Gloria Swanson at the time she made her first talkie, *The Trespasser* (1929), which Joe produced.
PHOTOFEST

Joe Kennedy's sons
imitated his womanizing,
with tragic results.
PHOTOFEST

Joe with the Marquis de la Falaise in France, 1929. At the time, he was
cuckolding the Marquis with his wife, Gloria Swanson.
COLLECTION OF LAWRENCE J. QUIRK

Actress Constance Bennett became one of Gloria Swanson's greatest rivals in matters of love. In 1930, in the latter stages of Gloria and Joe Kennedy's relationship, Connie had an affair with Joe behind Gloria's back. The next year, she snagged the Marquis de la Falaise on the heels of his divorce from Gloria.
POPPERFOTO

Owen Moore, one of the earliest male film stars, began his acting career for Biograph in 1908. Starring opposite Gloria Swanson in 1930's *What a Widow!*, he reportedly aroused Joe Kennedy's jealousy.

A charismatic and passionate actor in the 1920s, Walter Byron lost his "one big chance" as a leading man—opposite Gloria Swanson in the Joe Kennedy venture *Queen Kelly*—when production was halted halfway through shooting.

Phyllis Haver, silent-film star of *The Perfect Flapper* (1923) and *The Breath of Scandal* (1924), enjoyed a brief affair with Joe Kennedy before he left her for Evelyn Brent.

Mabel Normand blossomed into stardom in 1915 along with friend and co-star Charlie Chaplin. Later plagued by scandal, illness, and a drug habit, Mabel was dismissed by Joe Kennedy as "a hopeless drug addict" when friends appealed to him to give her a fresh chance in his studio.
ARCHIVE PHOTOS

Jack Pickford, Mary Pickford's
younger brother, achieved a fairly
prominent film career of his own in
the 1920s. Toward the end of his
career he became mired in drugs
and depression. In a failed effort to
help, Gloria Swanson tried to
convince Joe Kennedy to cast
Jack in *What a Widow!*

John Lodge, grandson of
renowned Massachusetts senator
Henry Cabot Lodge, starred with
Katharine Hepburn in *Little Women*
(1933) and with Marlene Dietrich in
The Scarlet Empress (1934).
Longstanding political animosity
between the Lodges and the Fitzgeralds
(and Kennedys) contributed to
Joe's resentment of Lodge's
Hollywood popularity.

Joe Kennedy took up with lovely screen star Nancy Carroll in 1931 after deserting Gloria Swanson.
PHOTOFEST

Producer Joe Kennedy gave Fred Thomson top billing in his ads. Thomson, who died young in 1928, was Joe's only hero.
PHOTOFEST

Fred Thomson trained his horse Silver King with wondrous expertise.
PHOTOFEST

Tom Mix, 1920s cowboy star, and his famous horse, Tony, worked under Joe Kennedy at FBO. Though Joe favored Fred Thomson in the cowboy-star department, he was impressed (and annoyed) with Tom's shrewd salary-negotiating ability.

Joan Crawford confided to me in 1956 that Joe had made a pass at her.
COLLECTION OF LAWRENCE J. QUIRK

Oscar-winning actress Joan Fontaine (*Suspicion*, *Rebecca*) dismissed Joe Kennedy's advances with amused disdain.
ARCHIVE PHOTOS

Despite his persistent attempts to add Greta Garbo to his list of conquests, Joe Kennedy finally had to admit that the reclusive actress would remain forever beyond his reach.
ARCHIVE PHOTOS

Twenty-two-year-old Jack Kennedy met Marlene Dietrich in Paris in 1939 at a party she gave for his father, then the U.S. ambassador to Great Britain. Although Joe had been pursuing her for years, the thirty-seven-year-old Dietrich seemed to take a greater interest in Jack, to Joe's flustered chagrin.
POPPERFOTO

Gloria Swanson and I became friends in 1949.
COLLECTION OF LAWRENCE J. QUIRK

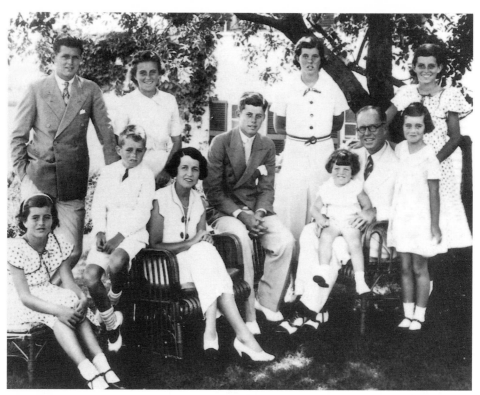

The Kennedy clan circa 1937
PHOTOFEST

Joe with his boys Joe Jr. and Jack.
PHOTOFEST

hands high" whom he would make famous as Silver King. He trained the horse to bow, kneel in prayer while bowing his head, dance, play dead, bare his teeth in anger or what passed (for a horse) as glee. Meanwhile Frances was busy writing hit silent screenplays for which she was well paid. Rugged, athletic, and "heart-stoppingly handsome," as Frances remembered, Fred found himself drawn (almost against his will, and to his regret, as she put it) into leading-man roles. Women across the country found him enthralling as Mary Pickford's romantic lead in the aptly titled *Lovelight*. Fred's career prospered, but romantic leads did not fulfill his spiritual needs, and he headed slowly but inexorably, along with his well-trained Silver King, toward the Westerns that would enable him to display what he called "a force for good, something decent to emulate, and to show kids that a man could fight and win fairly and cleanly and counter evil with positivism."

Hollywood was a little shocked that a man so *handsome* should be so utterly *decent*. Throughout his nine years of marriage to Frances, there was not a breath of scandal about Fred. "Drink, drugs, dissipation, these things were not for him," his friend and admirer King Vidor told me in 1956. "He was a really good man—a humble man—no sanctimoniousness, no hypocrisy, no ego, no posing." King recalled that Fred astonished him by declaring he wanted Silver King to be the star, not him, "and he meant it—really meant it," said King.

Unfortunately in 1926 the movie moguls wanted star personalities, not star horses, and Fred's Western movie projects smacked to them of too much *lack* of star ego. Frances and he were having trouble getting financing for their films.

Frances was always to remember her first meeting with Joe Kennedy, whom she had asked for an interview.

Accustomed to aloof moguls "who merely grunted or nodded" when one entered their offices, Frances and Fred found Joe Kennedy warm, accessible, and friendly. He congratulated Frances on her writing, then said, with what she recalled as unaffected boyish admiration, that he had followed Fred's career ever since he won the World's Decathlon Championship.

Joe was taken somewhat aback when Fred told him that he wanted to star his horse in a series of films. Frances was to recall the tact and persuasiveness that Joe employed as he so masterfully brought Fred over to his viewpoints: that a well-known actor wouldn't play second fiddle to a horse, so Fred had better star with the horse, especially since Fred had taught Silver King all his tricks, and who else could establish an equal simpatico with the horse?

Frances also remembered that Joe not only talked Fred into this but also got him to star in Universal's fifteen-episode serial, *The Eagle's Talons*. When Frances and Fred left the office that day, Fred's verdict on Joe was "a brilliant guy." Hers was "fascinating but smooth."

Fred and Frances were soon turning out Western fare for Joe Kennedy's FBO Productions. They were an immediate hit. Fred's deal brought him in time a salary of $10,000 a week. He followed Joe's suggestions about handling stunts, employing the best camera angles, creating sets at reasonable cost. Fred developed a profound respect for Joe as a producer.

When Rose Kennedy came to Hollywood later, she and Joe were guests of the Thomsons at their beautiful Spanish-style home above Beverly Hills, which they called "Enchanted Hill." Frances thought Rose "a good sensible person and morally, at least, the Kennedy family's *real* boss."

Frances, even though concerned that the biological clock was running against her, in her early forties presented

Fred with two sons, Fred Jr. and Richard. She was later to recall that their only arguments were about quarters for Fred's beloved horses and their grooms—and these were always restrained, friendly, and objective.

Joe began dropping by the Thomsons frequently, and Fred would take him riding. Joe learned that Fred didn't like off-color—even mildly off-color—jokes, yet Fred never expressed himself on "morality" issues in a priggish or holier-than-thou way. In 1927 when Fred learned—Hollywood gossip being relentless and universal—that Joe was playing around and had "made it" with the sad, rather vulnerable actress Evelyn Brent (also for a time on Joe's FBO payroll), Fred gently remonstrated, reminded Joe of the woman back east with the (then) seven kids and told him there was only unrest and unhappiness in a married man's womanizing.

At first impatient with Fred's observations on marriage and sex, Joe gradually became impressed with Fred's Beliefs. Following his usual habit, he hired private eyes to check out every aspect of Fred Thomson's life, and found absolutely nothing of a negative nature. True, Fred, an ordained Presbyterian minister, had in 1919 married Frances, a twice-divorced woman. Once Joe asked Fred about that. According to Frances, Fred said he felt no guilt, that anything done in the purest love was right and good, that he believed that churches ought to sanction divorce when both parties were unsuited to each other and making each other miserable, that there should be "second chances" in life. Fred went on to add that his marriage to Frances was the one and only time that he had put love above all else—and he felt no guilt about it. He told Joe that Frances had been miserable with her first two husbands, and he felt he had been sent to comfort her and teach her what love was truly about.

Joe once asked Fred if sex weren't a natural instinct? Weren't men chronic rovers, obsessed by curiosity? Could one woman ever be enough? Fred told him Frances was all he wanted or needed, that his two tiny boys were the great joys of his life, that the *sex* act alone was not enough, that for him it had to accompanied by *love* to make it whole and complete.

"From any other man," Joe later told Frances, "it would all have sounded like hypocritical, sanctimonious double-talk. But my God, Fred meant it—meant it, simply, sincerely, humbly!"

And so Fred Thomson became one of only two men Joe Kennedy sincerely respected and deeply loved as a friend. "I tell Fred things I wouldn't tell a priest," Frances recalled Joe saying to her. "I wish I had his spiritual decency, his goodness, but I don't." She recalled Joe saying this with a catch in his voice.

When Joe began his relationship with Gloria Swanson in 1928, he told Fred about it. Fred was deeply saddened. "Joe, it won't work—Evelyn Brent didn't work—none of it will *ever* work!" Joe tried to tell Fred that Rose's indifference to sex, coldness in bed, and Catholic-influenced ideas that sex was for procreation alone had driven him to feminine partners who could at least play back his physical enthusiasm. "But *emotionally*, Joe—*emotionally*, what are you feeling?" Fred asked. For this Joe had no answer. He just sat there saddened, puzzled.

Frances felt that had Fred lived, Joe might have tried to shape up more when it came to his womanizing. But by New Year's 1929, Fred Thomson, age thirty-eight, at the height of his stardom, loved by youngsters all across the country, a role model for many Americans tuned in to his spiritual qualities, was dead.

Frances was eloquently restrained when she wrote of Fred's death in her autobiography. Her words were all the more powerful for their omissions. In the late 1960s, when she spoke of Fred to me over a quiet little lunch in Hollywood, she burst into tears, tears that went on for minutes. "If there is an Eternity, if there is a God, if there is a Heaven, then I want to be with Fred," she said. "Just to be with *him* again—that is the only Heaven *I* ever want! . . . "

In her autobiography she tells of the week just before Christmas in 1928, the lighted trees on all the lawns, the delight in their two baby sons, ages two and one, and the hope they would react to the magic of the season. She and Fred went into their garden; from below sparkled the lights of Beverly Hills. As she put it: "We spoke of many things in the past which had changed the course of our own destinies. Fred's marriage to a divorced woman [Frances] and how we had tried to give each other up so that he might continue a career as a Presbyterian minister." She asked him if he had any regrets. With what she recalled as a sad, boyish honesty, he said that at first he had felt like a captain without a ship to guide, but not after realizing that his films with Silver King inspired millions of boys whose letters "fell upon him like blessings." Those letters contained phrases like these: "I'll never use guns when I grow up, Fred, because you never use guns to kill anybody." "You and Silver King capture the bad guys by tricks." And, "I'm kind to animals, Fred, on account of you're kind to animals." Of those letters from kids, Frances wrote: "Ten thousand, twelve thousand a week they poured in and among them were notes from little tykes who were saving their pennies in piggy banks so that someday they could buy one of Silver King's colts." Of this she remembered Fred saying: "If only Silver King could perform miracles!"

"Our minds met, our hearts touched, our hearts were one," she wrote. Fred put his arms around Frances and commented that Christmas 1928 would be their tenth happy Christmas together.

Frances noticed that as they walked into the house he was limping slightly. He had broken his leg a year before doing stunts, and she asked him if the leg were aching. He told her that he had stepped on a rusty nail and it bothered him a little.

Fred Thomson died on Christmas Night, 1928, from blood poisoning. "Blessed are little children," Frances wrote, "for they are spared the agonizing grief of parting from those we love. . . ."

Hedda Hopper knew and deeply loved Frances and Fred and had been comforted by friend Frances only the year before when she'd had to part from a married man she had deeply loved but who was not free to divorce his wife and marry her (a man who committed suicide shortly thereafter). Hedda was among the first to reach Frances. Hedda recalled in 1964 that vast outpouring of grief over Fred's death—"and on Christmas Night! Christmas Night!" Hedda said misty eyed, though some thirty-five years had by then passed. She remembered Frances devastated by grief, hugging her babies close to her, saying over and over, "Without Fred there is no life—no life." Hedda reminded her that she had two sons to love, two images of her beloved, and that she could honor Fred's memory by raising them in the way their father would have wanted. "She nodded; I knew that had gotten through to her, but for a long time grief ruled her heart," Hedda remembered.

Hedda opined that Frances had entered her fourth and final marriage, to the director George William Hill in 1930, because the loneliness had gotten to be too much for her, even in the face of her brilliant Oscar-winning career, and because she felt that George, who had also collaborated with her on screenplays and who had won a name directing films like *Tell It to the Marines* (1927) and *Min and Bill* (1930), would also prove a surrogate father to Fred's two small boys. But the marriage lasted only a year. George Hill was no Fred Thomson. He had his own excruciating inner demons to fight—usually he lost. Emotionally unstable, bisexual (and tormented by the ambivalence implicit in that), George had turned to drink and drugs. In 1934, three years after Frances—once more disillusioned with a husband—had sadly obtained a divorce, George committed suicide at his beach house.

Hedda, Adela St. Johns, and other firm and long-standing friends of Frances watched her go from triumph to triumph—writing great films, raising her boys well and faithfully. But as was obvious from my talks with Frances decades later, when Fred had disappeared so suddenly from her life on that 1928 Christmas Day "the light of the whole world had died, when love was done," to paraphrase the poet.

And Joe Kennedy? What had been *his* reaction when his favorite male star—and his favorite male person—Fred Thomson died? Hedda quoted Frances as saying that when Joe came to condole with Frances, "he wept and wept—couldn't stop weeping," and that "he kissed and hugged Fred's baby boys and swore to Frances that they would always have *him* to rely upon, no matter what came!" Hedda said Frances told her that Joe always remembered them on birthdays and at Christmas, and that when he visited them, he would say, "I loved your daddy so—he was the best, the *very* best guy I ever knew!"

Could Fred Thomson have spared Joe Kennedy the hurt and strain and tension that came later, the ulcers and other physical symptoms, the sorrow and loneliness that underlay his endless womanizing? Could Fred have taught

Joe by his example how important the influence of a father on his sons was, how the sins of that father were often visited on his sons?

Did Joe think of long-lost Fred when he lay immobilized by his stroke, when he sat in his wheelchair in mute, agonized grief as first Jack, then Bobby, was murdered? Did he think of him when Teddy was involved in the death of the young woman at Chappaquiddick, only a few months before Joe's own death in 1969? Did Fred haunt his friend Joe Kennedy; was he tormented by the might-have-beens, the lost beneficence that pure Fred's friendship might have given him? Did he think of all the talks never had, all the consolations never to be accorded?

I once asked Frances about Fred's favorite philosophical quotes, the aphorism that had most appealed to him.

She thought awhile. "Yes, there *was* one," she said. "*My strength is as the strength of ten because my heart is pure.*" Then Frances, Frances of the long loneliness, burst into tears.

SEVEN

Joe in the 1930s

B y mid-1932, with the Democratic national convention off and running, Joe Kennedy was set for a fresh start on new ground. The ulcers had healed, the call girls of West Fifty-Eighth Street (the firm was sold within a year of silent partner Jimmy Quirk's death) had worked miracles with his tensions, and he was looking for new fields to conquer. He had all the millions he thought appropriate (that $10 million fortune of 1932 would in time mushroom to more than $400 million), and he was looking for new endeavors.

At this time he renewed his friendship (if that were the term for it) with the genial but cynical Franklin D. Roosevelt, governor of New York, who was bucking intently and ruthlessly for the Democratic nomination for president of the United States. It was commonly felt in the summer of 1932 that whoever got that Democratic nomination would be a shoo-in for the nation's highest office, as Republican Herbert Hoover's do-nothing policies and false applications of what later came to be known as trickle-down methods had done nothing to ameliorate the horrific conditions brought about by a depression that by 1932 had dragged on for nearly three years.

Of course, Joe and FDR had an acquaintance going back nearly two decades when FDR had been assistant secretary of the navy and Joe managed the Bethlehem Shipyard at Fore River in Massachusetts. Joe had seen FDR's take-charge, expeditious, problem-solving methods firsthand, and he had become a keen Roosevelt admirer. Joe saw FDR as a man who could get things done, a man not afraid to cut corners, a man who could get the needed answers in a country that in 1932 was crying out for answers so agonizingly that a Communist takeover had ceased to be a distant threat and was increasingly on the minds of the press and public.

Soon Joe was taking an active part in getting FDR nominated. He did FDR a signal favor (which he never let FDR forget) by persuading his friend William Randolph Hearst, who controlled the delegations from Texas and California, to switch his political allegiance from John Nance Garner of Texas (who was later consoled with the vice presidency) to Roosevelt. William G. McAdoo, the senator from California, was also brought over to Roosevelt's side, again courtesy of Joe's frantic lobbying. Rewarded with a post on the Roosevelt executive committee to assure the New York governor's election, Joe delivered in fine style, lending large sums of money ($50,000 being a typical figure) to the campaign and later writing off the debt as what he called a "love contribution." Since love seemed to be something Joe Kennedy knew nothing about, Joe's generosities were promptly dubbed by other committee members "Joe K's Investment Contributions."

As the Roosevelts and their aides anticipated, upon FDR's election in November 1932, Joe began to put out feelers as to posts, suitable for his talents, in the new administration that would commence March 4, 1933. One of his ideas, promptly shot down by Roosevelt aides, was that he should be Secretary of the Treasury. After all, who knew more about money than Joe? Hadn't he weathered the crash, risen above all the desperate people who were down and out on the streets and who had jumped out of windows? If he could do this for himself, and had run up a $10 million kitty, then think what he could do for his fellow citizens? One author was later to say of Joe's treasury bid: "[As Secretary of the Treasury] Joe could keep an eye on the country's money and, at the same time, his own."

Joe went to Palm Beach, where he enjoyed his palatial new estate—and the attentions of some "high-class" ladies (or they were according to Eddie Moore) who were "loosely generous with their favors." There was silence for months from Roosevelt headquarters.

When the Roosevelt camp finally sent Joe Kennedy an offer, the ambassadorship to Ireland, Joe regarded the offer as insulting and indicated to family and friends that he had no intention of accepting it. Hadn't he discouraged too much Irish identification for his family; hadn't he tried to expunge mention of it from his record; hadn't he sent his children to aristocratic schools; hadn't he done everything possible to dissociate himself from the "cheap pols" and "muckers" who in his view overpopulated the Irish contingent? The answer went from Palm Beach to Washington: No!

Joe Kennedy knew that there were two people in the Roosevelt camp who did not particularly care for him: one was the First Lady, Eleanor Roosevelt, and the other was Louis Henry Howe, close confidant to the new president, who Joe suspected, with Eleanor's connivance, had stressed to FDR that a man so crassly and openly associated with underhanded financial chicaneries should be kept as far as possible from any governmental decision-making posts. (Eleanor Roosevelt was reported to be appalled at Joe's tastelessness in trying to put FDR on the phone to London and Gloria Swanson to elicit her congratulations on his nomination.) Joe guessed correctly that Eleanor had pushed the Irish diplomatic post as a message to him: go back to the muckerland you came from!

Soon Joe was back full force in the business that had brought him such phenomenal early profits: the booze trade. Roosevelt played into Joe hands by forcing the repeal of the Eighteenth Amendment, which meant that the sale of liquor was again legal. The new law went into effect in December 1933, during Roosevelt's first term as president. The underhanded chicaneries, sordid illegal ties, and gang-affiliated wheeler-dealings were now over for Joe; he could surface into the bright clean air of open liquor salesmanship and entrepreneurship.

Soon Joe had FDR's son Jimmy Roosevelt in tow and got Jimmy into the liquor business. They made a trip to England together, and with the direct cachet of Jimmy Roosevelt's name, Joe facilitated new deals from such European firms as Gordon's, Dewar's, and Haig and Haig, all big on the liquor scene abroad.

Joe was still pining away for a substantive, prestigious post in the Roosevelt administration. His impatience was finally rewarded; in early 1934 Roosevelt named him chairman of the new Securities and Exchange Commission.

There were ironies implicit in the appointment. After all, Joe had strong Wall Street connections and had long had a reputation as one of the sharpest operators in that milieu. But Roosevelt's reasoning went that it took one to control one or it would take a fox to keep the other foxes out of the chicken coop. "The Judas of Wall Street," as Joe was promptly dubbed by his former hotshot financial associates, turned out to be a sharp disciplinarian who controlled the money market sharks admirably. "*In* it, but not *of* it" had always been Joe's credo in dealing with his financial peers. Now he would function superbly as the governmental emissary of the man in the White House who had been dubbed "a traitor to his class" and "an enemy of the rich." That Roosevelt's radical reforms were aimed at saving capitalism from its excesses, not abolishing it, that his policies averted successfully a Communist threat, were never appreciated, let alone taken seriously into account, by his social and financial peers.

Moreover, in 1934 Joe Kennedy had all the money he wanted and could afford to play the role of government housecleaner and big shot from Washington—in fact he relished it keenly.

As one writer put it, "Joe Kennedy [as SEC chairman] performed well. He possessed genuine executive ability, self-discipline and phenomenal drive. This was the most powerful office he had ever held. Now he was in a position to put a brokerage firm out of business, or close down a major exchange, if he saw fit. All of a sudden brokers and bond salesmen and stock, bond and commodity exchange officials were inundated with government forms to fill out and saw their office invaded by scores of SEC men, bent on investigating their files and procedures."

Many former associates of Joe Kennedy were to be thoroughly humiliated over the next year, and Joe enjoyed it all hugely. There was a bonus: he got—through his government enforcement procedures—intimate insights into the chicaneries and manipulations of his former rivals, and if he could pick a cherry of revenge here and there, why so much the better and the bigger the bonus. Money, for once, was not Joe Kennedy's primary motivation as SEC commissioner. First came the satisfaction of pleasing his boss FDR; second came the satisfaction of embarrassing former rivals and learning their secrets; and third, the sheer power of the position satisfied one of his most visceral needs.

In later years it was generally agreed that Joe did a fine job as SEC chairman. His ruthless measures helped stabilize the economy, keep markets on target, and protect the public from corruption and fraud. Many of the safety measures (safety in the public interest) that Joe Kennedy initiated are still being applied today.

By 1936, his SEC salvage accomplished, Joe had moved on. He ingratiated himself further with Roosevelt by writing a book, *I'm for Roosevelt*, which was a useful tool for Roosevelt campaigners and henchmen during the 1936 campaign, which Roosevelt won handily.

In *I'm for Roosevelt*, Joe told the bankers and brokers that instead of reviling Roosevelt for his draconian measures to regulate the economy and eliminate waste and fraud, they should be humbly thanking him. A planned economy, heightened business regulations—this was the ticket for the future, Joe insisted in his book. Though as adept in business practices as any of the sharks and crooks he reviled, and though he had earned his own fortune employing many of their measures, indeed originating a few, Joe always held big business in contempt. "These people reminded him of his own dark side," an associate recalled. He knew in retrospect some of the things he himself had had to do to ensure his and his family's prosperity and future prospects. While not a drinker himself, Joe knew his liquor interests had furthered a habit that many religionists and reformers considered a scourge. But through the years Joe had an overriding

philosophy: make the money first, no matter how many corners had to be cut; then, with money you had dignity and
freedom and mobility; you could tell anyone to go to hell;
you were beholden to no man. To Joe, a life without the
security and power of money was no life at all.

This philosophy in 1931 had enabled Joe to leave the
movie business many times richer than when he came in.
And after resigning the SEC post (having done all he felt he
could do and restless as always to move on), Joe found himself suddenly back in the movie business—after a fashion.

It was 1936. RKO, the studio he had helped put into
existence, had run into serious financial difficulties. With
the noise of his SEC triumphs loud in the land and reaching all the way to California, Joe found his old associate
David Sarnoff on the wire one day. RKO needed a complete overhauling; he asked Joe to come up with new operating methods that would put RKO back in the black. Joe
thought it might be fun to visit in California again, but let
it be known to the anxious Sarnoff that a $150,000 consul-
tant's fee would be expected, and possibly more later, "if I
get too deep into this thing." Also Joe decided it might be
fun to renew his acquaintance with some of RKO's hottest
stars of 1936, particularly Ginger Rogers and Katharine
Hepburn. While in Hollywood ruthlessly ridding RKO of
deadwood and recommending wholesale trimmings and
numerous firings, which won him a whole new passel of
enemies, Joe did get to renew his acquaintance with both
Ginger and Kate, whom he had met in New York years
before. Sarnoff and his executives were a little nervous
about his interest in the two ladies because both were
strong egoists with minds of their own. Sarnoff knew they
were not equipped by temper or makeup to tolerate Joe's
skirt-chasing manipulations.

In 1936 Joe Kennedy was a healthy, hearty forty-eight, and he kept Eddie Moore busy finding likely ladies to accommodate his voracious sexual needs.

Ginger, whom he met on the set of one of her Fred Astaire-co-starring musicals, was having none of his nonsense, he soon found out. She was a big star now, twenty-five years old, had weathered a marriage to Lew Ayres, and had been linked with Jimmy Stewart and many other men. Despite her prissy "Christian" attitudes and stances, Ginger was a red-hot gal, sexually, who was to ring up a number of marriages, some of them impulsive and some of them disastrous to both her image and her finances.

Joe, she felt, was too old for her speed—anything above thirty-five gave Ginger pause. When he asked her to dinner, she brought her mother Lela along, to his great annoyance. Joe asked RKO director George Stevens about her. Stevens, though short enough with people he felt beneath him, was not of a mind to tell RKO's financial lifesaver of 1936 that Ginger found him repellent. Ginger had indeed told Stevens that the "dirty old man" had kept a tight hand on her arm when he joined her on a set "and he would have made for my breasts next, the way he was eyeing them!"

Stevens and Joe went to lunch. "What is the matter with Ginger!" Joe asked him. "Why is she so distant with me? And why in hell did she bring that bossy, brash mother of hers along to dinner?"

Stevens was a shrewd man and long a devotee of the famed old saw that the quickest and easiest way to get someone off someone else's back (in this case Ginger's) was to give the would-be stalker the idea that *he* was getting rid of her. "Ginger's very troubled just now," George told Joe, putting on a face complete with hand gestures that would have earned him at least an Oscar nomination had he applied it to acting. "She's been very hurt by one guy. And another says he'll beat up any guy he sees coming after her."

Joe's face turned serious. "But George, I have never heard about any of this, or read it anywhere."

"Oh, you know Louella and the others, Joe, they'd never allude to anything like that; the studios pressure Louella to protect stars, keep the dirt out of the papers. Then they reward her with perks—you know how it is, Joe."

Then George applied the clincher. "I'm afraid, too, that Ginger has caught a dose [translated, caught syphilis] from one of these guys."

Joe got up as if he had made a decision: "I guess she is one dame to be left alone, after all." George remembered Joe throwing the money for the lunch on the table and stalking out.

"I gave the biggest sigh of relief—you could hear it to Santa Monica," George told Perry Lieber (who years later told me that story). "Not only had I sidestepped Joe's anger and saved his pride, but I had done Ginger a favor she would not soon forget."

Next on Joe's list was Katharine Hepburn. She'd had some sensational romances such as Leland Hayward (Margaret Sullavan was to steal Hayward away from her and marry him), and her constant traveling with close women friends had won her (from Sullavan) the sobriquet of "Krazy Kate and her Giddy Girlfriends." Joe was mightily intrigued with Kate. Was she a woman who liked other women as much as she did men? What would she be like to know more intimately?

Joe soon found out that Kate was a tough lady to take when she didn't like someone—and she didn't like Joe. Financially shrewd, tough with a buck, Kate came from an old-line Connecticut family with the automatic entree that upward-climber Joe had always envied yet was never quite to achieve—at least in his own mind. She was more direct than Ginger, who for all her toughness didn't like to make enemies and needed intermediaries to "do the dirty work." When Joe asked Kate to dinner, she told him she was much too busy, that her current movie took up all her time and energies. Kate later told George Cukor that she thought Joe Kennedy "low class" and knew all about the cavalier treatments of Gloria Swanson, Nancy Carroll, Connie Bennett, and others. "I nip it in the bud," she told Cukor. "I don't accept a first date, then salve them over and let them down lightly. I'm cruel in order to be—well, not kind, but expeditious."

"Kate had a contempt for Joe Kennedy—a real, genuine contempt," George Cukor later said. "She thought he was pushy, crass, vulgar. Possessing as she did all the aristocratic lineage and noblesse oblige by right of birth that Joe could never aspire to, she was very direct in her rebuff."

Joe didn't take the slight lightly. "Well isn't *she* the Connecticut snob!" he fulminated to Pandro Berman, Kate's producer. "Who does she think she is? And isn't it true her brother committed suicide?" (Joe was referring to the 1921 death of Kate's fifteen-year-old brother, Tom, who had hanged himself in the attic of a house he and Kate had been visiting in New York. She had been thirteen at the time. After his death she had been in a blue funk for months; later, strangely, she forsook her own birthday, May 12, and took on Tom's, November 9. She did not throw off her depression about Tom until her life at Bryn Mawr, when her burgeoning stage ambitions redirected her spirit.)

Soon Joe was looking over the other possibly available RKO contingent. He took a shine to Lucille Ball, but she froze him out in short order. Then he got a thing for the new young actress, Andrea Leeds, but found that she was so "plumb scared of him" (as George Stevens remembered) that a combination of chivalry and guilt (or at least Joe Kennedy's brand of guilt, which was more like caution) caused him to give up on her, too.

Soon after this, Joe took down the numbers of high-class houses of prostitution in Hollywood, Chicago, and New York, which George Stevens gave him, and decided, at least for the time being, that *paying* for it was not only the path of least resistance but the route of least *bother*, too. While in Hollywood, he did take note—in passing—of the girlish charms of the then nineteen-year-old Joan Fontaine, younger sister of Errol Flynn's fast-rising Warner leading lady, Olivia de Havilland, but did not further the fleeting encounter he had with her. Joan Fontaine would pop up in his life again—a decade and a half later—and under rather amusing circumstances.

In 1936 Irving Thalberg, plagued with a bad heart, died at a premature thirty-seven while at the height of his career as MGM's prestige producer. His widow, Norma Shearer, was left with two young children, millions of dollars, and later, a whole new career at MGM, where she had signed a lucrative contract; after all, "the Widow Thalberg" owned a good share of Loew's stock. Joe had met Norma in his early days in Hollywood and now was intrigued by her glamor, money, and availability, or so he thought. But Norma was not in the market for forty-eight-year-olds; she liked 'em younger and hunkier. Eddie Mannix remembered that Norma complained that Joe sent her letters, flowers, and made a number of phone calls after Irving's death, following the same pattern he had with May Allison after her husband Jimmy Quirk died. According to Eddie, Norma had put Joe's nose out of joint by asking him about his wife and kids, and saying she would just *love* to entertain Rose if Joe ever brought him with her to Hollywood. That was Norma's (admittedly more tactful and gentle) method of getting rid of married men—bring up the wife, deflate the come-on, as an old Hollywood apothegm had it.

Soon Joe had other Hollywood matters to occupy his mind. Paramount in 1936 was a mess; even Mae West, the racy, sexy, buxom headliner hadn't managed to rescue it with box-office grosses that, especially after the Legion of Decency watered down her scripts, were falling off. Paramount executives brought in Joe to cut out the dead-wood. He began to cut salaries, lop off jobs, get rid of hang-ers-on and relatives of relatives. For this venture Kennedy, in deference (if that is the word) to what he discovered in the books Paramount accountants made available to his shrewd eye, mollified (and indeed astonished) the Paramount execs by asking what was for him a generously scaled-down fee indeed: $50,000.

Joe did fail completely when he tried to cut star salaries. Fred MacMurray, who even at twenty-eight demonstrated the sound business sense that eventually was to make him a multimillionaire through shrewd investments (he died in his eighties one of the richest men in the country), asked Joe to lunch and out-argued him by detailing all the expenses that went with being an up-and-coming leading man, adding that his weekly stipend was not all that great considering the weight of his fan letters in the Paramount mail room. Joe was impressed with Fred's hardheadedness. "Okay, your salary stays as is," he said, "but if you ever leave acting and try business, look me up—I might have a job for you!"

Claudette Colbert, another Paramount star, was a no-nonsense woman who made it plain to Joe that while her salary was high, she earned every cent of it and indeed was one of the studio's financial life belts. Joe left her alone, too.

Asked by Eddie Moore what his personal impression of Claudette was, Joe replied: "Too tough, too hardheaded for a woman—not my type at all!"

William Le Baron, who worked for Paramount for years as a producer-director, was a rich fountainhead of information for me on all this (as were others), when I interviewed him years ago for a biography on Jimmy Quirk, whom he had known well.

As Bill Le Baron put it, Joe's most hilarious encounter was with Mae West, who had a business sense as tough and shrewd as his. "Honey, I've earned every cent of what Paramount pays me," she told him, "and I could earn more if you, Joe Kennedy, would get those damned Legion of Decency bluenoses off my butt. They are ruining my dialogue; all my best jokes go out the window. Now I ask you, do those hypocrites understand good business?" Joe told Le Baron that he left Mae's salary alone, too, though the bluenoses left him powerless. "I agreed with her that the movies now are too damned prissy," Joe said, "but why take on all those church hypocrites and moral-crusade phonies. Now that is *not* good business. They're a large part of the audience!"

The author of such famed Westisms as "a hard man is good to find" and "is that a gun in your pocket or are you just glad to see me?" later told one of her directors, Eddie Sutherland (who repeated it to me in 1960): "Joe Kennedy is one of the world's prize phonies; I don't like him, and he has no respect for women, especially *ladies!* And I'm a *lady!* I made him understand that!"

It would be hard to imagine Joe Kennedy being taken with Mae West personally. For his tastes, Mae was too crude, too aggressive, and too fat. Joe liked his women lissome. But from what is known of their brief association, he did respect her business—and money—sense.

Soon it was apparent that Joe's services as "consultant" to hard-up companies were in demand, word having gotten around that he was a ruthless but effective cost-cutter and organizational genius. When word from Paramount executives, enthralled with Joe's streamlining of their financial and budget affairs, finally reached Joe's old friend William Randolph Hearst, Joe was summoned to an imperial audience at San Simeon.

It seemed that Hearst had serious troubles in 1936 in all financial departments. His fleet of newspapers was losing money; he had spent with profligacy on his San Simeon estate, buying statues and antiques, and transporting old castles stone by stone to California; he had also lost much money on the films of his longtime (since 1917) lover Marion Davies, who was (as per Joe's advice) to make her last film in 1937. Years later, according to Margaret Ettinger, when Louella Parsons (Margaret's cousin) asked Marion if she in any way blamed Joe Kennedy's financial advice for the termination of her career, Marion, replete with her charming, characteristic stutter, replied that she was, if anything, relieved: "I was almost glad—in fact I *was* glad," she told Louella. "I was forty years old, and I only kept on doing it to please Poopsie [one of her pet names for Hearst]. If Joe hadn't knocked sense into his head, he would have gone on losing money on my movies and I would have had a prize feeling of guilt!"

In 1937 Marion proved her loyalty to Hearst, then seventy-four and in dire financial straits, by giving him a million dollars. "It came from you and now it goes back to you" were the words she used when presenting Hearst with the check. Joe always liked Marion, though rumors that they'd had a fling were actually untrue. Joe didn't need a hassle with the jealous Hearst (who kept a close eye on such handsome Davies leading men as Dick Powell, who feared the mogul of

San Simeon mightily), and anyway, Marion was in the Mae
West category in Joe's parlance—a shade too old, too blowsy,
and too "used goods" for Joe's taste. But over the years Joe
and Marion kept their friendship alive, and after Hearst's
death in 1951, Joe advised her wisely on her investments. In
gratitude she presented him, in 1955, with a gold watch that
reportedly cost $25,000. "But no inscription," Marion stut-
tered charmingly to Hedda Hopper. "I wouldn't want Rose
to get the wrong idea if she found it in the bedroom or
someplace." Coincidentally, Marion was to die at age sixty-
four in 1961, the same year that Joe had the debilitating
stroke that left him half-paralyzed and seriously disabled
until his death in 1969.

Hounded by creditors from all sides in 1936 and 1937,
Hearst turned abjectly (for him) to Joe Kennedy. He was to
remain grateful to Joe for the remaining fourteen years of his
life. His editor, Walter Howey, who presided over the Hearst
Boston papers, told me years later that had it not been for
Joe, Hearst would really have gone down the drain. Joe
asked for a going salary of a reported $10,000 a week, and
proceeded to sell off useless Hearst real estate and put a stop
to any expenditures (the flow of statues and rugs and ancient
knickknacks from Europe ceased abruptly). Hearst had once
earned many millions per year—in his more prosperous period in the early 1930s, his income had soared to a reputed
$15 million a year. Now he was cash poor, in spades, and his
capital resources were paralyzed.

Joe Kennedy cut down the number of Hearst newspapers across the land, retaining only those that promised to be
profitable (like the Boston papers where Walter Howey
presided) and Hearst's flagship paper the *San Francisco
Examiner*. Joe was particularly concerned about the *New York
American*, which in 1937 was losing more than a million a
year. He did some drastic cost cutting and firing and made

new deals with paper firms and other services, especially after Hearst begged him not to kill his New York flagship paper. "Joe saved WR's pride," Walter Howey later told me, "but economy was the watchword on *that* paper henceforth—on all of them, for that matter!"

"Joe, and Joe alone, saved the Hearst empire in 1937" was Walter's final verdict to me on the matter in 1952.

Although on intimate and friendly terms with my father's brother, Jimmy Quirk, Joe Kennedy did not particularly like my mother's brother, Congressman William P. Connery Jr. of Massachusetts Seventh District, who had started, Ronald Reagan-style, as an actor, before becoming a World War I hero and later, a successful politician. A Democrat, Uncle Billy Connery had come into his own after the Roosevelt electoral landslide of 1932 and rose to become chairman of the House Labor Committee and coauthor of legislation highly favorable to labor, including the Wagner-Connery Bill (later the Wagner Act), the Black-Connery Bill (future Supreme Court Justice Hugo Black was his partner in this), and the National Labor Relations Act.

When Joe Kennedy was on the Securities and Exchange Commission, he crossed paths with Billy Connery frequently at Washington parties, and the substance of their encounters was always the same. Joe would ask him why he insisted on lopsidedly favoring labor at the expense of that same big business that, left unfettered, made jobs possible through the trickle-down economic system. Uncle Billy would always rejoinder that the working people got the short end of the stick when the big-shot entrepreneurs stacked the cards in their favor.

"They were always at it," my uncle and namesake Larry Connery (himself later a congressman) would relate. "Joe relentlessly and unswervingly on the side of Big Business and Billy on the side of the Worker and the Little Fellow."

"It's business acumen that makes the country move and prosper," Joe repetitively maintained, and when Billy tried to make the point that many dishonest, manipulative big-business types on Wall Street and elsewhere were rooking the "little guy" over and over, Joe's features would turn beet red.

Joe Kennedy, who had made a fortune as a bootlegger, had also disliked my maternal grandfather, William P. Connery Sr.—my grandfather had closed down all the saloons when he was mayor of Lynn in the 1911–1912 period, after which liquor interests saw to it that he failed of reelection. My grandfather later ran several Temperance and Total Abstinence societies. "People need their comforts and their escapes," Joe loved to repeat. "They like to drink, smoke, *escape* from their drab lives, and you're never going to legislate or change human nature."

Grandfather Connery, who had seen in his native Lynn the horrors of alcoholism and its effect on family life, believed in the ancient Irish curse on dispensers of spirits. That curse took the form of a retarded child in families that went into the liquor business. My grandfather's sister, Annie Connery, had married William H. Hennessey, who made his money in the liquor business, and they had a retarded son, Joe. The Kennedys had produced Rosemary, whom her father had lobotomized in order to calm her increasingly loose and unpredictable behavior. He had done this behind Rose's back, and when she found out about it years later, she never forgave Joe for keeping her out of so crucial a family decision.

Gloria Swanson remembered that when she had brought up Rosemary, Joe's personality had abruptly changed, and he made it plain he did not want Rosemary to be discussed. Did Joe have in mind the Irish curse—retardation to a member of the liquor-dispensing family? It is certain that he did. Rosemary was forever to remind him that he had engaged—for profits, profits, and more profits—in a business that was in some odd, mystical way hexed. It troubled him through the years more than he would admit. Only a few, including Eddie Moore, knew his private feelings on the matter. Rose didn't like the fact that the family had made money in booze dispensing, either, and liked to quote to Joe the Biblical observation about it not profiting a man to gain the whole world and lose his immortal soul.

But Joe had the last word on my uncle Billy, the defender of the downtrodden. Once when he talked with the actor William Powell, who mentioned that he had worked in stock with Uncle Billy when the latter was a young actor, Joe snapped; "I wish the hell Billy had stayed in acting and stayed out of politics, then a lot of the labor bullshit would never have happened!" William Powell found it amusing that he had gotten such a rise out of Joe on the matter.

EIGHT

Marlene

Joe Kennedy's relationship with Marlene Dietrich was more extended and more complex than most chroniclers have as yet discovered. They first met in 1930 in Hollywood; fresh from her triumph in *The Blue Angel*, the German film in which she was a cynical, depraved cabaret girl who makes a colossal fool out of fat, masochistic schoolteacher Emil Jannings, Marlene was working with Gary Cooper on *Morocco*, her first American film. *The Blue Angel* had been released in the United States, and Marlene, with her saucy stares, well-placed legs of surpasssing beauty, and luscious shape, had become an instant *cause célèbre*, "more notorious than famous," as an initially hostile and disgusted Louella Parsons, the prominent Hearst columnist, sniffed. Louella at the time, and indeed throughout her career, followed the Hearst party line in print, tending to be put-downish about actresses who were too sexually blatant (Hearst some years later was to term Mae West a "filmic horror"). Many insiders laughed that Hearst's public prissiness was guilt overcompensation because he had virtually abandoned his wife to live openly in Hollywood and elsewhere with his mistress, Marion Davies. But as Adela Rogers St. Johns told me, Marion was far from being the Susan Alexander of what she called Orson Welles's "travesty" of Hearst, the 1941 *Citizen Kane*, which Hearst did everything to sandbag, unsuccessfully. Unlike Welles's Susan, a nice but untalented girl forced into a operatic career for which she was hopelessly unsuited, Marion was one of the most talented comediennes on the screen, and in Adela's opinion (many shared that opinion), Marion would have won major stardom (as a comedienne) without the heavy assist an obsessed Hearst forced on her. The problem was that Hearst didn't want Marion to appear in any "racy' roles, barely tolerated her comedic stints, and wanted her to be a dignified dramatic actress. When MGM refused to let Marion play Elizabeth Barrett Browning and handed the role to the far more suitable dramatic star Norma Shearer, Hearst in high dudgeon abandoned his production deal with MGM and took Marion over to Warners, where, as usual, she proved only passable in dramatic concoctions and sparkling in comedy roles. Many later wondered why Hearst had bothered to make the move from Culver City to Burbank at all.

Guilt ridden as he was over his relationship with Marion, whom he wouldn't marry because, despite protestations otherwise, he didn't *want* a divorce from his wife, Hearst really went after Marlene Dietrich, whom he saw as a harlot-of-harlots whose influence on the American screen of the early thirties was "unwholesome."

Joe Kennedy, however, was mightily intrigued by Marlene and asked Jimmy Quirk, who was on one of his annual Hollywood trips, to introduce them. Joe was a little put off because her Svengali director, Josef Von Sternberg, insisted on being present at the meeting. Because Joe and

Gloria Swanson had come to a parting of the ways by late 1930, Joe was in the market for another big female star to take up the slack. Marlene made him feel naughty and mischievous (there was more than a little of the lascivious small boy in Joe), and he tried to isolate her from Von Sternberg, who was having none of it. The fact that Marlene had a husband, Rudy Sieber, and a small daughter, didn't faze Joe at all. After all, hadn't the star he was currently dumping, Gloria Swanson, had a husband, two ex-husbands, and two kids?

Marlene asked around about Joe Kennedy. She knew he was wealthy, but she had known men she felt were far wealthier and more powerful, so that was no lure. She asked May Allison (Mrs. Jimmy Quirk) about him, and May counseled her that she should give him a wide berth. Von advised her that Joe loved to get new notches in his belt when it came to secret (but well-gossiped-about) liaisons with movie actresses.

Joe also liked the fact that Dietrich, under contract to Paramount in 1930, would not need his "expertise" as producer-mentor, and it relieved him that Paramount execs could do the worrying about her career while he, hopefully, enjoyed her favors.

Jimmy Quirk advised Joe to lay off Dietrich, that his dumping of Gloria had left a bad taste in some of her friends' mouths and he should cool it for a while. So, early 1931 found Joe taking advantage of Nancy Carroll's falling-out with her husband Jack Kirkland (famed for *Tobacco Road*) and he proceeded to add the Carroll notch to his belt—for a time.

Dietrich and Von Sternberg had heard all about the *Queen Kelly* disaster of a year or so before, and they found amusing Swanson's horror over the scene in which her leading man, Walter Byron, ran her panties across his nose. Marlene couldn't help teasing Joe on the matter, and when he protested (Hearstian hypocrite that he was) that the panties-under-the-nose scene *was* a little extreme, she turned her famous sloe-eyed gaze on him (as May Allison laughingly remembered) and told him there had been a nearly identical scene in *The Blue Angel* in which she had thrown *her* panties into silly old fool Emil Jannings's face, so, she wanted to know, what was all this prudish nonsense about—if scenes like that had made her an international sensation and brought her to Hollywood and the Paramount star buildup, why couldn't a similar scene in Gloria's abortive movie have brought equally felicitous results to Gloria?

Joe lamely and haltingly tried to point out that censorship restrictions in America would have given *Queen Kelly* a hard time, whereas the *German* film was out of Hays Office jurisdiction when it was made, but Dietrich topped his ace by reminding him that the controversial scene remained *in* when *The Blue Angel* was released in America. For this Joe had no answer.

As Adela St. Johns recalled it, Joe felt he had been subtly rebuffed personally—and worse, out-argued professionally—by Dietrich. He "ceased and desisted" from his overtures to her but then ridiculed her to his Horsemen and other cronies as "that German bitch whose lousy accent will never win over American audiences" and spread stories about her frantic weight-loss programs, knowing as she did that American audiences liked them slim. "She won't last," Joe sour-graped. "And she'll never talk the King's English either—not with a thousand voice and diction coaches in her corner!" (Ruth Waterbury later remarked that Joe Kennedy could gossip as bitchily as any fishwife—especially when he was angry, affronted, or rejected. "And considering that freaky Boston accent that Gloria may have found cute but few other people did, Joe was no one to talk about speech patterns!" Ruth added.)

Ruth remembered that in early 1931 she had gotten a call from Joe Kennedy in which he offered to give her some "startling, hot exclusives" if she could persuade Jimmy Quirk to run another major article on him in *Photoplay*. Jimmy's first on Joe, written by Terry Ramsaye and published in the September 1927 issue, had played up his movie mogul activities *and* his family life with Rose and his kids. Joe told Ruth that he would give her his "inside" opinions of "the pants-presser's" production methods around 1931, and their "lack of vision," and so forth. Ruth demurred on this, saying such articles had become common. Then Joe came up with another idea "probably one born of desperation—this was one mad power-seeking publicity hound." How would she like to interview him on the ten most beautiful women on the screen? Ruth reported this idea back to Jimmy, who got Joe on the phone and in as friendly and tactful a manner as possible reminded him that Rose might not go for *that* idea and that the insiders who knew about him and Swanson and Evelyn Brent and all the others might make cruel jokes about such an article. Joe backed off.

After Joe left Hollywood in 1931, with added millions in his kitty but otherwise with his tail between his legs, stinging from the gossip his enemies enjoyed spreading (many of Gloria Swanson's friends felt he had treated Gloria shabbily and were out to retaliate), his opportunities for more mischief-making were limited.

Joe and Marlene were, however, to meet briefly and superficially over the next five years, and around 1936 he showed his sour grapes by telling Paramount executives, when he was serving as economic advisor, that Dietrich was a box-office liability and didn't rate her high salary; significantly, Dietrich's 1937 movie, *Angel*, was to be her last Paramount film for ten years. Later Joe spread the "I told you sos" to his Hollywood associates and the Horsemen when in early 1938 Dietrich was named one of the box-office-poison stars in a widely discussed industry poll that included such formidable names as Mae West and Joan Crawford.

Certainly in early 1939 Dietrich was "on vacation" in Paris and on the Riviera, having not made a picture in two years. She had gotten into a controversial, newsworthy tizzy when she had absolutely refused Adolf Hitler's plea for her to return and become Germany's biggest star. Despising Hitler and all he stood for, Dietrich instead had taken out American citizenship. Now in 1939 she was floating around France in the company of Noel Coward and her rumored "romance," Jean Gabin, while husband Sieber as usual stayed discreetly in the background. At this time (mid-1939) Dietrich was also carrying on a flaming liaison with Erich Maria Remarque, of *All Quiet on the Western Front* fame, who was also in bad with the Nazis.

Joe Kennedy was by 1939 United States ambassador to Great Britain, and that summer he and son John, then twenty-two, were in Paris. Josef Von Sternberg had joined the Dietrich-Remarque-Sieber-Gabin circle in Paris. When Noel Coward, who amused Dietrich with his bitchy witticisms and who also liked ironic, contrapuntal pairings, suggested that they give Joe a cocktail party, Dietrich shrugged (she knew exactly what Noel was up to) and said why not? John Kennedy was to remember that party. He told Lem Billings later that Dietrich (then thirty-seven) was a bit too self-consciously remote and unhealthily in love with her image; he also boasted that from the way she looked at him,

alternating her glances from his twenty-two-year-old face to
his crotch, he was sure she would have bedded him at the
first opportunity. "Jack has a manner," she told the flustered
Joe Kennedy later, "perhaps he should be an actor. And he
has a great smile!" Surveying Jack's slim, youthful figure (Joe
in 1939 was fifty-one and getting a little jowly and heavy
around the middle), he determined (father-son rivalry style)
that Marlene would never get within a mile of his boy. Jack,
as he told Lem later, sensed his father's discomfiture and the
hidden reasons for it, but he couldn't have cared less; he did-
n't find Dietrich his type; moreover, she was fifteen years his
senior. "Look close and you'll see her eyes are already crin-
kling around the edges," he told Lem.

Dietrich and Joe Kennedy then had a resumption of
what was always to be (by her choice and to his chagrin) a
platonic relationship. She introduced her daughter Maria, by
then a teenager, to Jack; they saw each other briefly and
innocently, without romantic involvement.

Marlene had an agenda in her renewed encounter with
Joe Kennedy. She had read and heard a great deal about his
Nazi appeasement stances, which were winning him the
beginnings of a vast unpopularity in England; she did not
agree with him on this, and she and Joe had some lively discussions on the matter. Joe found Marlene more informed
and well-read on historical and political matters than he had
suspected. Sometimes their arguments got heated. Marlene
told Joe that of course all Irishmen hated England and as an
Irish-American he was trying to humiliate the English before
their enemies the Germans, and he countered that she was
German born and German educated and didn't she ever have
pangs of conscience for having deserted her native land,
scorned its leader, and taken out American citizenship.
Hitler was after all the legally recognized and internationally

accepted leader of Germany, so why couldn't she accept him even if his politics repelled her?

Marlene would have answered him on all this even more sharply and pointedly, thus putting them back on each other's enemies list, but she had something else to discuss with him. Marlene was, if nothing else, a lady of consummate flexibility—her early years in Germany had taught her how to handle men like Joe, whether romantically or platonically—and she brought up the fact that she had not made a film, either in America or in Europe, for two years and that she thought a French film pairing her with Raimu, the noted character star of the French theater and movies, would be just the ticket. Raimu was later noted for his superb character portrayals for director Marcel Pagnol. Orson Welles once called this freakishly individualistic performer "the greatest actor who ever lived" (lavish praise indeed from the usually cynical and sardonic Orson, who prized no other actor's talent more than his own; he later maintained a professional association with Marlene).

Joe Kennedy did not turn her down, as she had half-expected. Despite his earlier film experiences, he was still game for more adventures, and this film would be made far from Hollywood, in France. "Of course you could help find investors for it and you wouldn't have to put money into it," Von Sternberg remembered Marlene saying to Joe, "or if you did put some money into it, you wouldn't have to have your name on it as *producer*."

Joe gave Marlene a sharp look, and as Von Sternberg remembered it, said, "Why wouldn't I want to be your producer *right there on the credits?* I am an up-front man, and it would be an honor to produce, openly, a movie with two artists like you and Raimu." Joe then phoned Raimu, and they engaged in talk about a prospective screenwriter. With his Horsemen and other aides, Joe even carried the discussions to the point of budget estimates and shooting locations. That they didn't even have a plot yet didn't seem to faze him. He approached Von Sternberg about directing it. "But what about the story—there is none," Von observed.

"Oh, with two hot personalities like that we can dream up the right story" was Joe's cavalier response.

But two events forestalled these burgeoning plans. War between Germany and allied England and France was on the verge of breaking out, and Dietrich suddenly got a Hollywood comeback offer. She was down to limited financial resources, and it couldn't have happened at a more fortuitous moment.

Joe Pasternak was planning to produce a Western with Jimmy Stewart—*Destry Rides Again*. He proposed to Marlene (whom he had known from the early days in Berlin) during a transatlantic phone call that she needed a dramatic reinvention of her screen image—from remote, inscrutable love goddess to blowsy, brassy saloon singer. He wanted Marlene to get a fresh hold on American audiences by appealing to their more—well, earthy sensibilities. "Down to brass tacks, Marlene," he told her, sporting one of the new American phrases he had acquired and savored. "I don't like the sound of words like 'brass tacks,'" he recalled her replying, but she needed the money, and it was Joe Kennedy, among others, who convinced her she should go back to Hollywood and try for a new image—and what turned out to be one of the great Hollywood comebacks.

"Joe knew the war was about to break out," Pasternak later recalled. "He was a little worried about Marlene batting around Europe with Hitler about to attack France, and what if she got captured?"

Joe Kennedy had another reason for wanting Marlene safely back in America. He jealously sensed that Marlene would have far preferred cradle-robbing bed play with slim, handsome Jack than with his bloating fifty-one-year-old self. *That*, as gossipy Clifton Webb recalled, would have proven the most fatal of humiliations for the man who proposed to show his sons all about the intricacies of romance. He wanted to be the all-potent teacher, not the forgotten also-ran.

Clifton Webb, years later in Hollywood, remembered that Joe was in a quandary, going two directions at once—wanting Marlene in Hollywood, wanting Jack back in America (Jack would graduate from Harvard the next year, 1940), and a continent between them.

Shortly Marlene was in Hollywood, where on the set of *Destry Rides Again*, she found that the boyish charms of manly twenty-two-year-old Jack Kennedy were quickly superseded by the boyish but more knowingly sophisticated charms of thirty-one-year-old Jimmy Stewart, whom she pursued with what Clifton later called "rampant abandon" on and off the set.

Marlene and the Kennedys were to cross paths socially often over the years that followed. Part of her never forgave Joe Kennedy for the appeasement policies that he had tried to force on England and America vis-à-vis Nazi Germany. Later, during the middle and later stages of World War II, when it had escalated into a worldwide confrontation involving the United States, Marlene visited army camps in Europe and was one of the more popular entertainers for American servicemen.

Joe Kennedy, whose ambassadorship to Great Britain had ended under something of a cloud in 1940, due to his unpopular stands, warned Marlene that she was risking her welfare by gallivanting around Europe with the troops, but she told him she considered herself as American as he was and, as an American citizen since 1939, she felt it her duty to heighten troop morale anywhere and everywhere.

"But Marlene, you're of *German* ancestry!" Joe continued to argue. "And *you* are an *Irishman!*" Marlene shot back. "German-American, Irish-American, what's the difference?" Joe got his dander up when Marlene reiterated that Irishmen, homegrown or transplanted, hated Britain as much as any German did, and insinuated that his appeasement policies had been influenced by that—she had posed this argument playfully in 1939, but with all that had happened to him in the ensuing five years, Joe in 1944 found that it really riled him. "Marlene said that Joe put the phone down on her after that," Adela St. Johns remembered. She and Marlene did a 1944 fan magazine article designed for *Photoplay*, but the editor at that time decided that Marlene, then out in *Kismet* with Ronald Colman and in need of what MGM's Howard Strickling called "the *right* publicity—all glamor, *no* politics," was much too frank about her and Joe and their political disagreements in the article to warrant its inclusion. The long hand of Howard Strickling was rightly suspected of killing the piece. "It is not an article that is right for a magazine such as *Photoplay*," Marlene's representatives were told. She promptly blamed Joe Kennedy. "But it was the MGM publicity department that killed it, not Joe," Adela remembered, "though I'm sure he would have agreed with MGM that it ought to be killed."

Also there was another factor in Joe's calculations after his oldest son, Joe Jr., was killed when his bomb-laden plane exploded off the English coast in 1944. Jack was the heir apparent; his PT-109 "exploit" had heightened him—somewhat—in American public awareness around 1943, and Joe was already looking ahead to the end of the war and Jack's incipient political career. He needed rehashings—by Marlene or anyone else—of his appeasement policies as ambassador to Great Britain in 1938–1940 like a hole in the head. In fact, Joe reasoned, he had better supply the money and clout but *play down* his own prior history when it came to getting Jack a political start.

Jack Kennedy and Marlene Dietrich had an encounter in Hollywood in 1940, the year after her *Destry Rides Again* triumph, that by tacit mutual consent they had not seen fit to apprise Joe. Marlene was making a picture called *Seven Sinners*, in which she was her most sultry, sirenish self, and Jack and Robert Stack, who knew everyone on the Universal lot, were dropping in on movie sets.

At twenty-three Jack, by then a Harvard grad, had penned *Why England Slept* (ghostwritten but with what Jack called his "idea inputs") and was a fledgling literary personality. *Why England Slept* was yet another of Joe Kennedy's gimmicks for putting his children prematurely ahead—on the shoulders and backs of more gifted ghost-writers and other toodies.

Jack had a pleasant session in Marlene Dietrich's dressing room. "With the co-stars you have in this film [among them superhunk John Wayne], I must seem like a kid to you," he said. According to Lem Billings, his confidant, her Mae Westian rejoinder was: "You are *definitely no kid!*" But she made no passes, he reported.

NINE

Lem the Adoring, Eddie the Faithful

There is no question but that Jack's roommate his sopho-more year at Choate, Kirk Le Moyne Billings, was in love with Jack all his life, adoring him unreservedly, unques-tioningly, while Jack was in love with Lem being in love with him and considered him the ideal follower-adorer.

Their friendship lasted until Jack's death. And, Lem confided in me, it was a friendship that included oral sex, with Jack always on the receiving end. Lem believed that this arrangement enabled Jack to sustain his self-delusion that straight men who received oral sex from other males were really only straights looking for a sexual release.

I first met Lem when I was helping in Jack's first con-gressional campaign in 1946. Lem was about thirty then. It was obvious that the whole Kennedy family loved him. At that time and in the years thereafter, I came to know Lem quite well, and that's when he shared with me many of the intimate details of his relationship with Jack.

Lem was a homosexual. The entire Kennedy family either knew it outright or suspected it covertly, but his devotion to Jack was to them so overwhelming, so total, that they made—for an essentially heterosexual family living by heterosexual standards in all departments—very generous allowances for Lem.

Lem in later years was to develop a fixation on Jack's charismatic sister Kathleen, "Kick" to her intimates, but she recognized his courtship for what it was—just another way of being even closer to Jack by marrying his sister—and she fobbed him off. She didn't laugh him off; the family took him too seriously for that. "Lem was no laughing matter," Eddie Moore once said. "His devotion to Jack had tragic, Shakespearean proportions."

Lem was not very good looking. His forehead was too high; his manner awkward and "grizzly-bearish" (as Kick once described it), and for all his physical strength, he had a high, nasal whine of a voice that instantly tabbed him as gay. At Choate, the dean had nervous reservations about Jack and Lem—especially when Lem deliberately held himself back a year because that meant one more year with Jack. Steps were taken to separate them, but Jack asked Old Joe to intervene. They remained roommates.

Old Joe had mixed feelings about Lem, but he considered him the lesser of two evils, the other potential evil being that Jack might go restlessly wandering abroad and get into more trouble than he was already in. But he found Lem's high, screechy laugh and doglike reactions to Jack's every word and move nerve-wracking, complaining (but only mildly) when Lem invariably accompanied Jack home on vacations, along the lines of "do we have to have that queer around all summer?"—such words were whispered covertly to Rose or Eddie Moore.

Joe Kennedy was not dumb about homo- and bisexuality. He had met a number of gay and bisexual men at Boston

Latin and Harvard, and because, as an Irishman in Yankee-dominated Boston, he felt himself a put-upon minority, his basic attitude was live-and-let-live where sexual preferences were concerned—so long as these did not intrude on him personally. He did not want Jack impregnating any of the girls he dated, and he was of the old-fashioned school that held that masturbation was sexually wasteful, so if Jack allowed Lem to pleasure him—well, worse things could happen to someone as undisciplined, rowdy, tomfoolery-perpetrating, and cynical as Jack was in his teen years and indeed into his twenties.

There was another element to Lem Billings that arrested Old Joe's attention and won his grudging respect: Lem's pedigree. Lem, homely, ungainly, and undignified in his slavish devotion to Jack, had the purest of Mayflower Yankee blood in his veins.

Lem's father, a respected Pittsburgh physician who died in 1933 when Lem was only in his teens, had lost his fortune in the 1929 crash, so Lem, suddenly impoverished along with other members of his family, was at Choate as a lowly scholarship student. Among Lem's ancestors on his father's side was a Brewster of Plymouth plantation who had later served as a seventeenth-century governor, and on his mother's side, the Le Moynes were noted physicians including Doctor Francis Le Moyne, who was a famed abolitionist and had fostered educational opportunities for blacks.

Yes, the blood ran blue for Lem, though he was humiliated by poverty, struggling on a scholarship, humbly grateful for crumbs of Kennedy hospitality. The combination of his lineage and his dependency undoubtedly appealed to Old Joe's sense of irony, given the Yankee put-downs of the Irish Joe had endured and festered over since boyhood.

Jack had inherited his father's attitude toward the Yankees, and he too enjoyed the irony of a Yankee aristocrat—in this case impoverished and powerless—serving him so loyally.

Lem also shared with Jack something that went to the core. They were both second sons who had for years submitted to the tyranny of bullying, patronizing older brothers. Fred Billings had been a football hero and class president. Joe Kennedy Jr. never let Jack forget who was boss. "Just because he came into the world a couple of years before me doesn't make Joe *God*," Jack would snivel at Lem, who invariably replied that he, too, had a brother who thought he was God.

Through the years Lem continued to service his beloved Jack in any and all ways that occurred to Jack. He was straight man to Jack, the brunt of his practical jokes. "But the family in time found Lem no joke," Stephen Smith later said. His all-out loyalty, a loyalty that persisted in the face of Jack's ambivalences, put-downs, practical jokes and whatnot, became to the family a touching and heroic thing. Even Old Joe was in spite of himself touched by it. When it came to Jack, Lem was without pride, never stood up for himself, but was not a doormat—not really. He just loved—loved, perhaps, too much, too unstintingly, too unquestioningly.

To me the Kennedys didn't seem patronizing toward him; rather they seemed protective—ruefully protective, but protective for all that. I felt Lem was a very lonely and unhappy man. "I'm not good-looking," he said to me once. "They make fun of my voice. People think me a joke. But I'm stuck with the Kennedys emotionally, and I will be to the end of my life." Lem was prophetic, for to the time of his death in 1981 at age sixty-five, he was loyal to the Kennedy mystique and legend. Sometimes he carried loyalty much too far. Essentially weak and a follower, he transferred his devotion, after Jack died, to his nephews, including Bobby Kennedy Jr. and Chris Lawford, and when these boys developed severe drug habits, instead of firmly helping them to combat their addictions, he *joined* them and became as big an addict as they were.

As Lem told me, he got into some jams indulging in what he called "men's room monkey business"—and the Kennedys repaid his devotion on a number of occasions by getting him off the hook legally and publicity-wise. Not particularly intellectual or well-read, Lem's lifetime obsession was Kennedy lore. He was particularly devoted to Eunice, whom he described to me on one occasion, "the Family Powerhouse." In the mid 1970s he was seriously considering an inside book on the Kennedys, as his finances were always, as he put it, "upsy-downsy." He had read and admired my 1968 book on Bobby Kennedy, *Robert Francis Kennedy*, and asked me once if I'd like to ghostwrite his book. Shortly after, he backtracked. "I can't do it," he told me. "Even if I said only nice positive things, I'd feel like a traitor to them!" I told him he was being too scrupulous, that he could offer provocative, illuminating insights that might make the clan more humanly understandable, but he shook his head sadly. "No, publishers want inside dirt—if I were under contract I'd be tempted by them to get too personal." And then he added: "They've been really good to me at times; I'd be an ingrate!" When I suggested that, having observed his devotion to Jack and the Kennedys since we first met in 1946, I felt *he* had been damned good to *them*, he shrugged his shoulders, looked at me sadly, and then said something that for twenty years I have remembered: "When I love . . . I *love!* It's just *me!*"

Some dozen years after Jack's death, Lem would burst into tears recalling their relationship. "Imagine," he would say with a kind of wondering breathlessness, "even when he became president, even when he was living in the White House, there was always a room reserved for *me!*" I had come to know Lem well enough by 1975 that I could afford to indulge the temptation to say that Jack had always needed a court jester and a superhenchman to help him feel good about himself, and then Lem would pout indignantly. "No, Larry," he said to me once, "he *needed* me. He was very lonely in his way, and he was never well, physically. And Bobby was right when he said Jack's back never stopped paining him!"

During the period when we were having talks about a possible book by Lem on JFK and company, I asked him about Jack's womanizing. "Oh, they all did that—all the Kennedys did—even Bobby. They took after the old man. I think in Jack's case it was loneliness and boredom." Then Lem recalled Jack saying that "getting it off with beautiful people was sort of reaffirming the life-force and escaping life's pressures all at the same time." He added, "It was part of Jack's cynical, lonely, don't-give-a-damn attitude. I know he wasn't just imitating his father—it went beyond that. Sex for Jack was an escapist addiction, just as drugs or alcohol are to others. Nor was he guilty about it. "I have to be *me*" was his attitude. Didn't Lem feel sorry that Jackie might be hurt about the infidelities? "Oh, she had her own life—she accepted it. I never felt sex was that important to Jackie—anyway, her father had been a rascal and womanizer and she had the sophisticated attitude (I think) that men were natural rovers and better to have it up front than kept secret."

Once I asked Lem about the story that Old Joe had given Jackie a million dollars to stay with Jack after she discovered the extent of his extramarital roving. Without answering directly, Lem said, "Oh, she had plenty of reasons to stay with him—the kids, the reflected glory of being married to a famous man, the beautiful clothes she could buy. I think she thought of her relationship with Jack as a *friendship*, and friends—well, they *tolerate* each other."

Jackie seemed to have used Lem as a confidant and shoulder to cry on more frequently than the record has disclosed. "Jackie always liked gay men, and found them in many ways more loyal and understanding than other women or straight men," Stephen Smith once said, and Lem told me that she had shared with him her views on some of the women who had in her words "gotten into Jack's shorts."

According to Lem, Jackie considered Marilyn Monroe a vulgar slut and publicity seeker, an egomaniac and self-promoter of a particularly vicious and unbalanced kind. Of all Jack's involvements, he said, she seemed to like best Gene Tierney, whose affair with Jack had, of course, preceded her own years with him. "Gene is so *tragic*," Jackie said to Lem. "That child born handicapped—I honestly would prefer *losing* a child, as I did Patrick [in 1963] to having one *handicapped!*" Lem had seized that occasion to bring up the unfortunate Rosemary, and Jackie said, flatly, tersely, "She was never really a functioning human being; she'd have been better off to have *died early!*"

Jackie's attitude toward Judith Exner (the woman involved with both Jack and Frank Sinatra) seems to have been contemptuous, according to Lem: "She was a user, a manipulator—common as dirt!" On Angie Dickinson? "Out for reflected glory." On Jayne Mansfield? "Her brains were in her boobs!"

Lem once asked Jackie what she hoped would happen to John-John (who in 1975 was turning fifteen) when it came to love, romance, marriage, whatever. She hoped he wouldn't be homosexual because it was a sad situation to be homosexual and famous. Jackie, he remembered, cited the case of a famous general's son who became totally anonymous and changed his name and hid away, "so he wouldn't have his gay lifestyle a tabloid plaything." Jackie told Lem that she didn't think homosexuality in itself was a tough lifestyle, but for someone in the public eye, it could be cruel and psychologically damaging. "Look at what you have had to go through," Jackie told Lem, "and you are not a directly famous person!" Then Lem asked Jackie how she would want John-John to behave with the women he got involved with. "Oh, I hope he marries someone devoted, but if there are involvements I just hope he will be fair and kind and do as little emotional harm as possible." (JFK Jr.'s involvements, now that he is thirty-five, are unanimous in describing him during and after his relationships as just that—fair and kind.)

With all the inside knowledge Lem had, he could have made a fine book out of it, and I am still sorry that I didn't ghostwrite it for him. Lem was very upset over stories that he was gay, and when a particularly vicious rumor had it, toward the close of his life, that he was in love with decades-younger Robert Kennedy Jr. and had aided and abetted his drug habit so as to personally control him and use him sexually, he told me he had the first of what he was sure were irregular heart spasms. I suspect these eventually killed him, for in his later years Lem's drinking and his overindulgence in drugs (his own private escape from unbearable loneliness and hurt) did drastically affect his heart, and he died in his sleep. Lem had had a series of painful unrequited involvements with actors and other handsome rascals who used him and then deserted him. "I even loved some of them, too," he said to me wistfully. "But the only man I ever loved totally and completely and for all my life was Jack Kennedy."

———————

When Edward Moore Kennedy, for thirty-three years now a United States senator, was born on February 22, 1932—the two hundredth anniversary of George Washington's birth—the loving and loyal aide who had served Joe Kennedy well for so long, Eddie Moore was given the ultimate honor a friend could expect from another friend: Joe Kennedy named his fourth and last son after him.

Joe in one of his earlier visits to Frances Marion had told her that had Fred lived, *he* would have been the godfather and *he* would have lent his name. Edward Moore Kennedy, had it not been for that death on Christmas Night, 1928, would have been Frederick Clifton Thomson Kennedy (Fred's full three names).

When Joe was asked once by his lost first son, Joe Jr., why he hadn't named Ted Fred anyway, despite the death (Joe Jr. adored Fred and his movies), Joe had sadly replied that to call his son "Fred" over and over through the years would have been like keeping a wound open and the blood flowing constantly. So Eddie Moore, certainly not by default—he had loved and served Joe Kennedy well for many years—got the namesake accolade which he had truly deserved.

"No one loved and served Joe Kennedy, unquestioningly and devotedly, constantly, eternally, more than Eddie Moore," Stephen Smith once said. Mary Moore, Eddie's wife, was a kind, motherly person who was always there for both Joe and Rose.

Eddie was a kind, simple person. "Judge not lest you *be* judged" was one of his favorite sayings. He knew Joe Kennedy as few men did. When several of Joe's entourage toward the close of his Hollywood adventure deserted him in 1931 to join a film studio that promised more of a future for them, repaying Joe's friendship with vicious gossip about Gloria, Nancy, Evelyn, and the other women in Joe's life, and exposing some of his more "corner-cutting" business practices, Eddie Moore told them off, accused them of betrayal, gross ingratitude, and weaselly back-knifing.

Eddie Moore was a great favorite of my uncle Jimmy Quirk, who said Eddie was one of the best friends any man could have. Jimmy told his aide, Kathryn Dougherty, who later told me, that Eddie was the salt of the earth, that he would have made a good priest or a social worker, that the greatest miracle of Joe's life was that he found Eddie.

Peter Lawford told me that Eddie "took a lot of shit from Joe," that he wondered, from all he had heard from the other Kennedys, how Eddie put up with it, so patiently and so long. Eddie did all the dirty-work detail: messenger boy between Joe and Gloria, Joe and Nancy, Joe and Evelyn; contact with less desirable mob elements who did the "booze-sale thing" with Joe. He got Joe out of scrapes, covered up for him, reportedly routed Joe out a window or back door and jumped into bed with one of Joe's gals-of-the-night when he heard of a raid or a jealous-lover assault being imminent (or when a frantic Joe phoned him with these and other bad-news rescue-me calls). Wife Mary was endlessly patient when Eddie leaped out of bed to jump to Joe's alarm ringing and endless demands, often in the middle of the night. Called unkindly "Joe Kennedy's slave-in-chief," the man for whom Ted Kennedy was named was far more than that—he gave that rarest of gifts: *unconditional love*.

There were those who felt Eddie carried that unconditional love to the point of outright masochism. Joe could approach sadism when commands were not obeyed to the letter, when bad situations were not straightened out in record time. "Eddie probably saved Joe's life—not physically but spiritually—with his common sense and decent instincts and protectiveness, always protectiveness," one friend said.

TEN

Jack Goes Hollywood

Among Jack's 1940 Hollywood playmates (in this case man-to-man platonic in their mutual pursuit of willing females) was the handsome young actor Robert Stack, scion of an aristocratic California family, who even before his twenty-first birthday had arrived had won a form of international fame for giving Deanna Durbin her first kiss in the film *First Love*. Bob Stack was a charming, affable fellow who wore his extreme good looks with casual ease, and I always enjoyed interviewing him. In 1958 in New York, he said of his old Hollywood pal John Kennedy (then running for his second Senate term—the presidency was two years in the future), "He was quite a guy with the women in those days! He was only twenty-three or so when I knew him [Bob was twenty-one] but did they take to him! He should have been an actor, with that charisma and charm, but then they say politics is a form of acting, too, and he has certainly done well enough in *that*, hasn't he? . . ."

Bob Stack, after that *First Love* debut at twenty, proved to be no Hollywood flash-in-the-pan. He went on to a num-

ber of nice-boy leads before serving in the navy in World
War II. He then went on to a solid Hollywood career, with
critic-pleasing stints in such winners as *The Bullfighter and
the Lady* (1951), *The High and the Mighty* (1954), and his
Oscar-nominated supporting role in *Written on the Wind*.
(Dorothy Malone, his co-star in the latter film, said to me in
1964: "Bob is a much finer actor than people bemused by his
good looks will admit!")

In the 1960s Bob went on to win television acclaim as
Eliot Ness in *The Untouchables*, winning an Emmy for it, and
also starred in such television series as *The Name of the Game*,
Most Wanted, *Strike Force*, and *Unsolved Mysteries*.

In his 1980 autobiography, Straight Shooting, Bob
wrote of Jack Kennedy:

> I've known many of the great Hollywood stars, and only
> a very few of them seemed to hold the attraction for
> women that JFK did, even before he entered the political
> arena. He'd just look at them and they'd tumble. I often
> wondered (in subsequent years) why he wasted his time on
> politics when he could have made it big in an important
> business like motion pictures.

Introduced by mutual friends in early 1940 in Hollywood, Bob and Jack soon were what was known on the
Hollywood circuit as a "cruise team"—meaning they spent
much of their time cruising after Hollywood's most attractive
ladies. Bob to this day (he is now seventy-seven) has a vivid
memory of a place he dubbed the Flag Room. He and Jack
used the room as a base, in more ways than one.

Bob recalled that it was on Whitley Terrace, "a small
curving street wandering into the Hollywood Hills, midway
between Highland and Cahuenga." It involved what he called
"a cul-de-sac of jumbled apartments irregularly stacked on top
of each other like building blocks put together by a drunk."

In his autobiography Bob had more to say about the Flag Room: "Each apartment was perched dangerously on its neighbor. Over each apartment grew a luxurious, tangled web of vines creating a veritable Garden of Eden effect." According to Bob: "It was here that I learned about the birds, the bees, the barracudas and other forms of Hollywood wildlife." A friend of Bob's, Alfredo de la Vega, had, in Bob's words: "come up with the idea that we should convince our mothers we needed a hideaway for meditation and study. When our mothers surprisingly agreed to this arrangement, we promised ourselves to study our favorite subjects even harder than before."

The high point of Bob and Jack's hideaway was the full-size bed in a room with a ceiling too low to permit an adult to stand upright. The walls were plastered with flags from any and all nations on the globe. Bob devised, for his and Jack's continued delectation, a game that required the evening's leading lady to memorize all the flags on the ceiling or pay the penalty. As Bob recalled: "Since she was already in a horizontal position (given the low ceiling) paying the penalty was usually no problem!" Just to keep things zinging along, Bob, Jack, and the others on hand kept switching flags around so that it would be difficult to memorize them—thus giving added impetus to the amorous maneuverings.

In his autobiography, Bob particularly recalled the landlord:

> . . . a one-legged boozer of prodigious capacity who never seemed to mind the racket downstairs as long as the door was open. Around the shank of the morning, say two or three o'clock, we would hear the clump, clump, clump of his wooden leg as he came to collect his toll, a beer glass of straight scotch.

Bob concluded his remarks on the Flag Room as follows: "I am happy to say that Jack Kennedy found occasion to further his geopolitical studies and gain future constituents at our little pad on Whitley Terrace," adding that when Jack later campaigned for the presidency and talked about international relations, he never brought up the Flag Room. Yet Bob and Alfredo always believed that they were to be held accountable "in some small way" for Jack Kennedy's training in what flag belonged to what country.

Bob Stack has another memory concerning the Kennedys—one not so pleasant. He found himself haplessly cast opposite a lady who has been termed "the world's worst actress"—Princess Lee Radziwill, now wife of the director Herbert Ross. The project was a television remake of the classic *Laura*. David Susskind, Bob recalled, talked him into it. "It's a great piece of natural casting," David remarked, adding that they'd get ratings that would skyrocket with Jackie Kennedy's sister in the lead. Bob asked if Lee had ever acted before. David quoted Truman Capote to the effect that Lee was a "natural." Bob later reflected that the words *natural* and *amateur* are interchangeable.

Bob's first impression of Lee Bouvier, as she chose to call herself professionally, was not favorable. He remembered her "frosted brown hair, the unmistakable Bouvier eyes set wide apart, and a slightly pointed chin." And she was dressed, dressed, dressed. Translate *that*: overdressed.

Soon, Bob realized that supporting-sustaining-carrying the supremely untalented Lee Bouvier was a task with which to reckon. George Sanders, Arlene Francis, and Farley Granger, also caught in the mess, summoned what dignity they could as the affair proceeded. Bob remembered the horror of Lee's first reading: "She sounded as if she were reading: 'the gray cat jumped over the spotted dog.'" He then discovered that Lee knew nothing about how to move, walking, as he recalled, "like a mechanical doll, a dead giveaway of an amateur."

Bob in retrospect blamed Michael Cacoyannis, director of *Zorba the Greek*, and the ubiquitous, ever mischievous Truman Capote for talking Lee into acting, telling her, "You *are* Laura." Later Capote, no doubt realizing the magnitude of his mistake and facing public embarrassment (just one of the many embarrassments for hapless, bungling Truman), backed out of his deal to write the screenplay and took off for the Bahamas.

The time was the 1960s, and since Lee was the sister-in-law of a president of the United States, even the nay-sayers of her acting conceded that curiosity value alone would bring the public to their television sets.

David Susskind began to get alarmed over his stone-faced, unresponsive star. Finally he begged Bob to "scare the hell out of her" to get *some* kind of reaction.

Bob recalled what happened next:

> I don't think Godzilla at his worst could have broken down Princess Radziwill's cafe-society cool, but I did manage to induce a faint expression of surprise when I suddenly threw a chair across the room and began pounding on the table and bellowing at her. After twenty-two takes we were running out of chairs, my hand hurt, and I'd lost my voice entirely. But Susskind got the rudimentary beginnings of a scene!

Bob recalled that the only thanks or acknowledgment for his help Lee gave him was when she murmured: "You kiss better than Farley Granger." And when asked later if she appreciated the cast's help, imperious Princess Radziwill replied, "No, they just did their job, no more!"

Years later I asked Farley Granger what it had been like to work with, let alone kiss, Lee Radziwill. He fixed me with the frostiest of looks and snapped, "No comment!" There were, of course, other rumors concerning Truman Capote's withdrawal as writer for the piece. This may be news to Bob and Farley, but he was said to have had secret, unrequited crushes on both of them, and told a friend, "It was *torture* being near *two of the most beautiful men in the world* constantly, I had to exit!"

Unlike Tennessee Williams, who according to Gore Vidal had a wild crush on Jack Kennedy ("Jack thought it was a horselaugh—he was greatly amused!" was Gore's description of Jack's response), Truman Capote never "thrilled and throbbed to the manly charms" (Truman's pet phrase) of Jack Kennedy. "He's an Irish clunk," Truman said. "Oh, I admit he has a vulgar appeal—but then the Kennedys are such a vulgar family!"

While in Hollywood in 1940, Jack, through various connections, wangled his way to the Universal lot and appeared one day on Margaret Sullavan's *Back Street* set, where they were photographed together. "A beautiful, beautiful man," Margaret Sullavan told me years later. "Even in his early twenties he had all that cocky masculine charm." She added (possibly joking, possibly not) that had she not been married (to Leland Hayward) and pregnant with her son Bill while making the film, she would have made a play for the twenty-three-year-old Jack. Jack, unfortunately, never knew what he was missing, for as I recounted in my 1986 Margaret Sullavan biography, she had a unique ability to make the men she dallied with (and there were many) feel good—really good. Lem Billings recalled later that Jack said he thought the unknowns and "starlets" were even more enticing than stars, being "so eager, so anxious to please."

ELEVEN

The Poignant Gene Tierney

One of the most poignant of Jack Kennedy's relationships with Hollywood actresses was his affair with Gene Tierney.

When they met on the set of *Dragonwyck* in February 1946, Jack was twenty-eight and Gene was twenty-five. Jack was in the early stages of the campaign that would win him his first term in Congress, and at that point he found himself introduced around as "Ambassador Kennedy's son"—notwithstanding that his father resigned his post as ambassador to Great Britain for more than five years before and that Jack had won some attention (his detractors called it notoriety) for his PT-109 navy mishap, which his father had barnstormed into an act of heroism. *Why England Slept*, Jack's first book, was also some five years in the past. Jack in early 1946 was known (slightly) as a naval officer who had suffered a back injury in the Pacific and had spent months in a military hospital. Gene, on the other hand, was a world-famous star who had won an Academy Award nomination for her recent, highly celebrated *Leave Her to Heaven*. As a woman who "loves too much" and even resorts to murder to hang on to her hapless husband's exclusive love, Gene showed she could be an actress as well as a beauty and personality.

The year before she had won top stardom in the celebrated *Laura*, in which she became the obsession of detective Dana Andrews, who thinks she is a murder victim and falls in love with her portrait, only to discover that she is alive and is herself a murder suspect.

At the time she met Jack, Gene was separated from her husband, Oleg Cassini, a film designer of eccentric cast with a strange, narrow face; both were playing the field. They shared a common sorrow: the retardation, blindness, and deafness of their three-year-old child, Daria.

Although she had won top fame, and was sought after by many men, including her sometime co-star Tyrone Power, and although she enjoyed all the accoutrements of stardom, being well-liked by her Twentieth Century-Fox boss Darryl Zanuck ("because," as he put it, "she isn't temperamental and demanding and never gives me trouble"), Gene was a lonely, troubled, and unhappy woman. She was given to depressive mood cycles and insecurities, and she lived in fear of what she conceived to be a propensity for mental illness that ran in her family.

That she was deeply in love with Jack Kennedy went without question. And in this one instance, Jack might have approached, for once in his life, a corresponding feeling for her. He was going with Gene all through 1946 when I first met him, and I recall that when her name came up and the usual joshing and kidding ensued, he would sharply correct all comers; "This isn't a joke or a fun thing," he said to Joe Kane and others who knew of his relationship with Gene. "She's a nice lady, a *real* lady, and I'm honored that she has taken me as seriously as she has."

Joe, Lem Billings, and others were struck at the time by his respectful attitude toward Gene. "I think he felt great sympathy for her," Lem Billings told me years later. "She had gone through a terrible tragedy with her retarded daughter, and Jack told me he had talked with her a lot about it and reminded her of his retarded sister Rosemary and counseled her on bearing what had to be borne." Joe Kane and others felt that Gene brought out Jack's best side, that "best side" involving chivalry, concern, and a profound sympathy that Jack could display if he felt that the object of sympathy was worth it.

I personally saw Jack's sympathy and concern at work firsthand as he commented on the poverty and desolation of the many underprivileged families he encountered during his 1946 congressional campaign. "I've been a very lucky guy— *very* lucky," he said one time. "Harvard education, first book at twenty-three, wonderful travel opportunities, every form of privilege one can imagine. And then I see how so many poor souls pulled themselves up by their bootstraps—and how many failed and gave up because the bleakness and defeatism proved too much for them. . . ." This was a side of Jack that Gene encountered full force—as did the constituents who elected him that first time in 1946. Much has been made of Jack, the spoiled, rich boy whose ambitious daddy bought him connections, political office, votes, and power, but there was so much more than that to the Jack I and others knew in those early years.

When Gene, later in their relationship, took him to meet her uppity, conservative, Irish *Republican* family—who were Episcopalians, to boot—Gene's mother commented on the "trashy commonness" of the Irish political henchmen with whom Jack surrounded himself during the throes of the 1946 campaign. Jack had a ready answer to that: politics involves meeting and knowing all kinds of people, learning their needs, identifying with their wants and their struggles. "I learned a lot about that in the navy, and now I'm really learning about it. And it's good for me. It opens me up; makes me a better person."

Gene's brother Howard, known as "Butch," resented Jack Kennedy. He had known Jack slightly at Harvard, where Butch in 1940 had done his graduate work, and he liked neither Jack's politics nor his general attitude. As Gene Tierney later recalled, on one occasion when she took Jack up to the Tierneys, Butch would not even let her in the door. "He did not feel, he made clear, that there was any future in my dating a Catholic. 'Any girl who is going through a divorce,' he lectured me, 'and has a retarded child, has no business looking to have her heart broken any more.'" Butch added, "I don't admire you or [Jack] for getting mixed up with each other."

Gene later gave her own analysis of Jack Kennedy: "I am not sure I can explain the nature of Jack's charm, but he took life just as it came. He didn't try to hide. He never worried about making an impression. He made you feel very secure." Gene never remembered seeing Jack angry, recalling: "He was good with people in a way that went beyond politics, thoughtful in more than a material way." Gifts and flowers were not his style (when he was courting a woman). Instead, Gene remembered, "He gave you his interest. He knew the strength of the phrase, 'What do *you* think?'"

The husband she was then unloading, the playboy dilettante and sometime designer Oleg Cassini, had tried several times to warn Gene about Jack Kennedy, telling her that Jack would never dignify their relationship with a marital proposal because he was a Catholic and his family had ambitions for him and would never allow it.

Gene said she had always felt in her subconscious that the romance was doomed, but went on with it anyway "because I was under the spell of Jack's charm and because I—how shall I put it—went on hoping against hope." Then she added, "Foolish, foolish me."

Jack always kept his special respect and regard for Gene Tierney. She was definitely not one of his easy Hollywood lays. She was no overly accommodating starlet or all-too-willing bimbo, and he let his father know it in no uncertain terms.

One time up on the Cape in the summer of 1946, between confabs on election strategy, Old Joe began kidding Jack about Gene Tierney. Joe's attitude toward Hollywood actresses was what it had always been—cavalier, faintly contemptuous—and his attitude that women should be sources more of pleasure than of sincerity, commitment, or caring sometimes irritated Jack mightily. "I understand Gene is going through a divorce," Joe cackled. "So she needs some good lays, and you're the man to give them to her!" A memory may have intruded into Jack's consciousness at that moment—that summer day in 1929 when twelve-year-old Jack caught his father and Gloria Swanson making out on the family yacht. He replied sharply, "Gene is a lady, Dad. A *lady*. Don't treat her name lightly." Then, as Lem Billings later remembered, he drove a knife into Old Joe with the observation that Gene had the retarded child—"later she may be well beyond lobotomizing!" As Lem remembered it, Joe got up suddenly, red faced and glowering, and went into the house.

That scene in 1929 was always to be there, unspoken and ominous, a sinister presence outside of allusion or speech. Jack let his father know that he was respectful, dutiful, and willing to take over for the departed Joe Jr., and part

of Jack enjoyed the human contact and admiration and political power plays. Joe knew he had his son's deferential, even
awed respect and that Jack even enjoyed watching Joe's
manipulations and maneuverings on his behalf. But deep
down Joe knew that he had lost his son's *love* long ago on
that yacht, and it galled and humiliated him.

Jack went on with his political campaigning, and he and
Gene were often separated geographically during 1946. She
recalled going to see him on the floor of Congress after his
election in the following year. "We tried to keep our
romance out of the gossip columns," she remembered, "and
for the most part we succeeded. I visited him once in
Washington [where in 1947 he was a freshman congressman]
and sat quietly in the guest balcony while Congress was in
session. A reporter spotted me and asked me what I was
doing there. Thinking quickly, I said that I was studying the
government. 'Oh, some kind of movie project?' he asked."
Gene nodded: "Something like that."

Gene's mother continued to be annoyed by the company Jack kept politically. "I could see the drive he had," Gene
recalled, "the sense of power acquired from being steeped
early in Boston Irish politics." Gene recalled yet another
occasion when Jack came to visit her family at Greens Farms,
Connecticut.

> Jack would have with him one of his ward heelers:
> hearty, rumpled men who left cigar stubs in [Mother's]
> ashtrays. Mother fed Jack milk and cookies in the kitchen,
> but (yet again) she could not mask her distaste for his com-
> panions and didn't try. Once she asked [Gene's sister] Pat,
> "Why can't [Jack] get a better class of people around him?"
> Pat laughed and said, "Mother, he's a politician. He's not
> on a polo team."

After that Gene's mother gave up once and for all on Jack's
political aspirations and companions. "But I know she

thought it all very *déclassé*," Gene later remembered. She and Butch thought the privileged and wealthy should mingle only with the privileged and wealthy, that this avoided jealousies and misunderstandings that were bound to crop up. "But that was one of the things I liked about Jack—he had the common touch. Oh he knew he was privileged, had a powerful and wealthy father who could open any doors he wanted; inescapably he took on some of the tinctures of the privileged. But he was not like that, really—not in his deepest heart."

I did a number of interviews with Gene Tierney in my years as a movie fan-mag editor and freelance journalist. As the 1950s advanced, I noted the steady deterioration in her personality, the haunted look she often had, the erratic conversational shifts. By 1955, at the time of her Humphrey Bogart co-starrer, *The Left Hand of God*, it was obvious something was going wrong. This was all the sadder because she was only thirty-five that year and would have given some wonderful, possibly Oscar-winning performances in her mature years. But she was cut off, spending years in mental hospitals, totally unable to cope with life, released to her family only to revert to institutional care again and again. No one was happier than I when wonderful Howard Lee, the Texas millionaire, came into her life and gave her, through their felicitous marriage, a form of security and caring she had never known before in an intimate context.

In a 1955 interview, she said sadly, "I have had a very lucky life, but I know the bad must come with the good. I don't know what the future will bring, but whatever it is, it is my destiny, and I believe that, somehow, destiny is foreordained. . . ."

In late 1946 Gene was at the height of her career, co-starring with Tyrone Power in *The Razor's Edge*, replete with a lavish premiere in New York with parties and fetes galore. Jack Kennedy, having won his first election to Congress that November, was planning to see Gene on the Cape. He seemed happier that November than I had ever known him to be—a new congressman in love with Hollywood's then brightest star. Meanwhile in New York, Tyrone Power, divorced from Annabella and a romantic free agent, was laying romantic siege to Gene. As she later recalled it, "Ty asked if he could stop by my suite after the party. He said he had a small gift for me. My mother and sister ducked discreetly into the bedroom when Ty arrived. He did not stay long. After a few minutes, I said, 'You know, Ty, I'm going up to the Cape tomorrow to visit a friend of my mother's. While I'm there I hope to see Jack Kennedy!'" She recalled the awkward silence that ensued as she opened her hands, palms up (one of her most characteristic gestures since childhood, as she once told me). She then whispered to Ty: "That's the gist of it." She remembered him leaving, not angrily but quietly. She opened Ty's gift. It was a beautiful silk scarf with the word *love* embroidered on it. She kept the scarf for years, but never wore it. She finally gave it to her sister. Her final wrap-up on *that* would-be triangle was: "Ty was warm and considerate. He had a beautiful face. But I could not fall in love with Ty Power, having met Jack Kennedy."

Late in 1947, still wrapped in her romantic dream about Jack Kennedy, Gene was having lunch with him. According to Lem Billings they had already become lovers, and it was the happiest time of Gene's life. Suddenly Jack lowered the boom. "You know, Gene," she recalled him saying, "I can never marry you." Her heart went stony and cold. She knew it was one of life's endings. When it was time for him to catch his flight to Washington, she said, "Bye-bye, Jack." "That sounds kind of final," she recalled him saying. "It is," she rejoindered. She remembered them looking at each other for "a long, timeless moment." Then he was gone, permanently out of her life—at least romantically.

Not that Jack didn't try again. Five years later, in 1952, she met him at Maxim's in Paris, where she was having dinner with Michele Morgan and her husband. They danced. He asked if they could start seeing each other again. Her answer was no. She knew that the future would hold nothing but hurt for her. The following year, 1953, she read of his marriage to Jacqueline Bouvier, single, aristocratic, stylish, poised—and the recipient of the all-out approval of Joe Kennedy and his family.

After she had gone through her first bout with mental illness, Jack and Gene met again in New York. The year was 1956. He had heard about her travails and had gone to see her. Her mother wouldn't leave her alone with him, he being a married man and all that. Jack, she remembered, found it amusing considering that he was only on hand, he said, as a sincere friend inquiring about her welfare.

To the end of his life, Gene Tierney was one of Jack Kennedy's earnest defenders and apologists. She denied he had used her, then dumped her. "No one really broke up our relationship," she later explained, "not Jack's father nor his mother nor my family. I did not date him again because I knew the consequences would not be happy ones. In truth ours was a sweet but short-lived romance. When I met him he was a serious young man with a dream. He was *not* a womanizer, not as *I* understand the term!"

Gene claimed that whenever she heard gossip about Jack's alleged private didoes or came across some woman's "revelations" about him in print, she recalled what her grandfather once said about President Warren Harding: that the media, the public, and the bluenoses were persecuting him because he had a mistress. Her grandfather called Harding "an unhappy man," adding, "I don't believe a man's morals have anything to do with his statesmanship."

When Jack was elected president in 1960, Gene sent him a telegram that read: "Congratulations! I knew you would make it!" She later laughed over the irony intrinsic in this gesture; "due to the conservative influence of my upbringing," she said, she had actually voted for Richard Nixon.

Gene saw Jack Kennedy one last time, in 1962, when the movie *Advise and Consent*, in which she had a role, premiered in Washington. With director Otto Preminger, other cast members, and husband Howard Lee, the forty-two-year-old Gene was asked to lunch with Jack, then forty-five, at the White House. She saw the warm concern in his eyes. He knew of her recent heroic battles against mental illness. When he asked her how she was doing, she made him and Howard laugh with her rejoinder: "I'm a very lucky woman, Jack. I have a husband who loves me even when I'm crazy!"

Gene was always haunted by her first child Daria's condition. It had broken her heart to put Daria into an institution, but a doctor had counseled her that to devote herself to such a child under at-home conditions would demoralize them both. "It was the hardest decision I ever had to make," Gene said years later. "It tore me apart." She always claimed that the seeds of mental illness lie in the psyche of many sensitive, fragile people, and it takes a succession of negatives in their personal lives to get the seeds growing, finally blossoming into full psychosis. Gene claimed that her father's desertion of her mother for another woman had been the first chink in her armor of self-discipline and self-possession. The second had been the revelation of Daria's hopeless retardation, blindness, and deafness. And she remembered the third and final trauma had come when a woman years later confessed that she had come to see Gene during a wartime event carrying the germ of German measles contracted from service contacts—Gene had been pregnant with Daria at the time. She remembered not bothering to tell the woman the shock this news produced and instead simply walked away. So it had all cumulated relentlessly—the father who had proved financially shifty and adulterous toward her mother, the retarded daughter, the cruel accident of the German measles contraction. "After that, I guess the full blooming of my psychosis was inevitable," she reminisced sadly.

In the years when I knew her, I found Gene Tierney a woman of considerable refinement, well-educated, cultured, understanding, kind. But I always sensed in her eyes the traumas life had inflicted; she once said that she had never had the gift of losing herself in her work to forget her troubles and that she envied fellow artists who had that ability. "I always let it wash over me, dominate me, paralyze me. I was no good at seeking escape. I wish I had been!"

In 1979, when her autobiography, *Self-Portrait*, came out, I had my last interview with Gene. "I think it helped to get it all out—all of it," she said. "I didn't do the book to wallow in self-pity or self-dramatization. I know now that I did it to get some form of cathartic escape—to find peace, to find out about myself." Of Jack Kennedy she said that year: "It is hard to believe that so vital a spirit has been gone for more than fifteen years. His death was so cruel and senseless. He had so much more of a contribution to make."

Did she wish they had defied family, religion, public opinion, and all of it to marry? "It was not to be," she said, "and think of what a burden my later illnesses would have been to Jack! He and his family had already known the sorrow of their poor sweet retarded Rosemary. To have had my lost Daria as a stepdaughter—wouldn't that have been over-load for him? What will be will be; what will not be—well, that is just as well. . . ." She claimed that she believed in destiny, in the law of compensation. "Without a wound the heart is hollow" was one of her favorite quotations. "And with many wounds the heart, hopefully, becomes full and deep and compassionate and loving—in the true meaning of loving," she said.

Asked in 1979 about her husband, Howard Lee, who had stuck by her, remaining loyal and loving toward her throughout the years, she referred me to the quotation in her dedication to him for *Self-Portrait*. It was from William Shakespeare's thirtieth sonnet, and it went:

But if the while I think on thee, dear friend,
All losses are restored, and sorrows end.

TWELVE

Peter Lawford: Friday's Child

Peter Lawford's ultimate decline and destruction was undoubtedly one of the greatest tragedies that resulted from seventy-odd years of Kennedy Hollywood adventurism.

Peter and I were born two days apart, in 1923. He arrived on the seventh of September, a Friday, and I showed up on the ninth, a Sunday. Peter used to kid me about it. "*I'm* the Friday's Child who's full of woe and *you're* the Sunday Kid who's gonna have it made on all counts," he'd laugh.

I met Peter in 1948 during one of my sojourns on the West Coast, when I did my first of many interviews with him. We were both twenty-five then. At the time, I remember, *I* felt like Friday and *he* seemed positively guaranteed to be a Sunday all his life.

At twenty-five, Peter seemed to have everything: looks, charm, social flair, mammoth popularity with the opposite sex, major studio backing from an aggressive MGM, and sufficient natural acting talent to take him on to wherever his will and motivation dictated. In that long-gone 1948 of our first meeting, he seemed indeed the up-and-coming golden boy of MGM, adored by the females and liked (and as it later turned out, loved and lusted for) by the males, cooperative and courteous with directors and coworkers, always reliable and prompt on the set, invariably on time for portrait sittings and interviews, and forever at the beck and call of the MGM publicity department that set him up on "dates" with female personalities who were bucking for needed fan and press attention.

I knew for a fact, then and in subsequent years, that Peter's premarital "womanizing" was largely specious press-agery; most of the women he knew and cared about—Elizabeth Taylor, June Allyson—were friends and no more. Of course he was compelled to make love in actuality to a number of the women he involved himself with. They expected it and he needed it, needed it for pleasure, for his image's sake, and to help dispel the rumors about his relationships with men—and there were a number of them. These relationships worried him; they were often a sexual release rather than a romance. When he fell in love with or entertained romantic feelings toward a man, Peter grew inescapably depressed. This side of his erotic life he found ominous, threatening, baleful, yet he needed it, too.

Peter was born in London. His father, Sir Sidney Lawford, was a knighted general of the First World War who spent his later years with his wife, Lady May, in retirement in California. Privately tutored, Peter got into movies early, as a boy of eight, in the 1931 British film, *Poor Old Bill*. Visiting with his family in California at fifteen in 1938, he had a small supporting role in the film *Lord Jeff*, but at eighteen in 1942 he blossomed into various bits at MGM in films like *Mrs. Miniver* and *Random Harvest*. The roles got better with *The White Cliffs of Dover* (1944) and *The Picture of Dorian Gray* (1945); by the time I met him he was a leading

MGM juvenile who had won a feminine following from movies like *Good News*.

The Peter I came to know as a friend in 1948 was to me oddly lacking in conceit or narcissism of any kind. I remember during our first interview the look of sudden sadness in his handsome face as he remarked suddenly: "Good looks. Charm. They can be *burdens*. Often one finds oneself attracting, without intending to, people one doesn't want to hurt—*dreads* to hurt—and then there are those who think anyone they consider 'attractive,' such as myself, can get anything or anyone he wants, so they descend into mean jealousy and petty sniping. . . ."

While admittedly he worked hard—and played hard—to earn his reputation, I have always thought it oddly unfair that the image of Peter Lawford most people persist in holding in their minds is that of a playboy, boozer, druggie, Kennedy pimp, abject Rat Pack member, and stooge supreme for Frank Sinatra and his gang. The Peter I knew in those early years was devoted to his parents, coped patiently with his perverse-minded and difficult mother, Lady May (who later shockingly betrayed her son's homosexual side to Louis B. Mayer). He bought them a nice house in Bel-Air with his MGM earnings, which at the time were not that great, and it seemed to me he put up with a great deal from them. Even his father, whom he sincerely loved and respected (and whom he feared was being mistreated and neglected by his mother) was in many ways a burden for the young man.

In Peter's twenties—for a time—he seemed to me full of hope, ambition, and life affirmation. And he was the most consummate gentleman I ever knew. Despite his aristocratic lineage and clipped British accent, he was essentially humble, down-to-earth, thoughtful of others and sensitive to their feelings. "I know what it feels like to be hurt—and hurt deeply—myself," he told me once, "and I can always sense hurt in others, even when the hurt comes through only faintly—I guess I have a sixth sense about it."

So often I have wanted to write Christopher Kennedy Lawford and his sisters and tell them what a wonderful, sweet, and decent guy their father was when I knew him in youth. I have wanted to tell Chris especially that the father he knew in later years was a lost soul afraid of the feelings and spontaneities he had so openly expressed in youth. I have wanted to tell them that life did things to their father and that I have hoped that in time, with a deeper knowledge of him, they will find forgiveness and love.

Peter's parents had lost their income from Britain upon the outbreak of World War II in 1939, and after they moved to Florida, where the living was (then) cheaper, Peter at seventeen took a variety of menial jobs to help out. The sudden shift from affluence to penury brought out his strongest side—even at seventeen. He told me, "Larry, I knew I couldn't buckle under then. My parents, especially my father, were along in years and I was their only child, and my father had done so much for me; with them I had seen the world on our many travels, and I knew I had to put my youth and my strength between them and their fears. . . ."

And then he added wistfully: "You know, it is often harder to have had some money in youth and then to have lost it, than never to have had it. When one has never had it, one doesn't have happier times to compare with a present reality."

"I have heard that said before, Peter," I replied. "My mother, who had had money growing up, and then lost it, used almost the same words as yours." He smiled. "Then you know," he said.

Over the years that followed, as I talked with him and conducted interviews on each of his inexorably downward steps, I often pondered what had happened to all the youthful positivism and valor, the self-discipline and strength, the sterling motivation and—yes—an odd kind of *innocence* that had so distinguished him at twenty-five.

In that 1944–1951 period, no one had the look of a future—and permanent—film star great more than Peter Lawford. He was romancing on film the top MGM female stars of that time—Elizabeth Taylor, Judy Garland, June Allyson—and had solid, rewarding roles in vehicles starring such greats as Greer Garson, Irene Dunne, and Deborah Kerr. He had been the lover of Lana Turner, the lover-lady of all time. (He told me once about Lana: "I felt so sorry for her—she was so vulnerable, so lost in a way. . . .") Louis B. Mayer had big plans for him in 1948. Peter had the burgeoning elegance of a Cary Grant (a fellow Britisher) and the acting promise of a future William Powell—both of whom he admired greatly. He was, in fact, naturally gifted with much greater latent talent than he has ever been given credit for.

Once he discussed with me his disappointment over not winning the title role in *The Picture of Dorian Gray* (Hurd Hatfield had been considered more suitable. They felt he had a more decadent aura). Peter felt *he* would have given the role greater dimension. This led to a discussion of homosexuality in general (the 1948 Kinsey Report, linking one-third of American males a to homosexual experience at some time in their lives, was on the tip of everyone's tongue). Peter said something that I have never forgotten and that might provide an enlightened explanation for his bisexuality then and later. "I think it's often like two chaps wanted to express their friendship-affection as concretely as they can, and physical interplay helps them do that," he said.

That was Peter at the height of his youthful vigor, positivism, and life affirmation—at twenty-five in 1948.

Then, tragically, at about age thirty (1953), Peter Lawford began to lose his grip. I noted the changes in their various stages, and I found them sad, even shocking. The Peter of 1948 was dynamic, selfless, helpful. I vividly remember him treating me not just as a journalist interviewing and studying him but as a friend. He took me to a friend's pool in Beverly Hills, helped me with my swimming strokes, advised me earnestly and caringly about toning up my physique. He drew me out, listened intently to the ups and downs of my own life story up to then, and counseled positivism, courage, and persistence.

By 1953 Peter, while always friendly and kind, had begun to withdraw into himself. He grew ever more jaded, cynical, life-weary. What had once come so naturally and spontaneously to him became mere rote, both in his art and in his life. He had taken up serious drinking by then, and that didn't help. Neither did his waning confidence in his acting future. And when his MGM contract ended during the Dore Schary regime that followed Mayer's, the loss of it seemed to knock the wind out of him. "I guess they felt I had run my course, that I had lost my freshness," he told me sadly in 1953. And then it was my turn to try to help, console, and hearten, but I felt somehow that in some subtle, inexorable way he had slipped beyond the reach of any real help or consolation.

In 1954 I felt for a while that his good role at Columbia with Judy Holliday in *It Should Happen to You* would give him a new lease on life, but it was to be his last film for five years. He then did a rather listless television series, *Dear Phoebe*, for two seasons, followed by *The Thin Man* on video, also for two seasons. Frank Sinatra, helpful as always to many colleagues he felt were slipping or needed shoring up, took him on for several films in which, unfortunately, Peter did not so much *act* as *cheerlead* for Frank and the other Rat Packers.

After that came character parts of ever decreasing importance in a number of forgettable films. When he had, at forty, a second lead in a Bette Davis film *Dead Ringer* (1964), the usually tart and waspish Bette called him out of his hearing, "that poor man."

Peter wed Patricia Kennedy in 1954 in an April ceremony widely publicized; marrying into the Kennedy family was the worst thing that ever happened to him. The Kennedys were not really Peter's style. Old Joe Kennedy was not keen on the union: an *actor*, an *Englishman*, a *non-Catholic*? He reportedly checked out Peter's personal life thoroughly, and when he learned his prospective son-in-law had a reputation as a womanizer, he seemed to find that reassuring. The FBI and other investigative services were brought into it and even questioned Louis B. Mayer about the gay rumors, which Mayer, obviously impressed by Peter's bedmanship with Lana Turner (whom Mayer had contacted) said were not true. Old Joe and his investigators' lack of thoroughness seems odd in retrospect, because by 1954 a number of males had enjoyed Peter's amatory favors. (The explanation for this oversight may well lie in the fact that "the closet" in the 1940s and 1950s was tightly locked.)

Joe always considered his son-in-law Peter an unstable also-ran, and Peter caught the vibes readily enough. Pat, who had inherited more than a little of her father's feistiness, had made him understand that it was Peter or no one, for she was deeply in love with him. Rose didn't care for the marriage either, even when Peter agreed any children would be raised as Catholics. Rose was haunted by memories of their lost Kathleen, who had married the British marquess of Hartington, who died in World War II. Kathleen had died later in a plane crash with a married lover. The British, in short, were bad news to the Kennedys by this time.

Stuck with him as they were, the family proceeded to patronize Peter; during the years of his marriage to Pat, I saw him take on a cowed, obsequious, smiling-Jim aura I had never seen in him before. Though he fathered a boy and three girls for Pat (who, to be fair to her, always wanted to help Peter but was bewildered by him), he was never considered appropriately "macho" by the male Kennedys, certainly not by their insensitive, energetic, touch-football standards. Jack Kennedy, who godfathered one of Pat and Peter's children, found him amusing and witty and highly versed in current Hollywood gossip (which Jack, especially when president, loved), but also tended to regard Peter with an affectionate contempt that he didn't bother to conceal. Once, when a photograph was published showing the president listening intently to Peter, JFK cruelly joshed, "Who would ever believe I was listening to *you*?"

When I was researching and interviewing for my book, *Robert Francis Kennedy*, published in 1968, I called Peter for some quotes on his brother-in-law, who was on the point of running for president (he was tragically shot and killed in June of that year). Peter, who several years before had been kicked out of the family after a divorce, sounded positively terrified. "I will always value your friendship, Larry, and please do not misunderstand," he said, "but please, please, don't even *mention* me in your book. It will only annoy them. I wish you luck with the book, but I don't want to be in it, Larry. I'm the last one they want to see in the book. Treat me, I beg you, as a nonperson."

I asked him if I could use other quotes he had given me during his marriage to Pat. "Not now—not just now—later sometime, maybe, but not now," he replied. "My boat's too rocky in that quarter as it is!" I respected Peter's wishes; he did not show up in the book.

In 1966 the Kennedy marriage went out with a bang on Pat's side, a whimper on Peter's (he had been unfaithful to her many times too often, and his drinking and drugging were becoming ever-increasing problems). Peter at forty-three was definitely on the skids on all fronts. When I saw him that year, he was tired, listless, jaded, and bored. Subsequent years held two brief, abortive marriages with younger women (in whom, perhaps, he hoped to find his own irretrievable youthful positivism) and some attempts at film producing (the pictures were at best forgettable), followed by a string of ever-more-infrequent character roles, some thrown to him by old friends (like Sinatra) hoping to pull him out of his alarming slump. And always the drinking (he always had a drink in his hand when I saw him). And after that, the drugs. Drugs to escape. Drugs to ease psychological pain. Drugs to blot it all out—if only for a time.

Peter was not a model father. With his children he was, I always felt, essentially ill at ease. He considered them more Kennedy than Lawford—or at any rate they had been, in his opinion, "brainwashed" to be. He worried about what other Kennedy family members told them about him. He was humiliated to the point of hysteria by the rumors and writings and mouthings that he had "pimped" for Jack and Bobby Kennedy with Marilyn Monroe and that he had been instrumental in helping to speed her death. He felt it all made him look like a "court fool," he said to me.

Once, in 1966, when I was talking with him quietly at the Polo Lounge of the Beverly Hills Hotel (he ordered four drinks in ninety minutes) and the conversation turned to his kids, his face darkened and he observed cuttingly, cryptically, "Ask their mother—she's homogenizing them all into

Kennedys!" Years later, when his son Chris, by then grown into an uncertain, confused young man of twenty, came to California hoping for loving advice and concerned paternal consolation about his own ever-more-menacing drug problem, Peter was distant and emotionally withdrawn. Finally with curt, dismissive words, he sent the unhappy and dangerously impressionable young Chris packing back east. Almost as emotionally vulnerable as his young son, Peter as a father consistently elected for self-protective aloofness.

In the 1970s, as he hit his fifties, Peter's film appearances were few. On talk shows he didn't always seem to know where he was, and his answers to questions were often incoherent. "Nothing matters," he told me sadly in 1976. "Nothing matters. I'm just trying to get by, from day to day. . . ." More sad years went by as Peter faded away, helplessly oblivious to the worries of those friends who still loved him, still cared.

And on Christmas Day, 1984, worn out by alcohol and drugs, beset by severe kidney and liver problems, harassed by money troubles so acute he had trouble paying his rent, Peter Lawford died at sixty-one.

In his final period he had married yet another Patricia, Patricia Seaton Lawford, who later wrote movingly of him in her own book; she was a young woman who had borne his self-destructive behavior with loving patience. Elizabeth Taylor, who had sat by his deathbed racked with poignant memories of the young, handsome, and vital man who had given her her first screen kiss thirty-six years before, paid for his funeral and got her lawyer to help settle his pitiful estate. Faithful to the end, Elizabeth had even gotten Peter a role in one of her television movies, but he had been too ill to complete it.

What happened to friend Peter, who entered this world with me in September 1923, who laughed that we'd toast

each other the week of our seventieth birthdays? I celebrated that seventieth nine years after he died. Did he have perhaps an instinctive awareness, even during that sunny,
youthful period, that in the end he would indeed be Friday's
Child?

From my knowledge of him over the years, I have
arrived at several conclusions. First, from the beginning of
his life to the end, Peter lacked essential self-confidence and
self-esteem. He knew in his youth that he was handsome,
charming, socially agreeable, but he never felt—deep down
where it counts—that he had genuine acting talent. I once
asked him why he didn't go on the stage, hone his style to a
fine, sharp edge, work and grow and learn. He smiled sadly
at me. "People say I have an acting gift, but I've never
believed it, never really. And because I don't really believe it,
I don't want to put in all the heartbreaking, disciplined effort
to make something out of what well may be *nothing*. . . ."

Second, Peter became opportunistic in the wrong way.
In 1954, with his career slipping badly, he married Pat
Kennedy, not because he was really in love with her (I never
believed he was), but because he liked her, enjoyed her company, and hoped that a glamorous marriage and the good
connections that came with it would help shore up his flag-
ging fortunes and wilting career.

He was, however passively and pathetically, opportunistic in letting himself play an abject—and finally discarded—
second fiddle to Frank Sinatra and his Rat Pack, with whom
he never had a real temperamental or cultural affinity. Again
he was going along for a free associational ride on the fame
of people he considered more important than himself, hoping with a kind of odd innocence mixed with craven guile,
that something of what they were would rub off on him. His
natural desire to be liked, respected, and needed had sadly
transformed him over the years into a fawning toady.

Third, he was self-destructive. A strong unconscious death wish showed up in much of what he said—and didn't say.

In one of our later meetings, Peter ruefully reminded me that he had quoted, during our first interview when we were twenty-five, Shakespeare's lines from *Cymbeline*: "Golden lads and girls all must, as chimney sweepers, come to dust." For all his surface aplomb and confidence, his romancing and friendships, Peter often seemed to me an alienated and frightened Englishman essentially alone in a strange and unpredictable American environment. Oh, he took on American ways, won many American friends, even, in time, became a citizen—and for a short while, the brother-in-law of the president of the United States. But I often sensed a poignant longing for England in him, for its people, its ways, its ambience.

He confessed to me in 1952 that he always felt a certain guilt that an injury to his arm sustained when he was four-teen had kept him out of both the British and American armed forces in World War II. "Why feel guilty, Peter?" I observed. "You were honestly disqualified physically and it was in no way your fault."

"It's kind of you to say that," he replied, "but I keep telling myself that maybe I could have just *bluffed* my way in, someway, somehow. I was having it bloody easy as a juvenile at MGM all during the time chaps my age were fighting, and dying terrible deaths."

"But there were your parents—they needed your help. Your earnings at MGM made their lives more comfortable and happy!" I reminded him. With a humility that I found so characteristic of him, he rejoindered: "Oh, *that* . . . well, a chap can always find excuses if he looks for them, can't he?" He said once he liked and appreciated my calling him "Peter" as they would in England. "Pete" he often answered to in America, but he confessed the nickname grated on him. I think guilt continued to assail him because after the relatively hard times from seventeen to nineteen, he felt everything had come too easy to him—the MGM contract, the leading roles, the love of many women, the friendship and intimacy with many men. Once, he bitterly observed of the 1948 Peter Lawford: "I was a halfway decent-looking English boy who looked nice in a drawing room standing by a piano."

And there was something else. Something that I felt tormented him all his life. He told me: "My parents didn't approve of the public school system in England. They felt places like Eton and Harrow and Winchester kept boys in situations together that were—well, unhealthily intimate and close." With a strange sadness in his eyes, he went on: "Of course I was too young to have any say about my education. They kept me working with private tutors, we traveled a lot, I saw much of the world, met many interesting people, but I had true intimates. I have always felt sad about that. The camaraderie, the closeness that fellows know in public school in England, it's something warm and beautiful and solid that stays with them all their lives. They call themselves 'old boys' with such pride. I have envied many fellows that. And having gone without it, I have never really felt that even in England, where I was born, I would ever have really *belonged*—that I would have been a perpetual outsider in my own native land. . . ."

Then a look of terrible sorrow came into Peter's eyes when he went on to speak of a young man who had once danced for Ziegfeld and whom Peter had met in Monte Carlo in 1935 when he was twelve—a man some fifteen years his senior. His name was Carl Randall. "He was my first real hero—there were other heroes for me along the way, but

Carl was my first real one. Carl taught me how to dance. I can still do some of the fancy steps he taught me; I even used them in some films."

And then he added, solemnly, "I had no brothers, no real friends ever, not at twelve, not at fourteen. A fellow needs a hero at that time of life."

"And forever afterward," I said. "Perhaps your life has been a search for a hero, among other things." Peter didn't answer. For about ten minutes there was silence on the patio where we sat. And then he said, roughly, as if knocking himself out of a painful reverie: "Let's go swimming, fellow! You're a terrible swimmer you know, and some of your strokes need pointing up!"

Later he was to speak again of Carl Randall, of how he wished they hadn't been separated when his parents resumed traveling, of how he thought of Carl often over the years. "He was twenty-seven to your twelve," I offered. "It's too bad you didn't have a buddy your own age."

"Oh, I was used to older people," he answered. "My parents were very old when I was growing up, you know. But however it might have been, or should have been, we can't replay the past, can we, fellow?"

Seeking to lighten Peter's mood, I joked: "Have I got a good title for a story on *this* session if I use it: *Sorrow—and Loss*." He didn't smile. He thought a moment, then replied with sudden sharpness, "No. . . not *that* . . . don't go into *that* at all . . . what I said about the English public schools . . . about Carl!"

"Why not? It's good copy, Peter," I replied. He leaned forward, folded his hands tightly, and stared at the floor. "No," he mused. "No, I was rambling on about that in a friendly, nostalgic way—but in print? Well, it would be—you know—misconstrued or something, and the MGM publicity boys would jump on me." I respected his wishes. I never ran it in print until now.

Opportunism—yes, that was one of his more destructive motivations. But the search for the hero—that came out of his better nature. Somehow I feel that all the "heroes" he focused on in America let him down: Jack and Bobby Kennedy, Frank Sinatra, Robert Walker, Dean Martin. Only one fellow actor understood him, really cared about him. That was Jackie Cooper, who for a while was his good friend. Van Johnson, too, offered Peter friendship and understanding. But somehow I feel that the ultimate hero always eluded Peter Lawford. And that loss was the salient, seminal cause for his ultimate tragedy.

At the end, besides the loyal and loving young woman who was his last wife, his best friend was Elizabeth Taylor—a steadfast heroine from his youth whose caring had in the end outweighed all the heroes of his youthful dreams. And he must have thought, at the end, of the other women who had passed thorough his life: Lana Turner, who had given him the ultimate gift of intimate passion. And June Allyson. And Judy Garland. He must have thought about his children and about young, confused Chris of the haunted Kennedys, with whom cruel fate and cruel fears had prevented him from getting truly close.

Those who scorn Peter Lawford today, who vilify him as playboy, opportunist, bisexual, nymphomaniac, drug addict, alcoholic, and pernicious sycophant, didn't know the Peter that *I* once knew. To me he always came through, over all the years, as essentially lonely, searching, wounded in self-image, lacking in long-term direction and decisive life-management. A broken spring. A broken heart.

What would have healed him? What would have inspired and galvanized him? What would have motivated him to make the most of what I always felt was an estimable acting gift? What? Or whom?

I think the answer to that lay in England in his boy-hood: an untold want, an untold need, an incompletion, a truncation, a road not taken. Feelings and longings left unexplored resulted in a spirit essentially *lost*—a sensitive, rare, delicate spirit for whom drugs, alcohol, promiscuous and compulsive bisexuality eased the surfaces of pain, but *only* the surfaces.

I feel very sad about friend Peter Lawford, Friday's Child. But at least now, and for the first time ever, he has found in death something that forever eluded him in life: *peace*.

THIRTEEN

Peter and Lana and Ava—and Bob

Peter Lawford's sex life was a bewildering blend of heterosexual and homosexual affairs, wild narcissistic binges, exhibitionism, and fellatio, which he enjoyed from both women and men and occasionally gave.

He was linked with a number of young men in his mid-1940s MGM period. He developed a big crush on young Robert Walker, who had made a splash in the Private Hargrove pictures and was licking his wounds in 1945 over his wife deserting him for David O. Selznick. Jennifer Jones, Mrs. Walker, had presented Bob with two sons, but after *The Song of Bernadette* and *Since You Went Away*, Jennifer's career far outstripped Bob's. "What's Hargrove up against a famous saint?" he commented to Peter in a moment of despair. Peter had seen Bob at the MGM commissary, and hearing that Bob was feeling down over Jennifer, he introduced himself. Soon Bob and Peter were going to films together, comparing acting notes, and soaking up sun at the beach.

Peter didn't take long to make his initial pitch. It happened at the beach, and there was temporary embarrassment when some acquaintances caught him with his arms around

Bob. Scrawny, nervous, unsure of his charm or his looks, Bob needed ego boosts chronically, and Peter's interest in him excited him and gave him a lift.

Peter always said that Bob gave, in his view, his all-time best performance opposite Farley Granger in Hitchcock's *Strangers on a Train*, in which, as a sinister young playboy of obvious homoerotic bent, he tries to make a reciprocal murder bargain with the hapless Farley character. "*That* was Bob," Peter said, "or rather, Bob as he'd like to be in real life—if he had the courage!"

Product of a dysfunctional childhood, Bob began drinking heavily, suffered several nervous breakdowns, entered into a six-week marriage to John Ford's daughter, Barbara, in 1948, then continued on a downward spiral that saw him arrested for drunken driving and institutionalized yet again for a nervous condition.

After giving what one critic called a perfect portrait of a "charming, perverted, murderous psychopath" in *Strangers on a Train*, Bob died before completing *My Son John* with Helen Hayes. A doctor had reportedly overdone dosages of sedatives administered to calm Bob's increasingly manic outbursts that summer of 1951, and he died suddenly.

Peter later felt guilt (of a sort) because he and Bob had continued their affair, off-and-on style, until near the time of Bob's death, and he wondered if Bob's confusion over his bisexual tendencies had only complicated his mental and emotional state further.

Another actor under contract to MGM in the mid 1940s who aroused a rather intense interest in Peter was Tom Drake. He was Judy Garland's boy-next-door in *Meet Me in St. Louis*, then went on to good parts in such films as *The Green Years* (1946), but his personality was deemed too quiet and repressed to warrant major stardom. With Peter,

Tom seems to have been anything *but* repressed. The pair jumped into a tempestuous affair that, as George Cukor later recalled, resulted in "Tom feeling more for Peter than Peter did for him, whereupon Tom became something of a stalker, hanging around Peter's driveway and waylaying him when he went out on errands. Peter finally had to literally punch him out to get rid of him."

Never high on self-confidence where his career was concerned, Tom went rapidly downhill. When his MGM contract ended, he did some television, then wound up as an automobile salesman. He died in 1982 at age sixty-four, completely forgotten. Peter always remembered the unrequited and obsessed Tom as "a handful" and joked about him along the lines of the famous sally about "it took him a while to get there but God help you when he got there!"

When he was on the womanizing side of the fence, Peter got into prime company, including Lana Turner, who he always recalled had a very high opinion of her charms; she refused to perform oral sex on him, loudly insisting that when she went to bed with a man, *he* was supposed to give *her* the maximum attention and not the other way around.

To Lana, he would always be profoundly grateful because, luckily for Peter, he was in the midst of an affair with her when his mother, Lady May Lawford, met privately with Louis B. Mayer and informed him that her son was bisexual and possibly a predominant homosexual. Her accusation was obviously an act of revenge for something Peter had done, and he later suspected it was for the time he had soundly castigated her for neglecting and mistreating his aged father. Lady May had doubtless seen him with some of his young men (he also had an affinity for bit actors and messengers, one or two of whom he brought around to the house when he thought his mother was out).

Mayer was upset—not that he wasn't accustomed to a long list of gay actors at MGM, a line dating from Ramon Novarro and Billy Haines in the 1920s. He called in Peter and suggested hormone shots. Outraged yet fearful, knowing full well that hormone injections would never affect his feelings or his physical urges, Peter gave the only Oscar-worthy performance of his career, insisting to Mayer that he was not gay. "Prove it!" was the substance of Mayer's sharp retort, so Peter frantically rang up Lana Turner and begged her to assure Mayer that in the sack Peter was one super woman-lover. Friendly and concerned, Lana did just that, and Mayer bought his story. Years later, when Joe Kennedy was trying to ascertain Peter's sexual orientation and had everyone from J. Edgar Hoover to a slew of private eyes zeroing in on him, Joe called Mayer and was reassured that Peter had run up a fine bed record with Lana Turner and others. Many believe that Peter went to George Cukor and begged George to lend him enough to pay off some of the nosier private eyes. In any event, their reports never reached Joe, at least the sections relating to Peter's gay liaisons. Since it was the mid 1950s, Peter was much more discreet about his male-male involvements, and the private eyes would have needed actual photos to convince Joe that his prospective son-in-law "messed with guys," Joe's phrase for homosexual behavior.

Not that Joe was that era's version of an anti-gay bigot. He had certainly been around, and he had known all about same-sex involvements among his Harvard friends and in the business world. If he did draw the line at a gay son-in-law, it was primarily because he didn't want Pat to be hurt. "Women don't understand that kind of thing as men do," he once said to Eddie Moore. Joe was slightly out of touch on this count; in fact, women were often kinder and more understanding toward (and in a way identified with) what Judy Garland once termed "Man-Mad Men."

Judy and Peter had had a hot but brief involvement in the early 1940s, and by 1948, when he was set to appear with Judy in *Easter Parade*, twenty-five-year-old Peter's original amorous curiosity had changed to a kind of brotherly concern and fear for her welfare. Judy's emotional state was very precarious at this time; her bewildering succession of drug dependencies and mental breakdowns were causing her intimates—among them Peter—to fear that she might try suicide.

Peter would talk to her by the hour, in person and on the phone, and she would wake him up at odd hours to burden him with her various fears and insecurities. Her marriage to Vinc0ente Minnelli was crashing down about her ears in the late 1940s. With Minnelli himself having emotional problems as well, he and Judy were soon removed from *Easter Parade*.

Peter always opined that the pressures the MGM bosses of the 1940s put on their more successful younger stars drove them into alcohol and drug dependencies and other childish escapes from reality. He said that it tore his heart out to see Judy in such straits. He even went to bed with her a number of times in the late 1940s "just to help her feel loved and secure." He added: "Good sex was a better tranquilizer than any of that poison MGM had its doctors injecting into Judy!"

During his MGM years Peter managed to "hit the sack" with an amazing number of women, even crossing the tricky "color line" when he engaged in a romance with the highly talented dancer-singer-actress Dorothy Dandridge. Dorothy had struggled up from dancing gigs to a regular spot on the television series, *Beulah*, then acquired an adoring audience of consistent fans. She entered films in small roles and reached her height of screen popularity in such 1950s films as *Carmen Jones* and *Porgy and Bess*. After her career faded and bad financial deals had depleted her funds, she committed suicide in 1965 at age forty-two.

Peter and Dorothy got together in the early 1950s; friends recalled him saying that it was his first involvement with a black woman and he was "thrilled" by her. Born the same year, at that time (1953) Dorothy and Peter were thirty; they had been around the track, and as one friend put it later, "It was surprising that they should have been so kiddie-romantic about each other—while it lasted." It was a time of heavy anti-black prejudice, and a white man dating a black woman risked not only social opprobrium but an outright beating. Peter would have friends pick her up, and they would pretend to "meet" at parties; others would have them come separately to beach house rendezvous, then leave them together. But Peter was hardly in the vanguard of any 1950s civil rights political crusading. (In fact, "that kind of pioneering didn't suit his temperament at all," as Tom Drake remembered decades later. "Even if it had been 1967 instead of 1953, Peter would have ducked it.") Finally both Peter and Dorothy agreed it should end; it had gotten too complicated on a number of counts. "But I know Peter felt bad when she died," Tom Drake remembered. "He broke down on the phone, blubbering how Dorothy had always led with her emotions instead of her head and had been taken advantage of, and so on. . . ."

Tom and other friends felt that Peter, insecure about his bisexual orientation and anxious to perpetuate a "stud about town" image, must surely have been making a list of all the famous Hollywood ladies who would enhance that image, if only for the moment. It also made good fodder for the proliferating fan magazines, and Peter loved telling his impressions of screen lovelies he had "dated" to such mavens of movieland gossip as Fredda Dudley Balling, Ruth Waterbury, Delight Evans, and of course the powerhouse duo, Louella Parsons and Hedda Hopper.

He targeted Rita Hayworth in 1946. Rita, separated from Orson Welles, was at the top of her fame (the blue-noses called it notoriety) as the heroine of the torrid *Gilda* and men-about-town regarded an involvement with Rita as the ultimate in "stud cachet," as Robert Walker called it.

Rita saw to it that her special private phone number was handed to Peter, who dutifully (and eagerly) showed up on Rita's doorstep. Rita was then twenty-eight, Peter was twenty-three. Peter's later reports on Rita were not flattering. He said she drank too much, ate too much, and was careless about her personal hygiene—"I licked her armpit and a lot of stinky sweat came off on my tongue" was one of his less complimentary references to the purveyor of *Gilda*'s immortal song number, "Put the Blame on Mame." Peter did not think much of Rita as a sex partner, calling her "aggressively passive" but "lousy at reciprocation." She acted as if any man in bed with her had hit the ultimate paradise of intimacy," he sneered, but it was "all a dud, a bore."

So much for the siren of Harry Cohn's Columbia Pictures. But with fellow MGM star Ava Gardner (*pre*-Frank Sinatra) Peter seemed to have better, more exciting encounters that made for spicier, more flattering (to Ava) narratives.

Ava, two years Peter's senior, had risen from second-rate MGM contract actress to wife of Mickey Rooney to racy "other woman" to star; at the height of her career in the 1950s, typical ad copy on Ava went: Ava is a Passionate Woman; She Will Love You as You Have Never Been Loved Before!

Peter had just hit his twenty-first birthday when he dated Ava Gardner for the first time in 1944. "She was never much of an intellectual; conversationally she could get tongue-tied, but her looks—oh those looks—and her actions, they spoke louder than words!" Such was Peter's capsulized verdict on Ava as lover supreme.

She was, he told Tom Drake later, the most man-obsessed gal he had ever met, and she made love with pristine hunger; even if she had been with another man only the night before, he recalled, "she came on with the male partner of the moment as if she hadn't had sex for a year!"

Peter liked to boast that he "intellectualized" Ava, cueing her in on the right books and the right music. Others say that they spent more time going to baseball games, indulging in wild joy rides up the coast, and dancing frenziedly at nightclubs.

Unfortunately for Peter, Ava liked variety, and he knew the Ava jig was up when singer Mel Torme walked in during one of his evenings with Ava and he was tactfully consigned to the driveway and his car.

In the years before he married Pat Kennedy in 1954, and after for that matter, Peter was determined to have the best stud scorecard in Hollywood. Nor did he neglect the men. Around 1944 he was rumored to have had a *ménage à trois* with Evie Wynn and her husband Keenan Wynn. Evie denies this today, but friends say she would hardly have found it flattering to her ego or consoling to her memories to admit that after the one-night stand she admitted to having with Peter, he had gone on to sample the manly charms of her husband.

Keenan Wynn was not the handsomest man in the world, but he demonstrated in his movie appearances and in real life that he had enormous sexual presence, and he and Peter had a romance that, as Tom Drake put it, "really burned up the road" during the period when Peter, Van Johnson, and Keenan were addicted to motorcycle riding (a pastime the studio finally put a stop to, reminding Peter especially that his "Pretty Pan" had to be preserved intact, accident free, if the women fans were to be expected to flood the MGM mails for a "future indefinite"). According to friends, Peter and Keenan would drive up the coast during their motorcycle phase, pick up a takeout lunch, and then make for lonely spots beside the highway.

Peter interspersed his relationships with men and women with quick affairs with girls he met at the beach, girls he encountered in restaurants, girls he picked up on the highway for impromptu motorcycle rides. "He must have had the worst case of VD—all kinds—in Hollywood," Jerry Asher later said to me, adding that he always wondered why Old Joe Kennedy hadn't checked his prospective son-in-law for *that*, knowing as he did of Peter's promiscuous life—the lady-side of it, anyway.

Peter liked to tell friends that director George Cukor was madly in love with him and was always trying to get him over to his beautiful house, "and not so he could show his etchings but so that I could show my family jewels," he told a friend.

George Cukor recalled Peter whining that he'd had only a subsidiary role in the 1945 MGM version of Oscar Wilde's *Picture of Dorian Gray*; Peter felt *he* should have played Dorian, but the part went to Hurd Hatfield largely, Jerry Asher remembered, because the studio wanted to keep Peter in the romantic running and they felt the role was too "morbid" for him. George assured Peter he would have made an admirable Dorian, "and given my personal experience with him, he *would* have!" George laughed.

George claimed that he *had* been to bed with Peter, who wanted to use him and hesitated to offend him. George's explanation for Peter denying any relationship had ever occurred was "Peter was as vain about his reputation as a man-lover as he was about his reputation as a woman-lover and he thought I was too old and unattractive to enhance his sexy reputation!" According to George, Peter had had no hesitancy in receiving oral sex from men he respected, admired, looked up to—and hoped to use. Noel Coward and Clifton Webb were two figures Peter hero-worshipped, and according to George, both of them "had Peter." Another report had Noel Coward angered because he thought he had picked up a "social disease" (as Noel called it) from Peter. This Peter huffily denied. Peter and Noel were not in communication after that.

"Peter was not a good lover—not at all," George Cukor remembered. "Of course his good looks helped create an illusion and he relied on that heavily. But he had difficulty being tender, spontaneous, affectionate. He preferred his sex direct and to the point."

According to Tom Drake, Peter had "a tall, thick case of chronic narcissism." He liked the impression he created nude and aroused. "He was a great one for watching his reflection in the mirror, too," Tom recalled, along the lines of "'I am Peter Lawford, and I am about to honor some lucky dame or some lucky bastard with my gift of intimacy.'"

Peter always hero-worshipped Jack Kennedy, but he did tend to get annoyed with Jack's constant efforts to use him as pimp and contact for Hollywood lovelies, a state of affairs that continued right up to the time of Jack's death.

"I should think you'd be flattered by Jack's using you as go-between that way," a friend once commented. "*Using* me—that's the phrase for it," Peter replied. He went on to speculate that, had it not been for his Hollywood connections, Jack Kennedy would have had no real use for him.

Certainly the Kennedys had Peter's number. Jack, Bobby, and Teddy had received Peter into the family readily enough in 1954, but to them he was weak, unfocused, too anxious to please, without a strong personality of his own. Billy Grady, the MGM talent executive who had helped the careers of many greats in their "climbing" years, told me once that Peter was handsome and charming but "tended to let people run all over him; he didn't stand up to people; he thought his looks and charm would do it all for him."

Certainly I always sensed this in Peter since my initial meeting with him. He did all that running around. He was hypersocial, dutiful to his parents, though he honestly disliked and distrusted his mother (with reason) and was almost neurotically overprotective of his father.

He once told me that he felt his mother was actually *jealous* of him, that she had never really wanted him in the first place, that she disparaged him as a child and patronized him in his teen years. Then, suddenly, Peter Lawford was a movie actor, handsome, popular, gregarious, and in his early and mid twenties, he seemed to have the world at his feet. Lady May Lawford was always consumed with the feeling that she had taken the wrong course in life, that she could have been a major celebrity in her own right had she "taken the right forks in the road," which she bitterly claimed later she hadn't.

And here was Peter, magnified a thousand times on the nation's screens, the lover of Hollywood's most beautiful people—Lady May had to tear it down somehow.

This is the real reason Lady May had gone to Mayer to expose her son's gay side—not to help him, not out of fear for his "image," not out of protective maternal concern—but out of pure and simple *jealousy*. Peter knew why she had done it and he never forgave her to the end of her life.

FOURTEEN

Chris Lawford's Lonely Journey

When Christopher Kennedy Lawford recently quit his largely unrewarding stint as Charlie in the soap opera *All My Children*, he was vague about his future plans, but mentioned that he wanted to continue his environmental work. He has been a supporter of the Hudson Riverkeeper Fund, which stresses the necessity of cleaning up New York's Hudson River. He also worked on his mother's Very Special Arts project for children with defects. He is now forty-one and the father of three young children with his wife, Jeannie Olsson, who is half Swedish and half Korean. Once a journalist, she now describes herself as a "committed wife, mother and homemaker."

Chris Lawford's life has been a largely unfulfilled one. Though he resembles his father physically, he isn't as handsome, nor is he as talented an actor as Peter was. His family trust fund share does not provide a sufficiently decent lifestyle for a family of six, and friends worry that Chris will begin to drift in middle age as he did in youth—a youth that was largely a nightmare of drugs and loose sexuality.

"Chris's tragedy is that he wanted to follow in his dad's footsteps, but his talent and drive were somewhat limited," a friend says. "He is still consumed with guilt over that druggie-sex-junkie youth." Others feel that Chris is bored with the husband-daddy routine and keeps to it only because it is for him the lesser of two evils. He does not want to repeat his father's tragic downhill course after middle age, yet a life as a second-rate actor and a staid if undistinguished family man seems stultifying—a dull, slow trip to Nowheresville.

Born March 29, 1955, in Santa Monica, Chris and his three younger sisters lived with Pat and Peter until their divorce when he was ten. Then Pat and her children moved to New York. There followed the usual third-generation Kennedy experiences: matriculation at Middlesex School in Concord, Massachusetts, summer and holiday vacations at the Cape Cod Kennedy compound, then Tufts University, from which Chris graduated in 1976. One family source said of him: "Chris, though intelligent, athletic, affably companionable, and good-looking, found himself caught between the show-business world his father represented and the Kennedy focus on politics." Worried about the spotlight his Kennedy connection forced on him, and for a while guilt ridden because he did not want to take on a third-generation role as perpetuator and furtherer of the Kennedy legacy, Chris in adolescence turned to drugs for escape from harsh realities that threatened to overwhelm him. From pot he progressed to hard drugs and by his own admission "made a mess of my life for some years."

Peter Lawford always found it difficult, indeed impossible, to express his love for his children, and when Chris visited him in Hollywood, his idea of father-son bonding was introducing Chris to cocaine. Indeed, on Chris's twenty-first birthday, Peter sent a cache of cocaine as a present, and Chris wrote his father a letter to the effect that the gift was welcome but disappeared in short order. His volunteer work for Very Special Arts, which his aunt, Jean Kennedy Smith, had founded to help mentally and physically disabled children, was sternly prescribed by Uncle Ted and others in order to divert Chris's attention to "more constructive aims," but his enthusiasm for that "family philanthropy stuff" was limited, and his cousin, the tragic, short-lived David Kennedy (who died of a drug overdose) quoted him as saying that it did little good to help others with *their* problems when "our own family problems are so bad that they should require our full attention!"

For a while David, Bobby Kennedy Jr., and Chris made up a private Kennedy drug culture. Unfortunately matters did not remain all that private. Chris was arrested on drug charges, but got off with a relative slap on the wrist because of family pressure.

Unlike other members of his family, Chris kept in constant touch with his feelings, "not that it did him all that much good," as his father Peter said to me. "It's safer to have no feelings at all in *that* goldfish bowl."

Since Pat Kennedy Lawford, after the divorce, seemed to retreat increasingly into a world of her own, Eunice and Ted tried to give Chris special attention. While still a Tufts undergraduate, Chris worked as an intern in Ted's Washington office. Ted tried to include him in various recreational projects and kept reminding him that he was always there for him, but Ted's own addiction to alcohol and his compulsive womanizing made him less than an admirable role model. Despite Chris's attempts to remain positive about his uncle, he found himself adopting the faintly contemptuous and condescending attitude of his cousins toward "Wild Uncle Ted." Lem Billings in his usual compulsive style tried to horn in on Chris's private life but Chris put him off, knowing full well Lem's predilections. When Lem began snorting coke with Bobby Jr. (whom Lem adored) and otherwise acting like just another Kennedy adolescent, Chris gave him an even wider berth.

"The trips to visit his father in California turned into nightmares," a friend said. "Not only did Peter keep him on drugs but got him womanizing at a fierce rate, and even enjoyed watching Chris have sex with one of Peter's girls-on-call. It never seemed to occur to Peter that playing voyeur to his son's sexual activities was far more incestuous, and far less innocent and affirmative, than expressing the love and concern for Chris that any son had a right to expect from his father—and which, to Chris's sorrow and frustration was sadly and constantly withheld."

There are several theories as to why and how Chris Lawford finally got his act together. Many credit Eunice's injunctions and constant supportive gestures toward him. Others give the credit to Kennedy family friend, former Attorney General Ramsey Clark, who enlisted Chris as an aide in his abortive U.S. senatorial campaign and had many fatherly talks with him as they enjoyed sports together. Ramsey Clark is credited with inciting Chris to go to law school.

But his ultimate rescuer was Jeannie Olsson, whom he met while at Boston College Law School in the early 1980s. He later said it was her supportive nurturing that kept him off drugs for keeps, checked his womanizing, and made possible his law degree, acquired by age twenty-eight in 1983. They were married in 1984.

Much has been made in recent years of Chris's determined efforts to counsel young people undergoing the same drug hassles he knew years before, but some who know him feel that he would prefer to avoid such work, as it arouses latent temptations he has worked hard, as a husband and father of three, to resist. And the memory of the loved cousin David Kennedy continues to haunt him. He named his firstborn son David.

Rendered inescapably melancholy, cautious, and guilt ridden because of his earlier drug and sexual excesses, Chris Lawford also has to live with the fact that his talent as an actor is essentially limited, as his role on the soap *All My Children* made inescapably clear. Nor was he startlingly noticeable in the small roles he did in films like *Impulse*, *Run*, and *The Doors*, and in some television commercials. About five years ago, he tried to interest himself in film producing and show-business law, but these efforts bore little fruit.

Two of his sisters got to the fringes of show business but only desultorily. Victoria has been a television coordinator for Very Special Arts and in 1987 married a Washington attorney, Robert Pender. Robin drifted to New York where she worked as a stage manager for productions off Broadway. A third sister, Sydney, married to Peter McKelvy, seems content with her role as homemaker.

Patricia Seaton Lawford, Peter's last wife, said of Peter's rejection of his children: "How terrible their pain must have been. How ironic that the man who freed me from my own suffering stemming from early child abuse could commit such emotional violence on his own children!" She added: "Unfortunately, withdrawing from responsibility and feelings was a common reaction for Peter when faced with emotional demands."

Patty Seaton Lawford quoted a letter to Peter from daughter Victoria. Dated July 11, 1978, (she was twenty) in reaction to her father's failure to visit her while in New York, it reads:

Dear Daddy,

I really don't know how to tell you this or how many times I've said this and meant it, but I love you.

I've never really had a chance to sit down and talk to you as father to daughter, but I guess I feel just as close to you as if I had.

I have to tell you I am very upset this year because last year I felt we got really close and then this year that all just fell apart. . . .

When I heard you were ill from Patty, I wanted to go see you so badly and yet couldn't tell you over the telephone.

I didn't understand what's going on this year when you sent us all a typed letter trying to explain that you were happy, busy, and in good health. All of that makes me happy, but I still don't understand it.

I love you, Daddy, and I never want you to forget it
　　　Your daughter, always,
　　　　　Victoria.

But what Victoria and her siblings did not understand was that Peter by age fifty-five in 1978, and with only six years left to live, was giving in rapidly to his darker, more self-destructive side. Impotent with his wives and with other women, besotted by drink and drugs, he had on occasion resorted to the sexual companionship of assorted male hustlers and had gotten on very friendly terms with a male madam who specialized in high-class call boys, meaning those with college degrees and some pretensions to culture and intellect. Peter once said that he didn't share the tendency of upper-class British men to consort with workingmen and other lowlifes, and that for him good looks had to be accompanied by some "polish," as he put it. But the quality of the men he turned to for solace could not have been as high as he hoped, for several of them beat and robbed him.

Chris as of 1996 seems to be at a crossroads (some would say an impasse). He is now a middle-aged man of forty-one; nothing he set out to do has turned out to be very successful—especially his acting. Law never really interested him that deeply. His mentor Ramsey Clark had persuaded him at the time that it was respectable and financially substantial if properly handled. He once reasoned that getting into show-business law might have given him the best of the two worlds inherited from his parents.

One producer suggested to Chris that he ought to hone his acting skills in summer stock and try for a whole new career as a character actor, but he is said to feel that if he wasn't that good at acting when he was younger, why parade his lack of genuine acting talent in middle age? But he must continue to earn a living, for there are those children to support.

What is the future going to hold for Chris Lawford, the only male heir of the ill-starred Peter?

Asked recently how he saw the future, he said: "I want to be a good husband and a good father. I want a life of some peace and self-respect. Beyond that—I will have to do my best and take my chances."

FIFTEEN

Frank and the Kennedys

Frank Sinatra's complicated relationship with the Kennedys has been covered extensively, indeed ad nauseam. He first began to edge toward the Kennedys when he co-starred with fellow MGM-contract player Peter Lawford in a movie called *It Happened in Brooklyn*. The movie dealt with an ambitious crew of young New Yorkers who covet musical success in show business, and on hand with Frank and Peter were Gloria Grahame, Kathryn Grayson, and Jimmy Durante. Tough, shrewd critic James Agee summed up the proceedings: "Aside from Sinatra and Durante, the show amounts to practically nothing, but there is a general kindliness about it which I enjoyed."

Peter, then twenty-four, fell almost immediately under thirty-one-year-old Frank's spell. He was to recall Frank later to me as "a dynamo of energy and talent and brash self-assurance. One felt that with Frank anything was possible, and he made anyone close to him feel he could lick the world, too!"

Frank and Peter continued their friendship through the years, and when Peter married Pat Kennedy in 1954, Pat became part of the Sinatra friendship circle. By 1960 Frank was helping the Kennedys with the campaign that elected Jack president, and through Frank a series of events resulted in President Jack Kennedy and Sam Giancana, the Chicago mob boss, sharing the same girlfriend, Judith Campbell Exner. Exner later served as go-between for Jack and Giancana and the mob when Jack wanted help with certain "tasks" including the much-discussed and much-tampered-with "plan" to assassinate Fidel Castro in order to get rid of what Jack called "that Cuban nuisance."

Bobby Kennedy as attorney general in the 1961–1963 period was always "out to get the mob," and this did not sit well with the boys. While Frank was not actually a part of the mob, he had many mobster friends; Bobby knew this, and when the president visited California in 1962, Bobby upset Jack's plan to stay with Sinatra. The ostensible reason given was that Bing Crosby, who got to play host, had an estate up against a hill that made secret service protection much easier, whereas the Frank Sinatra compound was not as easily guarded.

Frank did not buy this rationalization and blamed Peter Lawford, who until that time had been the main contact between Frank and the Kennedys. Up to 1962, Frank, usually cocky, arrogant, and autocratic, had shown an almost abject devotion to the Kennedys, claiming he had helped in the election through his contacts with mob figures who in the presidential primaries had helped bring West Virginia into line. Frank had been a frequent White house guest, had entertained there, had hobnobbed with the Kennedys socially, and had reveled in the class and prestige the connection brought him.

After Jack Kennedy, upon the urgent advice of Bobby and others, had chosen Bing's place over Frank's, it was never the same between Frank and the Kennedys. Earlier, in 1961, Old Joe (before the stroke that sidelined him later that year) had blown hot and cold on Frank, rescinding invitations to Kennedy affairs, then reinstating them. Old Joe and Frank were too much alike to be enduring friends—both of them being consummately egocentric and power-driven.

Peter Lawford, meanwhile, had been enjoying being part of Sinatra's famed Rat Pack that followed the Sinatra party line devotedly and loyally. The Rat Pack was a sort of offshoot of the Humphrey Bogart-Lauren Bacall Brat Pack which had more or less disintegrated after Bogart's death in 1957. Frank gave it a whole new spin, with a special code language, inside sexual lingo, an informal but definite set of rules about who was in and who was out and what kind of fun was to be had on what occasion. Peter in the 1947–1962 period had become mesmerized by Frank, who was his opposite when it came to such traits as confidence, upward mobility, self-containment, and leadership. Frank also accelerated Peter's womanizing proclivities and introduced him to willing female partners, famous, not-so-famous, and downright obscure—but all sexually delectable and "cream of the crop," as Peter put it. Peter's gay involvements, of course, were obtained strictly on his own, as Frank, while tolerant of gays (he had known many of them throughout his career) was not "into" gayness and at times grew impatient and even angry when it was flaunted in his vicinity, as Monty Clift was to do on one disastrous occasion, with the result that Monty got the heave-ho from Frank's inner circle. (Monty had made a flagrant pass at a fellow actor he thought was gay at a party Frank threw at the conclusion of *From Here to Eternity*, the picture that restored Frank to popular favor in 1953 after Frank had endured a dry spell.)

Peter always felt deeply his ouster by Frank, which only became conclusive after the Bing Crosby-as-presidential-host instance. Peter had gotten in dutch with Frank on other occasions, but had somehow wheedled, pleaded, and "brown-nosed" (as Dean Martin put it) his way back into the pack. On another occasion Peter had incurred Frank's wrath after having a strictly platonic, consolatory meal with Ava Gardner, the second Mrs. Sinatra, then estranged from Blue Eyes. Nothing Peter could do or say would convince Frank, at least for some time, that Peter wasn't trying to "muscle in on my woman territory," as Frank put it. Ava herself tried to make Frank see reason, reminding him that she and Peter were old friends from the MGM days. Intermediaries for Peter spent hours trying to make Frank see the true state of affairs between Peter and Ava. Finally it all blew over, but Frank never felt quite as close to Peter again.

In 1962 after Frank refused Peter's calls, he declared that he would meet him only to give him a good punch in the face. When he cut Peter out of the pack's two projected movies, Peter realized once and for all that he was *persona non grata* in Sinatra circles.

"That seemed to be the beginning of the end for Peter," one friend recalled. Though Peter went on (he and Pat Kennedy divorced in 1966), he had lost a lot of spark. "I don't think he realized until Frank went out of his life how much reflected energy and dynamism Frank had gifted him with."

Frank later began to disregard Peter and the Kennedys altogether. Laying aside the "presidential host" affair, he even invited Bing Crosby to appear in one of his pack movies; his politics shifted over the years, too. "He felt the Kennedys had served their purpose," Dean Martin said, "and now it was time to move on to other contacts and other associations."

Over the years, Frank had been archconsoler, and at times lover, to Marilyn Monroe, giving her lavish gifts (perfect emeralds on one occasion) and assuring her that he was always on the other end of a phone line if she "got in trouble." For a while Marilyn had even hoped that Frank would marry her; later she told friends that for all his romancing and the thing with Ava Gardner and whatnot, she felt that Frank's basic emotional allegiance was to his first wife, Nancy, and their three kids. When Marilyn confided in Delight Evans that she was sure this was the case, Delight (as she later told me) laughed heartily and declared that, with all the women, serious and nonserious, sexual and romantic, trivial and one-night-standish, Frank would have had a hell of time convincing Nancy that she was, after all, still his one-and-only in his heart of hearts.

Obviously Joe DiMaggio, when he drew up the guest list of those invited to Marilyn's services after her death, didn't agree that Frank had been a positive influence on Marilyn. Frank, to his anger and deep chagrin, was among those excluded. Dean Martin told the story that Frank threatened to use his connections on Joe—Frankie Boy didn't take insults lightly—but Joe relayed back through mutual connections that *he* was Italian too and that he also had "contacts." Not that this gave Frank significant pause. He was always one to go the other guy better in matters great or small, but as a mutual friend put it, "Frank thought it best to declare the Monroe-DiMaggio situation 'neutral territory.' Joe knew where the bodies were buried, and he also had the inside info on Marilyn and Frank that wouldn't have helped anybody if broadcasted," as the friend put it. So Joe DiMaggio, at the time of Marilyn' funeral and forever after, tended to be treated by the press and public as Mr. Right, Marilyn's trusted friend, her knight and protector. However Frank might have felt about this, his philosophy essentially was let sleeping ballplayers have the last word—a compromise, a retreat, a neutralizing call-it-what-you-will approach that Frank Sinatra seldom employed during his long career. Another friend feels that Frank may have felt for years a lingering guilt over Marilyn, may have felt he could have done more for her, possibly saved her. Events have clearly proved over the years that not the pope, Mother Teresa, Dr. Joyce Brothers, or Billy Graham could have saved the pill-popping, booze-imbibing, self-hating, self-destructive Marilyn from the inevitable.

Dean Martin remembered that he and Frank had to listen for hours on one occasion when Marilyn rehashed at great length Clark Gable's death of a heart attack in 1960 at a relatively young fifty-nine. Had her absences and unpredictable behavior on the set of their co-starrer, *The Misfits*, figured in whatever tensions led to Clark's death? Frank remained silent, shrugging and frowning. Finally he went to get a drink, and Dean, fed up with Marilyn's rationalizations and self-dramatizations, told her flat-out: "No, Marilyn, your conduct *didn't* help Clark!" Upon which, Dean later reported, Marilyn burst into tears, then threw a drink at him.

Dean, for years one of the foremost members of the Sinatra Rat Pack, has since his recent death been falsely given credit for trying to save Marilyn's neck when she got fired (twice) from *Something's Got to Give*, the Twentieth Century-Fox movie he was doing with her in 1962 just before her death. Marilyn was as usual pleading sickness and absenting herself, holding up director George Cukor and the cast and crew with her unpredictable hi-jinks.

The story went that Dean said he would refuse to do *Something's Got to Give* with any co-star other than Marilyn. This resulted in the picture being permanently shut down, with plans for a new co-star shelved. George Cukor and others had a different take on this oft-repeated "canard," as George put it. According to George, Dean had only signed on for the picture because Marilyn's comeback venture (she had been off the screen for a year and a half, since *The Misfits*) promised to be a box-office hit, fans being curious to see her after so long a layoff. Dean wanted to bask in what he conceived would be the reflected glory of her renewed success. "He didn't refuse to do the picture without her for *her* benefit, but for *his own*," George said.

It was well-known that Jackie Kennedy had never cared much for Sinatra, though on occasion, on Jack's (and Peter's) pleadings, she had tolerated him. She considered him pushy, vulgar, opportunistic and, moreover, did not feel that the connections he had made available to her husband had been, over the long run, beneficial.

Frank Sinatra these days doesn't want to talk about the Kennedys—*or* Marilyn. "He had enough of them—long since—they're history, he feels," one friend said.

SIXTEEN

Marilyn

Over the years, there has been much canonization of Marilyn Monroe—Monroe, child of foster homes who rose above her environment; Monroe, used and mistreated by the male of the species; Monroe, exploited by her studio bosses, underpaid and overworked; Monroe, the prey of illness and a multitude of misfortunes. You name your favorite Monroe misfortune; it's all part of the long-standing national—indeed international—game of feel sorry for poor dear Marilyn.

Well, as one who knew and interviewed her over a dozen years, I don't buy any of it. Marilyn was not a very nice person—that is the long and short of it. Far from rising above her sordid beginnings, she leaned on them, dragged them in as excuses for the varieties of miscounduct she indulged in during her years of fame. She also tended to be monstrously self-pitying and self-dramatizing and regrettably hypocritical about sex—pretending to be horrified by blatant obscenity and profoundly regretful over her status as sex symbol *par excellence*, but in actuality reveling in the often vulgar and blatant persona that she deliberately cultivated.

She always considered herself a bad actress, so she compensated with gimmicks and self-parodies and grotesque exaggerations. Far from being exploited for her sex appeal, she deliberately exploited it. And far from being a lover of the male, she privately hated men, felt they had all the best of the American dream, and nursed years-long grievances against the assorted one-night stands, lovers, husbands, associates, and unrequited male adorers that populated her Hollywood world.

Chronically insecure, destructively unpredictable, and emotionally unstable, she developed an obsession with famous men. She married Joe DiMaggio for his baseball fame and Arthur Miller for his playwriting renown, and functioned as John Kennedy's courtesan-in-chief because she wanted the Kennedys' fame to rub off on her—for better or for worse, so long as it rubbed off and stuck. But in that case she got more than she bargained for, John Kennedy being a love-'em-and-leave-'em type who used her for years, then deserted her when she threatened to become a hot potato in more ways than one. Certainly JFK and Bobby made a crucial contribution to the chronic emotional instability, pill-popping, and alcoholic excesses that sped Marilyn to her tragic, premature end at age thirty-six.

After directing her for months in 1960 for her last release, *The Misfits* (so aptly titled), John Huston, who had endured Marilyn's hysterias, chronic lateness on the set, assorted insecurities, and at times, outright cruelties toward those she knew could not fight back, predicted that within a two-year period she'd be either dead or stark bonkers. As a prophet, Huston rated four stars.

She had been divorced in 1960 from Arthur Miller (the divorce became final in January 1961, a month before the national release of *The Misfits*). Miller had his own brand of ego. He felt that living with a deranged Monroe was sapping his creative energies, and that *The Misfits*, which he had written, represented him at his creative worst. After a distinguished career as author of such acclaimed plays as *All My Sons*, *Death of a Salesman*, and *The Crucible*, Arthur at the time was running out of gas, creatively and personally. It took the photographer Inge Morath, whom he married as soon as he had legally dumped Marilyn, to give him a new lease on life in all departments. Marilyn, it was obvious, was becoming bad news on all fronts.

Clark Gable, her co-star in *Misfits*, had overreached himself performing stunts with horses, had gotten his blood pressure sky-high coping with Marilyn's chronic lateness and manic moods, and had suffered a major heart attack in November 1960, from which he promptly died. Marilyn was assaulted from all sides as the bad-girl-on-set catalyst for Gable's demise, and she was ridden with what some called guilt but others (probably more correctly) called chagrin over the bad public relations for her that followed Gable's death. Earlier in 1960, on the set of *Let's Make Love* (another of her highly apt picture titles), Marilyn had made a superplay for the sophisticated French star Yves Montand, who, playing opposite her, took his share of Marilyn goodies until he'd had his fill, whereupon he went back to Paris and his waiting, not always patient wife, Simone Signoret. Marilyn professed to be highly upset that Yves, French-style, had cut her off clean without the usual apologies, but as Tony Perkins, who would appear with Yves and Ingrid Bergman in *Goodbye Again* (Yves's next film) put it to me: "What did Marilyn expect? She pretended to be jilted but my suspicion was she was as tired of him at the end as he was of her." Yves proceeded to make passes at Ingrid Bergman during *Goodbye Again* while Ingrid made passes at Tony.

In early 1961 Marilyn was reported to be involved with such Hollywood leading men as Marlon Brando (who got bored with her craziness and promptly dumped her—she wasn't his type anyway, as such ladies as Movita and Anna Kashfi could have told her) and Frank Sinatra, who gave her a big rush while maintaining to all comers that he felt sorry for her and wanted to ease her "loneliness" and give her the feeling of "being wanted by someone." Actually, as Dean Martin and other friends verified, Frank "was just satisfying his lustful curiosity." Meanwhile Marilyn was showing up on the Sinatra yacht and at his Las Vegas Sands Hotel engagements. Dean Martin, who felt sorry for Marilyn and was more than a little intrigued by her romantically, saw that she was thoroughly and intimately accepted by the Rat Pack, Sinatra's "Society of Congenial Cool Cats," as Sammy Davis Jr. once dubbed it. Dean's 1961 association with Marilyn resulted in a deal struck by his company for Marilyn to appear, under Twentieth Century-Fox auspices, in the ill-fated *Something's Got to Give*, for which she was able to complete only a few scenes before her death in the summer of 1962. As for Frank, he soon lost interest in Marilyn and went in pursuit of Juliet Prowse (they were briefly engaged) before moving on to other erotic adventures.

"Marilyn really was a fool about men, but she brought a lot of her troubles on herself," George Cukor told me after Marilyn's death. "She knew Montand, Sinatra, Brando, and the rest were guys with short attention spans romantically, yet she waded right in. She also wanted their name value to rub off on her."

Yet all through the DiMaggio and Miller marriages, Marilyn had been carrying on a "back street" affair with John F. Kennedy—at the time of her death it had persisted for eight years. JFK had seen her at a party in 1954 when she was hot on the heels of her success in *Gentlemen Prefer Blondes* (1953) and was by then a major star, noted more for her wrigglings and simperings and sexual innuendoes than for any demonstrated acting ability. All through the years, and to the great annoyance of both her husbands, Marilyn had been seeing JFK, trysting with him in various hotels, private homes, and on yachts.

Because of his bad back JFK liked to have the woman on top of him—it meant less movement. He also liked oral sex. Lem Billings told me, "He said that Marilyn gave great head—hers was a true labor of love."

Arthur Miller had married Marilyn in 1956, and later that year his disillusion with her began. In 1956 Marilyn attempted to showcase the New Marilyn, the Actor's Studio Marilyn, in the film *Bus Stop*. Don Murray told me that she was an unholy pain to work with in that. "She was taking herself much too seriously," he said. When she landed in England to appear with no less a co-star than Sir Laurence Olivier in *The Prince and the Showgirl*, she had really inflated ideas about what was essentially a pedestrian talent, and both Olivier and Miller began to find her a mean, bitchy egomaniac. George Cukor later told me that he didn't understand why Marilyn hadn't driven Olivier into a heart attack as she later did to Gable. "Sir Larry was made of sturdier stuff than Clark, I guess," he snickered.

Miller already had a shadow over his past. During his Marilyn marriage, he had been investigated by the Un-American Activities Committee of Congress for his alleged involvement with Communist groups earlier in his career and had given a lame, shifty impression during the proceedings. Friends of Marilyn felt she had been harmed by her association with Miller.

Marilyn's publicists always tried to present her as a sweet, put-upon, naive, rinso-white victim of life, fate, and men, but it is plain in retrospect that Marilyn knew exactly what she was doing. "Fame and notoriety are all the same to her," writer Jerry Asher once told me. "As long as her name is spelled right in the paper I don't think she gives a damn what they say as long as they keep on saying it!"

In retrospect it is amazing that the press let Jack Kennedy get away with his relationship with Marilyn without blowing the lid on it. "In 1954 he was only a senator, and senators were notoriously wayward husbands, but in 1961 he was *president*, for God's sake," publicist Helen Ferguson told me, "and his brazenness was as hubris as hubris can get!"

Jackie Kennedy knew of the affair, as she did about most of Jack's dalliances, but her basic attitude was apparent in advice she gave the more vulnerable and less resilient Joan Kennedy when Joan asked her how to cope with Teddy's infidelities. "Oh, Kennedy men are like that," Jackie said, "and it doesn't mean anything!" But apparently Jackie had her distinct limits of tolerance, for more than once she told Jack that if she were publicly humiliated or shamed unduly, she would make a real stink.

There was the oft-repeated story that Joe Kennedy had offered Jackie a million bucks in her own name to stay with Jack after she had gotten the full force of Jack's infidelity rampages; most informed folk feel that she did get the equivalent of that sum from Joe and the Kennedys in an unspoken agreement along those lines. Lem Billings spread, to me and others, a hilarious story that Jackie had retorted to Old Joe, "Okay, a million it is, but if he brings home to me any venereal diseases from these sluts, the price goes up to $20 million!" Old Joe, who then sported a $400 million-plus kitty, according to Lem, "retorted with surprising mildness, 'Okay, Jackie, if that happens, name your own price. We've got to elect our boy president, regardless of what it takes!'"

There was another story—again with a million-dollar tag on it—that Old Joe, shortly before his stroke, offered Marilyn a million bucks just to ensure her perpetual silence about the years-long, romantic-sexual hanky-panky she had been indulging in with Jack. Much was made later about Marilyn being relatively poor and cash short when she died, but given her extravagances and total lack of money sense, she could have dissipated whatever silence money Joe paid her long before her passing. It is surprising how many Kennedy insiders believe this story. "It's just that it was so characteristic of Joe to offer it—and so characteristic of Marilyn to take it," one source remarked.

Again according to Lem Billings, the new president saw Marilyn at every opportunity. "Oddly she continued to hold his interest as a mistress," Lem said. "She visited on him a variety of moods and sexual attitudes that excited his craving for variety." (Others called it JFK's jaded eroticism.) Lem Billings also told me that in 1938, when Jack, at twenty-one, was circumcised because of tight foreskin problems, Jack said, "When you're circumcised at a much later age like that, you think of it as a kind of castration, a threat to manhood, so you have to keep on proving 'it' is okay, by any means possible."

On one occasion Marilyn found herself next to Jackie Kennedy at a formal gathering. "Hi, Jackie," she said in a timid little-girl voice. According to Jerry Asher, Jackie stared coldly at Marilyn, and her look telegraphed loud and clear the words, "Get lost, slut!"

Peter Lawford played a large role in the Marilyn-JFK eight-year involvement. The pair often met secretly at Peter's Malibu house. Pat Kennedy Lawford reportedly was usually ambivalent but, at times, ashamed about Peter pimping for Jack and Marilyn. Accepting Jackie's "Kennedy men are like that" dictum on the family male shenanigans, she tolerated Peter's stratagems on Cupid's behalf, but reportedly was heartily disillusioned after Marilyn's death when Peter removed from Marilyn's house all traces of any Kennedy presence.

There has been much division of opinion, retrospectively, as to whether Bobby Kennedy was also, however briefly, the recipient of Marilyn's erotic favors. Said one friend, "When he was trying to calm her down just before her death and keep her from blabbing to the press about she and the president, he doubtless did what he thought would 'calm her down' and Marilyn cued him in on what would calm her by making crude jokes about 'Bobby Baby-Maker's Big Dick.'" (Bobby was to wind up with eleven children by Ethel.) Certainly in the last days of her life, in early August 1962, Bobby had been delegated not only to assure that Marilyn thoroughly understood that it was conclusively, finally, irrevocably over between her and JFK, but to get her in a frame of mind to be objectively acquiescent. "And if giving her his dick was part of the price, Bobby willingly, gladly paid it—he was a very *sensual* man," as publicist Jim Reid put it to me in 1964.

During 1962 things had been heating up to a dangerous point where Marilyn and the president were concerned. She had not only vulgarized his May 1962 birthday celebration at Madison Square Garden with her intimate singing of "Happy Birthday, Mr. President," replete with tight gown and swaying hips (Jackie had pointedly absented herself from this evening, knowing what was on tap), but her frequent obsessive calls to the president's private White House line and her reported threats to spill the beans at a press conference had made termination of the affair—and her silence—a must.

Marilyn was at the time tired of being a "back street" woman—however famous. And according to both Lem Billings and Peter Lawford, she also, earlier that summer of 1962, had aborted JFK's child in a secret operation. "She felt she wasn't getting enough respect from the Kennedy quarters," Jerry Asher recalled. "And she knew JFK was playing around with other women." But Jerry, a prominent fan-mag writer and publicist, never believed that the Kennedys had permanently "put her to sleep," nor does the evidence suggest such. Marilyn, by August 4, 1962, the night she died, was heavily into pills and alcohol, which she ingested indiscriminately and recklessly. She had made calls to Peter Lawford and others that telegraphed her distress.

She was, after all, under siege from many quarters in the last hours of her life. She had always been underpaid by her studio, Twentieth Century-Fox, which reportedly made a quarter million from her films but paid her a sliverous fraction of that. She had little cash reserve, was living (for a movie star) rather modestly, was heavily in debt, and worried about the future. After several false starts and despite glowing reports on the early rushes, the studio had finally closed down *Something's Got to Give* for keeps when her frequent absences, psychosomatic-illness spells, and irrational demands proved to be too much. She knew that JFK had permanently tired of her; that she was regarded by the Kennedys and their entourage as a liability; that even Pat and Peter, more loyal standbys than many others had been, were getting weary of her neurotic carryings-on.

Jerry Asher believed, as I do, that she overdosed on pills and alcohol and that, deep in her subconscious, was a sense that at thirty-six, her life, which had depended on youth and beauty and kittenish vibrancy, was over conclusively. Despite her acting pretensions, Marilyn was not a lady who would have taken aging well. "The forties would have been a horror for her," George Cukor felt. "She didn't have the integrity of a true actress—she would not have welcomed the richness of character interpretations, as a true actress would have. She was a star trading on certain gimmicks, and in her heart she knew it."

There was much criticism of her ex-husband Joe DiMaggio's refusal to admit to her services the people—co-stars, hangers-on, false pals, press agent toadies, and so forth—who he felt had hastened her inevitable end. But many objective insiders at the time felt that Joe had been honest in exposing Hollywood hypocrisy and indeed skull-duggery. In excluding those who enticed, for whatever sub-jective reasons, Marilyn into her steadily downhill path, he was making a statement that needed to be made.

It is a notable fact that press agent toadies and other hangers-on who loudly protested in later years any realistic appraisals of Marilyn Monroe's true character, thus drawing attention to themselves as her "defenders," were notably among the absent when she had *really* needed them.

This was also true of a Marilyn nemesis, Joan Crawford, who had won Marilyn's permanent enmity by ridiculing her "tasteless" and "sexy" conduct and attire during the 1953 Photoplay Magazine Awards, at which Marilyn was named outstanding newcomer of 1952. "I thought Joan was a caring older friend," Marilyn told me some years later. "Then she has me to her house, condescendingly and coldly advises me on clothes and personal conduct and the necessity of sleeking-up and streamlining any native crudities. I told her she was she and I was I and I was coming from a different direction and had to be myself. She was very mean and cutting to me after that—was probably jealous that *I* was in my mid twenties and *she* was in her early fifties!"

I interviewed Marilyn Monroe a number of times over the years when I was a fan-mag and general-media editor and writer. Though she was struggling for major attention in a series of supporting roles when I first met her and was a major star the last time we got together, I noted no essential change in her personality or outlook. Under the falsely kittenish surface and the little-girl voice and the slithery, supple mannerisms of face, body, and posturing, she seemed to me a ruthless egomaniac on a colossal compensation binge.

When I first knew her, she had played a hapless little sex kitten at the mercy of bristly, bitchy stage star Margo Channing, played by Bette Davis in 1950. I recognized at once that Marilyn shared with Bette a common emotion: *anger*. Anger in its perverse, roundabout way can be one of the great dynamics in a career—the kind of anger that leads to contempt for origins and people associated with those origins, anger that is ridden with overcompensatory drives to achieve the highest reaches of public fame and notoriety. This kind of anger has its own innate ruthlessness; it is not aimed at harming others so much as perpetuating, nourishing, and sustaining the self along the path to the heights—of fame, money, success, adulation. That both actresses sometimes failed to note the crucial difference between fame and notoriety went with the territory of upward career striving—

the usual perspective, balance, objectivity, and attempts at shrewd self-appraisal are sacrificed along the way, assuming that they ever existed in the first place.

In reviewing what Marilyn said to me in those interviews, I note striking similarities to the interview statements and personal confidences made to me by two other stars I knew well, Joan Crawford and Bette Davis.

The following are statements Marilyn made to me over the years:

> 1950: "I want to be the best there is. My daily routine, in matters great and small, is devoted to a larger goal: total self-fulfillment!"

> 1951: "I don't think there is anything wrong with sex. I am not ashamed to be thought sexy. Sex is a driving force in life. It is hypocritical, unrealistic, to downgrade it. It is a blessing. A blessing to be enjoyed, to be reveled in."

> 1952: "Between you and me, and you are not to print this, I think Ginger is jealous of me! [Marilyn and Ginger appeared in the film Monkey Business that year.] After all, I am in my mid twenties and Ginger is over forty, and I sympathize with her—but does she have to take it out on me?"

> 1953: "I like Jane Russell [who co-starred with her in her tremendous hit, Gentlemen Prefer Blondes] but Jane is thirty-two and over the hill and I am twenty-seven and just getting there in bigtime terms and I'm the one who brought in the audiences and I should have had first billing!"

> 1954: "Bob [Robert Mitchum, her co-star in River of No Return] is a nice guy but he should watch his bad breath and he is a lousy kisser! (Now, Larry, that is off the record!)"

1956: "It's mean and unfair that some people laugh at my efforts to improve my acting. I can't play the dumb blonde forever, you know. After all, I just turned thirty! Anyone who goes to Bus Stop and says 'that isn't the Marilyn I want to see,' well, I can only reply that we keep growing and moving on and I don't want to stay a silly sex symbol forever. That image did well by me once, but not now!"

1957: "I admire talent, and greatness. Why do they object to my marrying a literary genius [Arthur Miller] and acting with yet another genius [Sir Laurence Olivier in Prince and the Showgirl]. Is it so awful to want to improve oneself among one's betters?"

1960: "Jack Kennedy could have been a movie star himself. He had the charisma, the charm, that come-hither quality that can never be duplicated. Is it any wonder he got elected president?"

1961: "Why do they come down so hard on poor Monty [Montgomery Clift, one of her Misfits co-stars]? He had that horrible accident that ruined his face; he has been unwell. Why don't people understand what Monty and I understand? That one can have money and fame and still feel so alone. . . ."

Barbara Barondess MacLean, actress, top Hollywood fashion designer, and lately much loved humanitarian, was a fixture on the Hollywood scene from the early 1930s when, under MGM contract, she supported as an actress the likes of John, Ethel, and Lionel Barrymore, Greta Garbo, and Jean Harlow. Later married to the distinguished producer-actor Douglas MacLean, she moved to the top of Hollywood society and designed clothes for actresses such as Norma Shearer, Joan Crawford, and Gloria Swanson—apparel as timely and ultrafashionable today as it was fifty-odd years ago. Today, at eighty-nine, she is the donor of the Torch of Hope Awards, replete with a posh annual ceremony in New York that honors deserving people from all branches of the theatrical arts.

Barbara knew Marilyn Monroe very well in the years before her tragic end. To Barbara's way of thinking, Marilyn was a consummate self-seeker because she was following the law of self-preservation. To Barbara, Marilyn did "bad, self-destructive things"—like drugs, alcohol, undisciplined living and too many, far too many, men—because she was in eternal wild flight, eternal escape, forever the frightened child thrown on her own resources in sinister foster homes, afraid of the encroaching night, the threatening tomorrow. To Barbara, Marilyn was a victim of *men*—too trusting, too hopeful, and far too romantic. She wanted life with a man to be like a romantic film of the 1930s, with love and eternal togetherness triumphing over all odds. "She was such a sad case," Barbara says thoughtfully today. "Life was not kind, *men* were not kind, and it was not all *her* fault!"

Barbara feels that Marilyn's worst misfortune was becoming involved with the Kennedy men. She feels that Jack used and mistreated her and that Bobby was more the middleman caught between Jack and Marilyn. She feels that Marilyn and Jack were the lovers, *not* Marilyn and Bobby. While conceding that there might possibly have been sexual episodes between Bobby and Marilyn, she insists Bobby was not out to harm Marilyn but had simply gotten into another of those situations in which he was trying, as ever, to pull his adored brother Jack's chestnuts out of the fire.

Barbara to this day feels deeply sorry for Marilyn, and she has for sometime (and at eighty-nine yet) been planning to tell about her in a book. Barbara seems to hold Joe DiMaggio in high esteem—of all the men in Marilyn's life, she agrees, *he* tried to be helpful, constructive.

Helen Ferguson told me in 1964, two years after Marilyn's death, that Marilyn's greatest tragedy was not holding on to the marriage with Joe. She said that Marilyn once told her, "The sex was best with Joe—it had *meaning*, it fulfilled me." Helen was not at all surprised that it was Joe who came forward to give some dignity to Marilyn's services after her passing. Helen believed that the only man who really loved Marilyn was Joe DiMaggio. "Joe didn't think of her as another notch in his crotch belt like Jack Kennedy, or a glamorous conquest to embellish his escutcheon, like Arthur Miller. He gave her protective, concerned love, even after death." Helen was glad, she said, that "all those phonies were kept away from the poor darling's services."

Marilyn confessed to Helen that fellatio was her favorite sexual position with men, not that she didn't like penetration and other forms of expression. According to Helen, "Joe was a 'square' when it came to things like that—a missionary-position, macho Italian athlete, all the way." She added, "Marilyn felt her marriage to Joe really broke up because he didn't like to be fellated, and rebelled against her insistence along those lines. This fixation of Marilyn's scared Joe off."

Barbara and Sonia Wolfson, the Twentieth Century-Fox publicity woman who in the 1960s was like a mother to her female star clients, were to have the last word on Marilyn. To Barbara she was, and always will be, "a sad, lost child—forever victim of that terrible youth where men used her and twisted her out of shape for all her life." Sonia Wolfson told me in 1964: "Marilyn was the unhappiest girl I ever knew. She was heading for a tragic end—it was so apparent. Yes, she was immaturely self-seeking, and she hurt a number of people along the way. But Marilyn's worst enemy was—Marilyn."

Robert Stack, who had guided Jack Kennedy's 1940 Hollywood hegira sexually and romantically, never liked

Marilyn. When Gregory Speck, the prominent show-business journalist and author of the book *Hollywood Royalty*, asked him about her, Bob Stack spoke indignantly about her lateness and immature conduct that perhaps cost Bob's friend and mentor Clark Gable's life. Gregory Speck quotes Bob Stack in *Hollywood Royalty* thus:

> I had a hunch when Clark went up to do *The Misfits* that he wouldn't be coming back. I knew about Marilyn, about her compulsive lateness, and sometimes not showing up at all. She often didn't know her lines, and would get so sick she would throw up. By contrast, Clark was the total professional.

Perry Lieber, the top Twentieth Century-Fox publicist who had once been a young hot-to-trot protégé of my uncle Jimmy Quirk, gave me what I consider the definitive explanation of Marilyn's much-yakked-about and raked-over demise. Perry told me: "It was very simple. Her emotions caught up with her. She couldn't distinguish between reality and unreality any more. She mixed her pills, had no sense of what combinations were lethal, what were not. In a way she was a suicide; she was recklessly overindulging in anything and everything, drinks, pills, whatever she felt would kill the pain, the hurt, the shame she was feeling." He continued, "She knew she had muffed her last, best chance when she fouled up with *Something's Got to Give* and got herself fired. She just stopped caring. And she was scared—always scared. Of growing old, of being deserted, of failing in love. And subconsciously," Perry ended sadly, "I think she thought of death as—well, merciful oblivion."

Barbara never liked the Kennedys. She felt that their influence on Marilyn was "horrible," and that Old Joe got his just desserts when, after his 1961 stroke, he had to sit helpless, drooling, and mute in his wheelchair, quailing

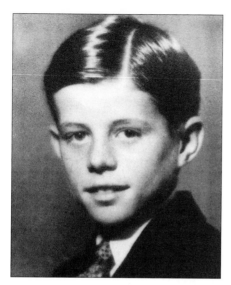

JFK as a boy.
PHOTOFEST

Young Joe Jr. and Jack.
PHOTOFEST

At twenty-two in 1939,
Jack Kennedy was
physically frail but
emotionally love-hungry.
PHOTOFEST

Jack and Joe Jr., here with their dad in 1938, were brutally competitive.
PHOTOFEST

Jack's PT-109 accident was built up as an heroic feat by his
father's relentless public relations campaign.
PHOTOFEST

Jack felt he hadn't really
earned the medal he received
for his PT-109 adventure.
PHOTOFEST

Jack Kennedy with Lem Billings, the man who loved him all his life, vacationing in Europe, 1937.
PHOTOFEST

Jack Kennedy's handsome Hollywood buddy, actor Robert Stack (with actress Dolores Moran at the Mocambo in 1942) was very much the man about town. In 1940, Stack helped Jack "go Hollywood" with a vengeance.
PHOTOFEST

Robert Stack gave
Deanna Durbin her first
screen kiss in *First Love*
(1939).
PHOTOFEST

Publicist and former silent-film actress Helen Ferguson told me that she had
once been secretly in love with Bob Stack (with her in 1946 at a Ciro's party for
Frank Sinatra) but felt that she was too old for him.
PHOTOFEST

Jack Kennedy in 1940 at age twenty-three: young, eager, and hot-to-trot with the
Hollywood ladies.

Jack was mesmerized by the charms of the lovely Angie Dickinson.
PHOTOFEST

Jack enjoyed a brief fling with the immensely popular ice skating actress, Sonja Henie, in 1946. Seven years Jack's senior (she was thirty-six, he twenty-nine), Sonja loved Jack's boyish charm.
ARCHIVE PHOTOS

Gene Tierney, once Jack Kennedy's love, gave birth to a handicapped child and later battled mental illness.
PHOTOFEST

Gene was still married to Oleg Cassini (with her above) when she romanced with Jack.
PHOTOFEST

Jack Kennedy broke Gene's heart when he told her he could never marry her.

During the 1946 congressional campaign, Jack marched in a parade in East Boston.
PHOTOFEST

The young congressman
waxes serious.
PHOTOFEST

Congressman JFK at a hearing.
PHOTOFEST

Intelligent, cultured, and refined, British actress Peggy Cummins (of 1947's *Moss Rose*) went out with Jack on several occasions, but she did not fall easy prey to his advances.
ARCHIVE PHOTOS

Jack Kennedy's 1946 dalliance with Peggy was short-lived. She was disappointed to discover that Jack did not consider her marriage material.
ARCHIVE PHOTOS

Jack Kennedy pursued actress June Allyson in the mid 1940s; she knew him
when he was only a "charming and fun-loving" young man who planned to
enter politics.

Soon after Peter Lawford arranged a Malibu tryst between
Bobby Kennedy and actress Lee Remick in 1961, Lee became
involved in a heavy affair with Peter. Her obsession with the
Kennedy clan (as well as her other extramarital involvements)
eventually destroyed her marriage to Bill Colleran.

Robert Walker, who
starred in Hitchcock's
Strangers on a Train, was
involved for a time with
fellow MGM actor Peter
Lawford in the mid 1940s.

Jack was always condescending to Peter.
COLLECTION OF LAWRENCE J. QUIRK

Peter Lawford (before Pat Kennedy) and Ava Gardner (before Frank Sinatra) had a brief but steamy relationship.
ARCHIVE PHOTOS

Actress Lana Turner, a
former love-interest of
Peter Lawford's,
testified to his prowess
in bed to dispel rumors
that he was gay.
ARCHIVE PHOTOS

Marrying into the Kennedy family was the beginning of Peter Lawford's
downfall. Peter's drinking and infidelities finally broke Pat's heart.
PHOTOFEST

JFK and Jackie on their wedding day. Widespread rumors had it that Joe later paid Jackie a million dollars to tolerate Jack's infidelities.
COLLECTION OF LAWRENCE J. QUIRK

Jack, here on his wedding day with Jackie (Teddy in rear), was a flagrantly unfaithful husband.
PHOTOFEST

Jack and Frank Sinatra had an upsy-downsy friendship.
PHOTOFEST

The Sinatra Rat Pack: Peter, Frank, Sammy Davis Jr., Joey Bishop, and Dean Martin.
PHOTOFEST

Marilyn's famous "come hither" look got her into a lot of mischief. She would find her Kennedy liaisons a curse.
PHOTOFEST

Alan Ladd, who resisted Marilyn's come-ons, congratulates her for winning the *Photoplay* Gold Medal for Most Promising New Film Personality, 1953.
PHOTOFEST

Sir Laurence Olivier found
Marilyn a pain to work with
during *The Prince and the
Showgirl* (1957).
PHOTOFEST

Marilyn the man-mad in 1960 was balancing her co-star boyfriend Yves Montand
against her then-hubby Arthur Miller—and romancing Jack Kennedy on the side.
PHOTOFEST

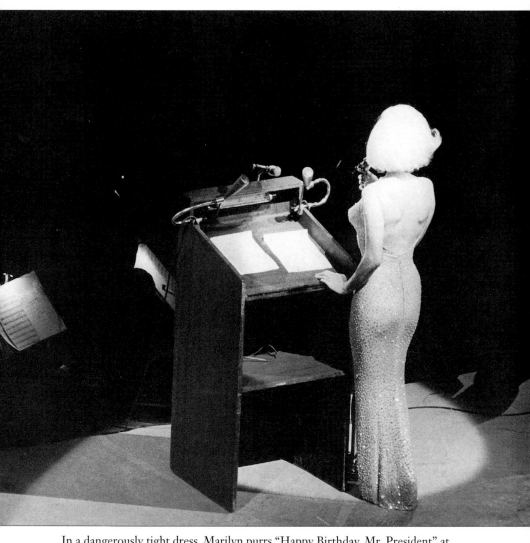

In a dangerously tight dress, Marilyn purrs "Happy Birthday, Mr. President" at Madison Square Garden in 1962. Jackie absented herself.
PHOTOFEST

Jayne Mansfield's peeing pups annoyed me during a 1957 interview. In many ways, Jayne tried to emulate Marilyn Monroe—including where JFK was concerned. With Peter Lawford as go-between, the pair finally got together in 1960.
COLLECTION OF LAWRENCE J. QUIRK

The three Kennedy brothers were to know variegated destinies.
PHOTOFEST

Pat, Jack, and Peter in a rare moment of mutual felicity in 1960.
PHOTOFEST

Steve Smith, the practical brother-in-law, and Peter Lawford, the wayward naughty-boy, with Jack in 1961.
PHOTOFEST

Jack and Jackie look haggard
and concerned after visiting Joe
after his stroke in 1961.
PHOTOFEST

Jack doted on
daughter Caroline.
PHOTOFEST

JFK as meditative
President.
PHOTOFEST

Jack on the golf course, 1963, with Jackie and Mrs. Ben Bradlee in the golf cart
behind him. Jack found golf to be a great tension reliever.
PHOTOFEST

Jackie thought Peter Lawford was a bad role model for aspiring actor JFK Jr.
Here are the three at Sydney Lawford's 1983 wedding.
PHOTOFEST

Peter (left) and Chris (right), here with Peter McKelvy at his wedding to Sydney Lawford, never really made it as father and son.
COLLECTION OF LAWRENCE J. QUIRK

John-John's relationship with Sally Munro did not endure.
COLLECTION OF LAWRENCE J. QUIRK

Daryl Hannah's idyll
with JFK Jr. did not win
Jackie's approval.
COLLECTION OF
LAWRENCE J. QUIRK

Jackie was afraid actress
Daryl Hannah would
encourage John to pursue
an "actor's lifestyle."
The relationship
eventually fizzled.
COLLECTION OF
LAWRENCE J. QUIRK

Teddy, Caroline, John-John, and Jackie (at Kennedy library) had their internecine disagreements but put up a united public front.
COLLECTION OF LAWRENCE J. QUIRK

John-John was Jackie's dutiful son and escort, but inwardly he often seethed with resentment.
COLLECTION OF LAWRENCE J. QUIRK

John-John loved to show off his body.
COLLECTION OF LAWRENCE J. QUIRK

Super-Body Boy Arnold
Schwarzenegger (here in
1985's *Commando*) won
Maria Shriver for his
own in 1986. They have
now lasted ten years as
husband and wife.
PHOTOFEST

Arnold escorted his then-girlfriend Maria Shriver to the 1984 Academy
Awards ceremony. The couple dated for nine years before tying the
knot in 1986.
ARCHIVE PHOTOS

Arnold Schwarzenegger (here with Maria placing his handprints in the sidewalk in front of Grauman's Chinese Theater) has not shifted his firmly Republican political views in spite of the influence of his in-laws.
ARCHIVE PHOTOS/LEE

JFK Jr. appears on Murphy Brown to plug his magazine, *George*, in 1995. Candice Bergen looks impressed by the cover (featuring her), but it was faked for the occasion.
PHOTOFEST

before the contempt in Rose's eyes, her satisfaction in seeing her often unfaithful, distant, absent husband potentially
at her mercy until death claimed him after eight long years.

She agreed with me that the Kennedy men's macho,
insensitive attitudes toward women were ridiculous and
repellent. "The Kennedy weakness is sex," Vicent Gardenia's
sinister, jowly J. Edgar Hoover proclaimed in a 1984 television miniseries. But then the Kennedys were themselves
caught in a pernicious American macho trap.

In this author's 1974 book, *The Great Romantic Films*, it
is noted that the prevalent dread among American males—
that they will be perceived as sissies or worse if they indulge
any creative bents they might have—has been responsible for
a scandalous loss of male artistic talent in this country.
Certainly the Kennedys, in the way they raised their sons,
were guilty not only of creativity thwarting—forcing talented actors to become lawyers, for instance—but of inculcating
ridiculously lopsided sexual and romantic values. That is, if
"romantic" were a word the Kennedy males understood at
all. Rose in later years laughed that getting Old Joe interested in opera was like dragging a reluctant mule to water, yet
once she saturated him in it, he came to love it, to become,
in later years, *addicted* to it.

I once told Helen Ferguson how Rose had finally gotten
Joe to enjoy opera, and she laughed. "If only her prayers, all
those Catholic prayers she was saying, had gotten those boys
to *behave* themselves with women—*that* would have helped
far more than force-feeding Joe opera!"

The Kennedy generations of men tended to ape each
other—in the wrong ways. Ted is involved with a woman's
drowning at Chappaquiddick, so young Joe the third gets
himself responsible for another woman being permanently
crippled in a car accident. David gets caught up in all the

druggie doings—his nascent creativity thwarted and ridiculed—and ends up at twenty-nine in the cemetery. Some escaped: Patrick stopped using drugs and made father Ted proud by becoming a congressman; Joe cleaned up his act and also became a congressman. But he also imitated Uncle Teddy by getting a divorce and remarrying. And so on and so on.

Teddy reportedly did some rather weak imitations of Jack in courting the Hollywood ladies, with Peter Lawford drafted, as usual, as pimp. According to Patricia Seaton Lawford's book about her husband Peter, Ted took a shine to her and suggested she join him in Washington for a love tryst. When she reported this to hubby Peter, then fargone and nearing death, he seemed unquestioningly to acquiesce—to her disgust.

To Barbara MacLean and others who knew Marilyn Monroe well, her final tragedy is not just *her* tragedy alone; the shades of Joe and Jack Kennedy share in it, as well—they and the wrongheaded values that all Rose's operas and prayers could never exorcise.

Stephen Jerome, curator of the Brookline Historical Society, reminds us, however, that while there may be bad in the best of us, there is also good in the worst of us—including the Kennedys. Stephen was Teddy Kennedy Jr.'s roommate at Wesleyan and watched Teddy weather heroically the loss of his leg after a cancer siege in his teens. Using prosthetics and a positive attitude, Teddy forged on to a hopeful adult life. Stephen also reminds me that Ted Sr. was the most loving and supportive of fathers when Ted Jr. underwent his hardships, as was his mother Joan.

Yes, Ted Kennedy Jr. is a heroic and admirable survivor—and so is Caroline Kennedy Schlossberg, who made a good life for herself as wife, homemaker, and mother, while functioning as an attorney and coauthor of several well-received, law-oriented books. I agree with my friend Stephen that it is important that we look for *good* in people—that there *are* good people, everywhere. Al Manski, a Boston writer and film historian, agrees. "Life is an uncertain journey, and a sad one," Al says. "The Kennedys have paid their dues for being part of the human condition." And for Al, too, Ted Kennedy Jr. and Caroline Kennedy Schlossberg are that tragic family's outstanding hero and heroine.

SEVENTEEN

Clowning Around with Jayne

One of Jack Kennedy's sillier romantic involvements was with Jayne Mansfield, who had staked her life and career in the 1950s—and beyond—on becoming not only the *poor man's* Marilyn Monroe but *Everyman's* answer to Marilyn Monroe. That Jayne's plans did not work out as she had hoped was due not only to the poor management and promotion of her cause but to her own self-destructive obsession with becoming an almost caricaturial Monroe. "Marilyn thinks of me as her rival—I know it unnerves her," she told me in 1957 during an interview at the Sherry-Netherland; at the table where we were lunching she sported her usual exaggerated-breasts outfit. When her noisy little dogs, whom she kept handing to me, first spit and then peed on me, far from apologizing, she thought it hilarious. Granted that the pee came out only in small droplets, which I quickly corrected in the men's room, I suspected it was the dog's commentary on all journalists that amused her—though she needed those same journalists to further the image she was after.

When I got back from the men's room, all spruced up and deodorized, the dogs had disappeared—some hep publicist must have seen the light—and Jane went on telling me about how Marilyn had gone *arty* but *she* was out to win the hearts of the public.

"I'll be here for the long haul—you'll see—I know just what I'm doing!" she told me. I asked her if she wanted these words in the published interview and reminded her that I was editing the fan magazine that would be using it, as well as writing the article on her. This seemed to discombobulate her, and she said, "You mean you *edit* as well as *write?*"

"Yes, Jayne, such double-jointed animals do exist," I rejoindered. At that she giggled and appeared to relax a bit, conveying that we were about to become coconspirators as to what she wanted the public to believe about her.

"I think sex is healthy, and there's too much guilt and hypocrisy about it," she continued. "Marilyn understood that, and so do I." Asked if she didn't feel it demeaning to attempt carbon-copying someone, she snapped back: "Oh, but I am merely *influenced* by Marilyn! Artists in all fields have original influences then they go on to put their own individual stamp on what they are offering their public!"

And what, I asked, was to be Jayne's original stamp in this instance? "Well, what with that Actor's Studio stuff Marilyn goes in for, and her acting with Laurence Olivier and all that, I want to strike out on the common trail; I want to be the ordinary man's conception of what a sexy, obliging, comradely, down-to-earth girlfriend ought to be." It was still repressed 1957; had it been a later decade, Jayne, I am sure, would have said "bed partner" or "lover" instead of "girlfriend." But I got the general drift and conveyed it duly in my article later.

There is a photograph of Jayne and me and the dogs at that table in the Sherry-Netherland in 1957. Jayne and the dogs are looking, well, busy and watchful, and *I* am looking puzzled and sardonic, as I would in a dozen other interviews with Jayne over the next few years.

Certainly, at that time, Jayne had cashed in on what she called Marilyn's "arty ideas." Twentieth Century-Fox, while recognizing that they had in Jayne a cruder, more elemental sexpot—subtlety was never one of Jayne's watchwords—felt that she could be milked not only for sexual titillation but for laughs, and Jayne did everything to aid and abet them. Her motto, as she confessed to me later (off the record), was: get the public's attention anyway you can. When I gently suggested that there was a subtle distinction between notoriety and fame, she shook her finger at me and interrupted with "but in Hollywood, notoriety *is* fame!"

And notoriety is what Jayne proceeded to win, year after year, until she ran out of gas.

Born Vera Jayne Palmer in 1933 in Bryn Mawr, Pennsylvania, she was married at sixteen and a mother at seventeen. After drifting (briefly) through drama classes at such places as the University of Texas and UCLA, she got into and won a number of beauty contests, did minor television work, then did her first notoriety shtick in Broadway's *Will Success Spoil Rock Hunter?*, in which she sashayed around in a tantalizingly loose Turkish towel. The dizzyblonde role she essayed in the play (obviously a somewhat cartoonish takeoff on Marilyn Monroe) she repeated in the 1957 movie version. After that, a succession of similar roles followed, until the inevitable downward slide in the 1960s. Having unloaded her early husband far back in the game, she married muscle-boy Mickey Hargitay in 1958 (they split in 1964), and later the Mansfield-Hargitay

THE KENNEDYS IN HOLLYWOOD

combine was reincarnated by Arnold Schwarzenegger and Loni Anderson in a 1980 television movie, *The Jayne Mansfield Story*.

Her third marriage, to director Matt Cimber, lasted only a couple of years in the 1960s. By the mid 1960s she had to resort to low-budget European movies, and after age thirty, her buxom blonde charms turned increasingly blowsy. She died at thirty-four in a car accident in New Orleans while on her way to a nightclub engagement. The original story that she had been decapitated was later proven untrue; she had lost her wig, was scalped, but died from general bodily traumas.

But for awhile, from 1955 to about 1960, Jayne seemed to be holding her own in such films as *The Girl Can't Help It*, *Kiss Them for Me*, and *It Happened in Athens*.

From the mid 1950s, Jayne had heard about the Jack Kennedy-Marilyn Monroe on-again, off-again affair, and as always, she heartily envied Marilyn for it. She pondered later, with considerable chagrin (as she told me off the record in 1959), Marilyn's talent for marrying "big shots" like Joe DiMaggio and Arthur Miller while she could only attract what she called "small-fry." She even said this within earshot of her then husband Mickey Hargitay, and I could tell from his scowl that he didn't appreciate it.

According to one of her publicists, Raymond Strait, who later authored two books on her, Jayne was determined to catch up with Marilyn where Jack Kennedy was concerned, and in 1960, the year he was elected president, she made it with him. As usual, Peter Lawford was the go-between. Peter himself mentioned it to me; he said Jack found Jayne's Marilyn-aping act amusing, adding that Jack thought that "Jayne's ass was as good as, if not better than, Marilyn's." "She's so anxious to *ape* Marilyn, *be* Marilyn, we'll add to her credentials by giving her a roll in the hay," Jack laughed.

Because in 1960 Marilyn was still married to Arthur Miller and the Millers were doing *The Misfits* together, Peter felt that there was time and room for Jack to experiment with Jayne. Peter also had a vixenish side and knew Marilyn would hear of it, get jealous, and soon want to be back in the main running in Jack's bedroom scheme.

Jack was in the early stages of his 1960 campaign and was still a senator from Massachusetts, so this gave him more mobility and "incognito opportunities" than he would know later as president (not that the presidency stopped Jack from attaining his objectives. Peter Lawford once said to me that when Jack wanted something, he wanted it, and even had he been *pope* he would have found a way to get it).

Raymond Strait remembered a call from a mysterious Mr. J (Jack) while he was vacationing in Palm Springs. Peter Lawford had given him all the phone numbers and addresses he would need in tracking down Jayne; Jack lost no time in availing himself of them. The first time, Jack and Jayne rendezvoused in Palm Springs; the second time, at Peter's beach house in Santa Monica. Peter was a master at keeping the *wrong* cast members off the stage at crucial times. Peter, Peter's wife, and the kids were away; there were no other visitors. Jack and Jayne had ample opportunity to test their mating skills.

Jayne later told Peter and others that Jack left something to be desired as a lover, preferring sex while on his back and pressing her to perform oral sex on him. "And once he's done, he's done; it's like you don't exist any more!" Peter reminded Jayne about Jack's bad back and the recurring pain he suffered, hence his preference for certain methods of intercourse. Jayne gave the most classic answer to this of all

Jack's lovers: "Okay, but couldn't he at least be a little *tender?*" Peter felt this was ironic coming from Jayne, since *tenderness* was distinctly not a part of her public persona, onscreen and off. "Greer Garson and Norma Shearer and Irene Dunne she ain't, never was, never will be!" Peter laughed.

Raymond Strait continued to be cued in on Jayne's encounters with Jack Kennedy. Another time, as he recalled it, Jayne dropped by his place for a chat and a cup of coffee and a cigarette and left a matchbook with the Presidential Seal on it.

Peter didn't think Jayne very discreet and told her so. "Why bother?" she snapped back. "Everyone in Hollywood and Washington knows about it anyway, and I like it that way! And I'll bet Marilyn's pissed as all get out!"

There was truth in Jayne's statement, for all amours and assignations of any kind were gossip fodder in Washington and Los Angeles, the two gossipiest towns in America—or the world for that matter. There were always prying chauffeurs and maids looking for stains and whatnot in beds, elevator operators and desk clerks, all with a sharp eye out, all hoping to sell whatever information they had. While this was the era of the *Confidential*-type tabloids, the info they had was even more valuable to the network of spies who could fit such stuff into their special-interest agendas.

But the strangest encounter, as Strait remembered (Peter Lawford and others corroborated Strait on this), was when Jayne was pregnant with her fourth child and was nearing birthing time. Jack told Strait he had to see Jayne; Strait said he'd do all he could. When Jayne heard that Jack wanted her to come down to Palm Springs, she rushed to get there. When Peter tried to remonstrate that with her big belly and bloated appearance Jack would hardly find her an inviting sight, she said, "Jack knows all about it; you don't know him as I know him; he'll find his own way to enjoy himself with me—he always does!"

Jayne later reported that she had performed oral sex on Jack while he stroked her belly. "Jack got a kick out of being 'done' by a woman almost ready to give birth—he was always looking for freaky variations on things," she laughed. Did she find their relative positions during the act uncomfortable? "Oh no," she said, "I managed—it was different and fun!"

Ruth Waterbury was one of Hollywood's prime interviewers and somewhat of a mother figure to stars she interviewed; she also played fair, and stars knew she would print material that was within what they called "decent limits." Ruth told me in 1964 of the Jayne-Jack interlude while she was pregnant. "If I dared print but one half of one percent of all I know about these people," Ruth chortled, "I'd be run out of Hollywood on a rail in five minutes flat!" When I asked Ruth why she felt Jack had this strange compulsion toward indiscriminate, often freaky, promiscuity, she answered, succinctly: "Power. Male nymphomania. And the cachet (which he savored) of fucking the famous!"

According to Strait, Jack once put Jayne's nose out of joint by telling her that her voice reminded him of the woman she was busily cuckolding—Jackie. Again according to Strait, Jayne found the comparison "insulting and depressing." But far from feeling even a tinge of guilt over her adultery, Jayne put the needle in Jackie, protesting angrily, "I don't sound like her! She doesn't sound like anything!"

Fred Otash, an associate of Raymond Strait's, was a detective often for hire and popular with notables in Washington, New York, and Hollywood, who for whatever reasons wanted to get the dirt on each other. Strait later claimed that he listened to an audiotape recording Otash had made secretly. Reportedly, Jack and Jayne's lovemaking noises—and their highly imaginative sexual imagery and fetishism, vocalized eloquently and noisily—rendered the audiotape a classic of its kind.

Peter Lawford, during the presidential years of Jack Kennedy, saw to it that Jayne met with Jack whenever he expressed a desire along those lines. Whether in or out of marriage, Jayne was always available. "I'm honored— *honored!*" she told Ruth Waterbury. "Why, think, I'll go down in history like that—what was her name—Madame O'Barry."

"Madame *Du* Barry," Ruth gently corrected Jayne, adding, "she was *French*, Jayne, not *Irish*!"

"Oh, whatever she was, I'm in good historical company, ain't I?" Jayne giggled.

Marilyn and Jayne, in the 1960–1962 period, occasionally ran into each other. "Marilyn was never cordial," Jayne told Ruth. "She was seeing Jack, too, and she hated me for being her rival." When Jayne heard shortly before Marilyn's death that Marilyn had aborted Jack's baby, she was miserly with the sympathy. "Why couldn't the silly dame have been more careful?" was her tart observation.

I brought up Jayne Mansfield several times to Marilyn Monroe when I interviewed her. Marilyn, I can testify, hated her. "All she does is imitate me—but her imitations are an insult to her as well as to myself." she snapped. "I know it's supposed to be flattering to be imitated, but she does it so grossly, so vulgarly—I wish I had some legal means to sue her."

"Sue her for what, Marilyn?" I asked.

"For degrading the image I worked for years to construct!" Marilyn shot back.

When Marilyn's death was reported on August 5, 1962, Jayne, according to Strait, Ruth Waterbury, and another of her confidants, Jerry Asher, the fan-mag writer, grew very nervous and fearful. "Maybe I'll be next!" she kept repeating, striding around her bedroom, smoking frantically. Peter Lawford tried to reassure her. "But Jayne," he reminded her, "you never gave Jack any problems. You never came on possessive or demanding; you never called him, as Marilyn did; you always waited for him to call you."

But Jayne would not be comforted. "Maybe I should go to Europe for a while," she said to Ruth. Ruth, who thought Jayne was melodramatizing things and making too much of it, suggested that if Jayne did go to Europe, she should visit Versailles outside Paris and roam around among the scenes associated with Madame Du Barry, Madame de Pompadour, and other extramarital consorts of French royalty. Ruth told me years later that Jayne vetoed this. "They're dead and I'm alive. *I'm* the one who has to do the worrying—it's just not funny."

In the last years of her life (1966–1967) Jayne toyed with writing her autobiography. Jerry Asher tried to make her understand that she wasn't the personality she had been, that it might not attract sufficient buyers. Always the realist, if an addle-headed and indiscreet one, Jayne asked what would happen to potential sales if she told all—meaning about her and Jack, among other encounters. "Then you will take the heat you have always been ducking," Jerry snapped back. "Don't be a fool, Jayne. Let sleeping dogs lie."

Always on hand with a humorous crack even in moments of tension, he recalled, Jayne said, "You mean let sleeping *wolves* lie."

In one of her interviews with me, Jayne once said she thought Teddy Kennedy was the cutest of the Kennedys and she had a crush on him but had never gotten to close quarters with him. At that time (1965) Jayne was thirty-two and Teddy was thirty-three. I made notes on this at the time, remarking that it was just as well Ted and Jayne stayed at a distance from each other; Jayne, being the kind of person she was, would have possibly done worse than drive Ted's wife Joan to drink—she might have driven her to suicide.

In 1965, Jerry Asher, who was writing for my fan magazines, told me Jayne was still begging him to ghostwrite her life story, but he had never liked ghostwriting. He suggested, "Why don't you ask my editor, Larry Quirk?" Jayne was soon on the phone.

I tried to let the lady down lightly: "Jayne, I'm editing four fan magazines at once, and writing for them, too, and where would I find the time?" I suggested writer-publicist Jim Reid, who was one of my contacts. "Oh, Jim's too nice— he wouldn't write it hard-boiled. And *I'm* hard-boiled." Jayne giggled.

EIGHTEEN

The Kennedys on Camera

The Kennedys over the years have heavily involved themselves with Hollywood performers and other artists from La-La Land, and they themselves have figured in numerous movies and television dramas, from *romans à clef* to dramatizations naming names and drawing directly from life.

They have always tried to involve themselves directly in these enterprises, either originating and promoting the projects, or using their considerable influence to suppress or water down projects that they have suspected might portray them in a less-than-flattering light.

The Kennedy manipulation of the media was going full force as far back as 1940 when Jack Kennedy published his ghostwritten *Why England Slept*. Old Joe saw to it that the book got major media coverage; Joe had put out his own book, *I'm for Roosevelt* in 1936, but that book had sold more on the Roosevelt name than on Kennedy pressure and manipulation, though that played some part in it. Jack's second book, *Profiles in Courage*, also got major promotion due to Kennedy manipulations. Joe worked to ensure that his son's book would be a bestseller by wining and dining influential critics while sending out staff members to certain bookstores—particularly those surveyed for the bestseller lists—to buy up as many copies as they could carry. Literally thousands upon thousands of these copies were stored in the attic of the Kennedy compound, but Joe's plan worked and it was assumed that the books had been actually snatched up by an eager public.

The Kennedys did the same for other projects designed to further their public relations program, but when it came to movies and television, they got mixed results over the years.

In 1961, before his debilitating stroke, Joe Kennedy had negotiated with Hollywood studios for movie versions of the books *The Enemy Within*, which dealt with Bobby's battles with the mob, and *PT-109*, about Jack's Pacific exploit in World War II.

Bobby had wanted Paul Newman, long known as a liberal Democrat of the deepest dye, to play the lead in *The Enemy Within*. Paul refused. He and Bobby did not have simpatico personally, and Newman's was a different brand of Democratic politics. Bobby reportedly never forgave Newman for passing on the project. During 1962 and 1963 Bobby looked at a number of actors to star in the projected film, but was satisfied with none of them. In 1963 I was pushing, in the fan mags I edited, a twenty-six-year-old actor named Jack Nicholson, who had been acting and writing for Roger Corman and had made something of a splash in a Corman picture with Boris Karloff, *The Terror*. Jack and I corresponded and talked on the phone about *The Enemy Within*—I felt he looked somewhat like Bobby, was a good actor, and could give weight to the picture. I contacted Bobby thorough his aides, and the word came back that they would look at some of Jack Nicholson's films and put him in the running. As it turned out, Jack didn't need *The Enemy Within* to put him over. After *Five Easy Pieces* six years later, he was on his way to becoming one of our greatest and most enduring stars.

After quite a lot of Kennedy-inspired hype and brouha-ha over Bobby's take-down-the-mob film, the project was abandoned, and for a complex of reasons, one of which was the new administration in Washington under Lyndon Johnson after JFK's assassination. Bobby, refusing the vice presidency under Johnson in 1964, would be running for the New York senatorship (he would later win), and such mob films seemed to carry more liabilities than assets on a number of counts.

The other project Old Joe had negotiated in 1961 *did* get off the ground. *PT-109* recounted JFK's much vaunted but suspect Pacific "heroics," the saving of one or more lives of his crew when his boat was rammed and sunk.

In a recent issue of *George*, John Kennedy Jr. interviewed Warren Beatty, who was active in Democratic politics and had worked speaking on behalf of Bobby Kennedy in the 1968 presidential campaign. Warren recalled that Bobby Kennedy in 1962 had specifically requested that he star as JFK in the PT-109 project and had sent Pierre Salinger with a script for Warren to look over. Beatty gave him a straight response: he didn't think the script was very good. Beatty in the *George* interview went on to mention that he had understood that Jacqueline Kennedy, who had admired his performance in *Splendor in the Grass*, had wanted him for the role, believing he would suggest the essence of the president as he was at twenty-six.

Beatty told John Jr., "I was thrilled to be asked, though I didn't want to do it," and recalled that JFK (after looking at the final result on screen) told Beatty, "You sure made the right decision on that one."

After Beatty refused the part, months of testing followed—the casting impasse continued. There was a strong Hollywood faction rooting for the then popular Ed Byrnes; at twenty-eight he was close to JFK's actual age when the action in the Pacific took place, and he looked somewhat like him and had features acceptably Irish looking. Next on the list was Peter Fonda, who had a Kennedy-esque look, especially when it came to facial bone structure, and again was the right age. But they passed on Peter, too.

Then word went out from the White House aides: "We want a man who subtly suggests the future greatness and eminence of this particular young navy lieutenant. We can find plenty of youngsters to put across physical courage and resourcefulness in war, but finding an actor who can suggest potential depth of spirit and future leadership of the highest order—well, that is something else."

The ukase from on high pounded home its primary point with the statement: "After all, this is the President of the United States we are portraying, regardless of what period of his life we are showing!"

JFK made the decisive choice. They had been running test after test on actors who aspired to the role, and when the president saw Cliff Robertson, he said: "That's the one!"

In retrospect, after thirty-four years, Cliff Robertson seems a strange choice to play JFK in *PT-109*. He was then thirty-seven; the president had been twenty-six at the time of the action. Cliff was of Scottish descent and a Protestant, and here he would be playing a young Irish-descended Catholic. They looked not a bit alike; Cliff's facial features were totally different from JFK's—the eyes, the bone structure, the expressions, entirely dissimilar.

JFK seemed to have been blind to all these considerations. He went along with the White House line—which *he* had initiated anyway—that this kid of twenty-six had to suggest "future greatness."

When the picture was released in 1963, it bombed with a vengeance. Typical of the critical reaction was that of Leslie Halliwell of the later famous *Film Guide*, who wrote: "[It was] an extraordinarily protracted and very dull action story which seemed to be overawed by its subject." In Leonard Maltin's 1996 *Movie and Video Guide*, thirty-three years later, *PT-109* gets only two stars and is dismissed as a "standard action film . . . neither here nor there."

I knew personally, or interviewed over time, most of the cast of the film version of *PT-109*—all of whom looked sheepish or embarrassed or cast eyes denigratively skyward when the movie came up. Ty Hardin remembered, "Hell, it went through three—count 'em *three*—directors!" Leslie Martinson, director number three, refused to be quoted on the subject.

Certainly it did nothing to enhance the inappropriately cast Cliff Robertson's career. The next year the Gore Vidal-originated *The Best Man* would give him a big boost upward, followed four years later by his Oscar-winning *Charlie*.

Lem Billings gave the most direct and honest estimate of *PT-109* to me—and the shortest: "It *sucked!*" For once, the longtime admirer and intimate of *PT-109*'s subject was right on target.

The *PT-109* disaster—disaster in real life and disaster supreme on the screen—did not in the least discourage those who decided, either on their own or through backstage Kennedy prodding, that the Kennedys and entourage were hot camera fodder, especially after the president's death, Bobby's disastrous ending, and Jackie's remarriage.

Among the numerous movies inspired by the Kennedys or their entourage was *Young Joe: The Forgotten Kennedy*, starring Peter Strauss. The telepic rendition of the short twenty-nine years of Joe Kennedy Jr.'s life, his early hopes and aspirations, his please-daddy strivings, his ambitious wanderings, and his tragic death in a bombing mission over the English Channel in August 1944, might have seemed to Peter a major opportunity at the time, but it took his career absolutely nowhere. The 1977 reviews were respectful but yawning. Richard T. Heffron, the director, refused an interview on the matter. Barbara Parkins, the television actress who had hoped it would "do something" for her when I talked with her during shooting, was "disappointed" a year later. Another actor, Lance Kerwin, who had figured in it somewhat peripherally, only shrugged when it was mentioned. A current movie guide tries to be nice about it, saying: "[Peter Strauss] gives sincere performance in tear-stained drama that strives to fulfill the public's never-ending fascination with the legendary Kennedy family." Then it labeled the ninety-seven-minute telepic "average."

As the years passed, it was no surprise to anyone that the Kennedy family member who seemed to get the most screen and telepic time was Jackie Kennedy Onassis. And the event that got played to death was, of course, the assassination.

In 1978 the public was treated to the movie *The Greek Tycoon*, J. Lee Thompson's thinly disguised look at the relationship between Jackie (played by the aptly first-named but imperfectly talented Jacqueline Bisset) and Aristotle Onassis, given the hale and hearty Zorba-the-Greek treatment by larger-than-life Anthony Quinn. James Franciscus, a good actor who had had a brief filmic heyday in the

1960s, played in the early scenes a JFK type named Cassidy (same number of letters in the name, same general sound, get it?) Although Quinn's portrayal of the Greek magnate was flattering in its virile and impressive rendering, according the original unhandsome Onassis a more charismatic persona than he deserved, the picture itself presented both people and events in a matter-of-fact style devoid of any depth. Despite evocative scenery and music and a transparent go-for-the-jugular entertainment appeal, *The Greek Tycoon* proved utterly superficial.

Three years later, television got back in the act with *Jacqueline Bouvier Kennedy*, which ended just at the point that *The Greek Tycoon* began. Jaclyn Smith wasn't as awful a Jackie Kennedy as everyone expected, but an Emmy-winning performance it was not. James Franciscus, by this time looking hapless, helpless, and bored, was again JFK. (Jim told me a year later: "I wish to hell I'd never done it—the role is a damned jinx for me. It leaves me with bad, bad vibes.") Rod Taylor won some praise for his Black Jack Bouvier, Jackie's rascally dad. Reviews, while kind to individual actors, tended to be perfunctory and dismissive.

The 1990s brought the inevitable and dourly predicted six-hour miniseries based on C. David Heymann's best-selling biography *A Woman Named Jackie*, which did better detailing the early courtship between Jackie and JFK (which hadn't been done to death in previous films) than with the depiction of the overly familiar and shopworn assassination and Onassis material. Stephen Collins and Josef Sommer did creditably as Jack Kennedy and Old Joe, respectively. The sequence where JFK dies in the Dallas hospital was effective and compelling, and the impersonations of Jackie and Marilyn Monroe were well-rendered also. Lalo Schiffrin did nicely with the musical score, but the whole project was second-rate in conception and execution, being often artificially forced and compressed.

The JFK assassination was fictionalized for the screen with David Miller's 1973 *Executive Action*. Dalton Trumbo's screenplay suggested that a group of right-wing extremists—not revolutionaries, mind you, but high-ranking government officials—conspired to execute the president (using Lee Harvey Oswald as a duped scapegoat) because they "felt Kennedy's liberal policies would lead to the destruction of the nation." Burt Lancaster and Robert Ryan—it was Ryan's last picture—were the stars, but the film was too crude and polemical (though not entirely unconvincing) to make much of an impact. The reviews were mixed, veering toward negative. *Variety* called it "a dodo bird of a movie, the winner of the *Tora Tora Tora* prize." Leslie Halliwell, the British critic, later labeled it "a rather messy mixture of fact and fiction." *Movie and TV Guide* later summed up the proceedings as "an excruciatingly dull thriller [that] promised to clear the air about JFK's assassination but was more successful at clearing theaters." In my publication *Quirk's Reviews* in 1973, the film was dismissed as "catering to the sensation-minded, boring for large stretches, then frenetic and rather screechy as it seeks to make its far-fetched points."

In 1974 Warren Beatty, who twelve years before had turned up his nose at playing JFK as PT-109 skipper, came out with a movie called *The Parallax View*, directed by Alan J. Pakula. One of Warren's more successful movies critically and popularly, it showcased him as a reporter out to investigate a senator's assassination. The story grows ever more scary and sinister as he encounters the perpetrators and unravels the truth behind the murder, piece by piece. Witnesses to the murder are killed off, one by one, with Beatty's journalist trying to reverse the inexorable train of events. The director, photographer, and production designer were later responsible for *All the President's Men*. Alan Pakula gave a penetrating if not always lucid analysis of the film later, writing: "It is terribly important to give an audience a lot of things they may not get as well as those they will, so that finally the film does take on a texture and is not just simplistic communication [*sic*]." Warren Beatty has always taken pride in this film and considers it one of his more worthy cinema outings.

In *George* John Kennedy Jr., while stating that he could not bring himself to view *JFK*, the controversial 1991 Oliver Stone film (and could one blame him, considering the personally painful subject matter?) said of the picture: "The ideas in [it] became fixed in the public psyche—for a year it seemed that was all anyone talked about—Jim Garrison, Johnson, my father, the CIA. In an odd way, it wasn't that different from the first hundred days of this Congress, when everyone was talking about the Contract with America—that ability of politics and film to get lots of people talking about the same thing."

JFK, which takes off on a number of tracks, some of them confusing and pointless, examines an alleged conspiracy to murder the president, focusing on real-life district attorney Jim Garrison (Kevin Costner) and his attempts to prosecute a homosexual businessman (Tommy Lee Jones) whom Garrison thinks is knee-deep in the plot to murder JFK. Despite Stone's grandiose claims, the movie does not in any sense solve the assassination "mystery" and indeed often rewrites and brazenly recasts history for dramatic effect. It does make for absorbing, colorful viewing. As many critics have felt necessary to stress, *JFK* is *not* documentary, just one more highly dramatized, fictional take on the notorious, much debated, much analyzed happening. Stone, as usual, goes off into wild flights of fancy, stretching matters out of all proportion and introducing half-baked, quite fantastical theories such as that the CIA, FBI, and the Establishment in general wanted JFK out of the way because of his Vietnam policies—policies, incidentally, that reached full fruition only under his successor, Lyndon Johnson. Stone, in his latest film, *Nixon*, exhibits the same imbalance on Richard Nixon, demonizing traits in RMN that are perfectly human and understandable in anyone, famous or obscure. The implication, for instance, that Nixon never matured beyond his adolescent angst could be applied to most human beings whose experiences, emotions—and traumas—of childhood and adolescence remain strong adult influences. One critic of Stone's much-too-harsh evaluation of Nixon remarked that Stone needed a crash course in human psychology, starting with endless variations on the old saw: "Show me what a boy is at twelve, and I'll tell you what he'll be for the rest of his life."

A new book on Kennedy and Nixon has propounded the thesis that Nixon and Kennedy, who started as freshmen congressmen in 1946, were devoted personal friends for long periods earlier in their careers. Doubtless a film about *that* will be coming along presently. But responsible critics and pundits fervently hope that Oliver Stone does *not* direct it. "Oliver has himself not grown beyond *his own* adolescent angst, pernicious and damaging to him as it was, and that is what gives his movies such pathological unreality and blatant denial of proven facts!" one critic has remarked. It is doubtful if most of the Kennedys really appreciate Stone's takeoffs on their most revered-cum-notorious family figure. "Let's hope Oliver doesn't decide to do a movie about JFK's sex life—*that* would be a season in *hell*, not just purgatory," one commentator noted, the phrasing being a takeoff on a Dominick Dunne novel about a Kennedy-connected unsolved murder.

After Dallas, Oswald, and the famous grassy knoll, the most infamous and bruited-to-death part of the JFK legend was his (and Bobby's) relationship with Marilyn Monroe. The year 1974 brought along the television film *The Sex Symbol*, starring Connie Stevens as sex bomb Kelly Williams. Its eventual broadcasting was delayed time and again after half a dozen libel suits were either filed or threatened by parties concerned about how they would be portrayed in this obvious *roman à clef* about MM.

Naturally the Kennedys were among those most concerned. The film was based on screenwriter Alvah Bessie's 1966 novel *The Symbol*, and it focused primarily on Kelly's affairs with several high-powered male figures, though it was careful not to go overboard in its nonetheless garish indiscretions in this regard. Stevens wasn't bad as Marilyn—pardon, *Kelly*—but Shelley Winters had the most fun as a catty gossip columnist who runs hot and cold on Kelly/Marilyn, depending on what the girl is up to—and with whom.

There were two more Monroe telepics in 1980: *Marilyn: The Untold Story* and *This Year's Blonde*—adapted from Garson Kanin's *Moviola*. Both focused primarily (some Kennedy aficionados whispered *mercifully*) on other aspects of the legendary movie star's life and romantic involvements, such as those with agent Johnny Hyde.

Then there was *Marilyn and Me* (1991)—a television adaptation of the ubiquitous, vulgarly insistent, and factually questionable book in which author Bob Slatzer insists that he had indeed been one of the earlier Mr. Marilyn Monroes. Several television movies that came along next fictionalized (in rather detailed form) the affair between Marilyn and

Bobby Kennedy. The whole JFK-Bobby-Marilyn interaction was also fictionalized literarily in Michael Korda's fascinating novel, *The Immortals*, which took us into the respective minds of these three superstars with some depth, compassion, and painstaking credibility. Despite the book's strong appeal, solid writing, and commercial viability (given its pre-occupation with the trans-American obsession with the Kennedys and Monroe), *The Immortals*, as noted by *Publisher's Weekly* in its year-end roundup, had comparatively disappointing sales and failed to emerge as the blockbuster its publishers hoped for, a doubly strange result considering Korda's track record. (Korda had generated several best-sellers including *Queenie*, a *roman à clef* on one of his uncle Alexander Korda's wives—Merle Oberon, no less). The talk along Publishers Row was that the Kennedys had somehow fixed the odds against the book's success in the same way they had once (positively) manipulated sales for *Profiles in Courage*.

Kennedy agents were much less successful suppressing the even more damaging *A Season in Purgatory* by Dominick Dunne, which did hit the bestseller lists. This *roman à clef* delves into a troubling real-life event in which a murder (in this case the killing of a young girl in Connecticut that implicated as a chief suspect Thomas Skakel, son of Ethel Kennedy's brother) was reportedly covered up with big bucks, paybacks, and heavy leaning on the authorities concerned. Dominick had changed names, events, situations, and so fourth, in the best *roman à clef* style, but everyone knew he was zeroing in on the Skakel case. A television drama based on the book appeared in early 1996. It was surprisingly frank and trenchant, with many sly "fictional" references to real-life Kennedy doings and with, it seems inexplicably, no family pressure applied.

Then there were the destructive cavortings of Ted Kennedy and their tragic long-range consequences, culminating in the film treatment of the little-seen *Chappaquiddick*, which advented in the 1980s but was quickly and efficiently suppressed. Rumors have abounded for years that the producers were paid off and that copies of the film were rounded up and systematically destroyed. It is like pulling teeth to get anyone in a position to know to spill the beans on this!

After Jackie and JFK, the most filmed Kennedy is John-John, who turned up (in disguise, but not much of one) in two television series that premiered in the fall of 1995. *Central Park West* was a new series from Darren Starr, the creator of *Beverly Hills 90210* and *Melrose Place*. CBS accorded it one of the biggest publicity campaigns ever mounted for a new show, but it never found its audience and later went on hiatus to be "retooled." Focusing on several media-oriented characters and their struggles and romantic entanglements in New York City, *CPW* featured a young lawyer clearly modeled on JFK Jr., played by John-John-type, handsome and gentlemanly John Barrowman (who in real life was one of the young May-November lovers of sixty-ish Angie Dickinson, who was allegedly one of the lovers of John-John's father).

Several of the *Central Park West* episodes centered on the John-John type's relationship with a young female reporter who dates him to get a story, only to realize that, under false pretensions and posturings, she is falling in love with him and is beginning to feel guilty about her manipulations. Like John-John, Barrowman's character has a deceased politician father, and of course he is portrayed in *CPW* as coming from one of the wealthiest, most prominent families in America. Not that John-John or his crew at *George* should take offense, really. The Barrowman character is shown as a really nice guy, a gentleman with women, a rinso-white hero of sorts, although he does bed his gals regularly (but what red-blooded, young, real-life guy would object to *that*?).

Even more blatant was the concurrently running 1995 weekly soap opera about a Kennedy-like political family which the producers had the amusing, tongue-in-cheek gall to call *The Monroes*. The pilot episode began with the youngest son being stopped by a traffic cop who decides not to write him a ticket when he learns who he is. The boy has the spurious grace to declare, "I'm just like everybody else!" The cop, mindful of a wife and kids to be fed and who knows his onions when it comes to *not* screwing with the well-connected, shakes his head ruefully and firmly rejoinders: "You are *not* like everybody else!"

The Joe Kennedy-like family patriarch (played with bite by William Devane) uses money and his unethical wiles to manipulate and control all about him, while his strong, takes-no-abuse wife (Susan Sullivan) castigates him, Rose-Jackie style, for his affairs.

Then—let's see—there's a do-gooder son who tries to stay out of the spotlight but winds up heading a high-profile mission for NASA (which his father brought about, naturally); a daughter and campaign manager who is having an affair with—one guess—the president; another daughter who seeks thrills and an escape from a husband straight from Dullsville. Then there is a Ted Kennedy-esque old son who has sex with his secretary in his Senate office and gets locked out in the hallway buck naked.

The Monroes are clearly meant to be the Kennedys—at least in an alternate television universe. The series was well acted and well scripted—one of the best new series of the season, in fact. But the real-life Kennedys were not amused. The show was abruptly canceled after only a half dozen episodes despite the fact that other shows with even lower ratings were given a chance to build an audience.

John-John to his credit displayed a sense of humor about it all. *The Monroes* was reviewed in the first issue of his magazine, *George*. The critic, Lisa Kogan, treading carefully, of course, implied, tongue-in-cheek, that since everyone knew the famous family that was the inspiration for the show, she didn't really have to name it, did she? But then, what the hell, she would. With a figurative wink at her readers, she mentioned a completely different political family altogether—the Coolidges.

Lisa then closed with a sort of benediction regarding *The Monroes*: "But in the end," she purred, "there's something rather winning about these adult children of Machiavellians. They have style, they have wit, and oh, God do they have sex. The question is, do they have what it takes to compete with *Seinfeld*?"

NINETEEN

Jackie, the Fan Mags, and Me

The Kennedys were always publicity conscious. They did not originate the popular old saw, "I don't care what you write about me, so long as you spell my name right," but if someone hadn't already thought about it, *they* would have. Of course they preferred favorable publicity to bad publicity, but Old Joe had often cited the thin line between notoriety and fame. He sensed before anyone else in the family that if the Kennedys became the nation's first living soap opera, an ordinary mortal, seeing much of himself in the Kennedys' trials and tribulations (even their naughtinesses and mischievousness), would give what he called "identificatory allegiance." He once told his friend Walter Howey that the public distrusted goody-goodies and people who led dull lives; "they feel those people look down on them; if they can feel close to a public figure because they know they share his faults even on a minor scale of social mobility, they can identify and still feel a little more superior."

Sometimes the Kennedy publicity bandwagon went just a little too far, adventuring in the wrong pastures. In the mid

1960s Jackie Kennedy and the rest of the family made much of a fuss over William Manchester's manuscript, *The Death of a President*, claiming it was too "intimate" and "tasteless" and "realistic in the *wrong* way" (whatever *that* meant). After arguing and conciliating, standing up to the Kennedys and backing down all in bewildering succession, Manchester found himself in the hospital with stress-related complaints. Eventually a "compromise" version of the book, which the Kennedys had originally authorized (and therefore thought they owned), was published in 1967.

While the Kennedys were fighting Manchester and his publisher tooth and nail often over the most minor points, they continued to my extreme puzzlement to totally ignore the tasteless coverlines and equally tasteless stories that the fan magazines began running by the carload starting in 1961.

I was editing several movie fan magazines in the 1950s and 1960s. For a while I was even writing all the copy. In 1957 Walter Winchell, whom my uncle had helped with many a scoop and who was always grateful, ran an item in his column: "The *Hollywood Stars* magazine is a one-man operation; completely written and edited by Larry Quirk." Later I moved on to bigger magazines with bigger budgets and soon was hiring top writers such as Fredda Dudley Balling, Mac St. Johns (son of Adela), Paul Denis, and Jerry Asher—all of whom kept me abreast of the most intimate doings in Hollywood and entertained me lavishly during my yearly trips to Hollywood.

In 1964 my publisher and I were adamantly in agreement on one point: we would *not* run Jackie Kennedy's picture on our cover, and we would *not* print a tasteless and mendacious story about her, no matter how juicy, no matter how big and connected the writer.

In a 1963 article on the fan magazines that appeared in *Variety*, I had excoriated other fan-mag editors for their obsessive "Jackie-ing," declaring that it all "smacked of execrable taste and editorial desperation and has caused observers to wonder if circulation-chasing has superseded common sense along fan-mag row these days."

In those days I was bucking to move on from *Screen Stars* and *Movie World*, the two magazines I edited along with several other "specials," to *Photoplay*, which I had long dreamed of editing. I believed that one could put out a quality magazine that would win respect yet still be lively, readable, and spicy. Though "a publication that doesn't make its readers mad has no vitality" was one of my uncle's more famous pronouncements, I knew that he would have drawn the line—as certainly I did—at using the First Lady of the land on a movie magazine cover, to say nothing of the mendacious and salaciously gossipy stories on the inside.

Yet *Photoplay* in the 1961–1968 period was the chief offender, running Jackie obsessively on covers. I went on Hy Gardner's television show to protest all this in 1964; other fan-mag editors, including the offenders, were invited, but they didn't show up, thereby leaving the field to me. Later, in a 1965 *Screen Stars* article in which I wondered publicly just when the fan mags of the 1960s were going to get back to the good old-fashioned business of building up *film* stars and leave the widow of our president in peace, I said of my uncle Jimmy Quirk: "If anyone had ever suggested to him in 1927 that he run Charles A. Lindbergh [on a movie magazine cover] just because Lindy was young and handsome and had just flown the Atlantic, or if anyone had suggested that he go trotting afield for Queen Marie of Romania as a movie mag cover subject just because Her Majesty, quite a glamor girl albeit a superannuated one, had visited the U.S. that year with much fanfare, he would have told them to jump in the lake. Or he would have suggested a strait jacket and a nice quiet rest in the country."

That 1965 I innocently assumed from informal contacts with the Kennedys, that they shared my ideas on the subject and wrote a follow-up article called "Why Don't They Leave Jackie Alone?" in which I predicted that Kennedy clout and disapproval would eventually bring the Jackie-fan-mag-cover trend to an end. Then I was amused but a little puzzled when I met Bobby Kennedy at a party in 1965. After congratulating me on carrying on the Quirk name in film journalism and acknowledging my fight to keep Jackie and the tasteless coverage under control, Bobby mentioned the 1927 *Photoplay* story in which my uncle had highlighted his father as an up-and-coming film producer and had even run photographic vignettes of him and his kids (Bobby was then two). I quickly pointed out to Bobby that Kennedy coverage in a 1927 *Photoplay* was warranted and legitimate as Joe Kennedy was a prominent film figure then. He let this pass with a shrug and a grin, but when I directly asked him about the rancid *Photoplay* coverage of Jackie in the mid 1960s, he said it was a complex matter of freedom of the press, but he would look into it, as he agreed that at times it had gone "perhaps a shade too far."

I should have taken my cue from that, but I followed up by writing to Ed Guthman, a former aide to Bobby who later became national editor of the *Los Angeles Times*. Ed called me several times; he was cordial and concerned, he said; then I got a formal letter from him that stated: "I have no reason to doubt that the fan magazine exploitation of Mrs. Kennedy is most distasteful to her and the family. But I don't believe there is anything they can do." Since the long arm of the Kennedys touched everyone and everything they cared to touch, I tended to doubt this statement. Joe Kennedy, because of his devastating stroke in 1961, was incapacitated. I missed Joe; I felt he would have had some solid advice for me were he in a position to give it.

Next I heard from Richard Drayne, at the time Teddy Kennedy's press aide, who opined: "Mrs. John F. Kennedy has no control over the use of her picture and her name by the kind of magazines to which you refer. She certainly does nothing to encourage this kind of publicity, but at the same time she is, unfortunately, unable to prevent it."

Shortly after this I ran into Steve Smith, Jean Kennedy's aggressive and feisty husband, who had taken over the family's financial and other affairs since Old Joe's incapacitation. We found ourselves sitting together at a charity event and had an extensive conversation, there and later over drinks, concerning the Jackie fan-mag coverage. He said he didn't care for it personally, but tended to agree with Bobby that the freedom-of-the-press angle created some fine lines that should be crossed only with caution. At the time (1965) he was very interested in my hopes to one day become editor of *Photoplay* and carry on my uncle's tradition, but gave as his opinion that instead of fighting the *Photoplay* powers-that-be on Jackie matters, I should be diplomatic if I ever hoped to get my chance at the helm over there. Though Steve had one of the hardest-headed minds of any of the Kennedys, he also seemed to me to value conciliation tactics and even quoted the old saw that "you catch more flies with honey than vinegar."

"Sometimes yes, sometimes no," I told him. "The honey and the vinegar need to be used selectively."

In any event, though we parted cordially, even warmly, that evening, I knew that I would be getting nowhere with Steve on the issue.

By 1967 I had decided that publication of an open letter to the Kennedys might do the trick, as by then the media was ridiculing the fan mags mercilessly on the Jackie matter, and because I was still editing fan mags, I wanted to set myself apart on the matter. The letter, addressed to Bobby and Teddy, read in part:

> As you know, I have fought consistently the use of your sister-in-law, Mrs. Jacqueline Kennedy, on movie magazine covers, have never run her on the cover of any magazine I have edited, and have fought this abuse of her at every turn. I have refused editorial posts at other fan magazines that would have meant a raise and even better facilities because they would not guarantee that Mrs. Kennedy would be left off the cover.
>
> However, I have grown increasingly mystified at the fact that while the Kennedy family has resorted to strong protests and legal suits and what-not with regard to the forthcoming book by William Manchester on your brother's assassination, the Kennedys have done nothing for six years to stop the far more tasteless—and often mendacious and distorted—invasion of Mrs. Kennedy's privacy by the fan magazines. Why is this so?

I then added:

> I myself have come to feel that perhaps Mrs. Kennedy finds that the publicity value of her pictures on countless fan magazine covers outweighs the tastelessness of cover-line and story approaches; if this be so, then why should I continue to refrain from editing magazines whose publishers insist she be used? Accordingly I am dropping my stand on this matter and will accept the next fan magazine editorship offered (that promises a better salary and better editorial resources) regardless of whether Mrs. Kennedy is used on the cover or not. And can you blame me?

A month after that I signed on with a fan magazine that offered me a better deal. To the publisher's credit, he said he respected my stand on Jackie, that she wasn't a movie star and didn't belong in the medium, and it was obvious that the Kennedys were grandstanding and indiscriminately garnering publicity.

By 1968, the year Bobby Kennedy began to campaign for the Democratic presidential nomination, I was getting feelers from the Kennedy camp about joining their public relations staff. I had just published my biography *Robert Francis Kennedy*, and Peter Lawford, during a New York jaunt, told me that Bobby liked the book. "Even the knocks in it give it an objectivity that keep people from thinking you're a Kennedy apologist and hagiographic flack," Peter said. Next I heard that Bobby's staff was buying extra copies of the book and spreading them around where they would do Bobby some good. I was amused by this, as I told Peter, because I had said some frank things in the book, the following being a good example:

> Certain conformist distrusts and rigidities creep into [Bobby and Ethel's] handling of the children [despite] their best intentions. Being neither especially imaginative nor creative themselves, Bobby and Ethel are apt to put negative constructions on any harmlessly imaginative divergence from the norm that their children might manifest. [David], for instance, developed a hobby: collecting wildflowers. Missing the obvious, that all the Kennedy boys can't be politicians and one just might make a botanist, Bobby informed his son that this was an unmanly pursuit and that he should desist from it.

I added:

> The only conclusion that can be drawn from the evidence is that if any Kennedy boy starts scribbling a la Gore Vidal or writing poetry a la Allen Ginsberg, he can expect an exile to darkest Siberia. Or maybe Bobby will send him to join Jimmy Hoffa!

Peter Lawford then surprised me with a call in which he told me that he had called the preceding passage to Bobby's attention and Bobby had said that he felt it was "thought-provoking" and had "some basic truths in it" and that "Larry writes so well he'd be a great man to have on staff—maybe writing speeches!" I told Peter that I didn't think I'd care to work for the Kennedys, though I knew their good points, and that I'd feel "neutralized" writing for them.

But I noticed that the Kennedys did begin playing down Jackie by early 1968, especially after absorbing such articles as one I wrote saying that the Kennedys might be trying to influence immature readers of fan mags with the long-range goal of getting them to march like zombies to the polls when they get to voting age and put their *X*s beside the name Kennedy. I suggested that this tolerance of Kennedy "garbage" publicity in fan mags might well be part of the Kennedy publicity steamroller, especially with Bobby running for president.

Rose Kennedy herself got into the act early in 1968 by calling *Women's Wear Daily* and asking them to "lay off" Jackie for a while. *WWD* didn't stoop quite as low as the fan mags in their coverage of Jackie, but it was gamy enough, and of course "more dignity publicly" became the watchword the year Bobby ran for president. His assassination on June 6 of that year changed the rules of the game considerably, and when Jackie Kennedy married Aristotle Onassis later that year, took the kids to Europe, and let out word that she "hated an America that killed Kennedys," her vogue went into the shade—for a while.

More Kennedy Lovers, Friends, Enemies

T he following is a roundup of other people who knew the Kennedys in Hollywood, either as lovers, rumored lovers, friends, associates, onlookers, enemies, whatever. They are an interesting bunch.

Marshall (Mickey) Neilan (1891–1958)

Mickey Neilan was one of my earliest guides and mentors in the film industry, and we were good friends during the last nine years of his life. He reminisced a great deal about the old Hollywood. Mickey had had a great career as a film director (he had helped Mary Pickford to stardom with his able handling of her early pictures). He started in films in 1911 as D. W. Griffith's assistant at Biograph, then went into acting at Kalem Studios in 1912. He combined acting with directing after 1914 and by 1917 won prominence as one of Mary Pickford's leading men.

By the early 1920s he was much sought after as a director and in 1922 married the beautiful screen star Blanche Sweet, who said to me later: "[Mickey] was a wonderful director but a terrible husband!" They divorced in 1929. Alcoholism and a playboyish irresponsibility, plus a tendency to womanize indiscriminately, sometimes with other men's wives, brought about his downfall in the 1930s. He directed his last feature film at forty-six in 1937 and after that bummed around Hollywood doing odd jobs, occasional writing stints, and even driving a cab, one of his specialties being to worm his way into film studios to put the touch on old friends.

Mickey never liked Joe Kennedy. He said that, back in the 1920s, Joe had abruptly refused him a job, calling him a "drunken bum." As he recalled it, he pulled Joe's glasses off and nailed one on him. One of Gloria Swanson's lovers in the early 1920s, Mickey felt the Swanson-Kennedy liaison would lead to trouble and warned Gloria about this, but he said she wouldn't listen.

Mickey died of cancer at the Motion Picture Country Home in 1958. Mary Pickford paid for his funeral.

Laura Hope Crews (1879–1942)

The famed character actress best known for her Aunt Pittypat in *Gone with the Wind* and her Prudence, Garbo's mentor in *Camille*, came to know Joe Kennedy well while she was coaching Gloria Swanson's diction in *The Trespasser* (1929).

Laura debuted in stock in 1883 at age four and by twenty-two was a prominent leading lady on the stage; her unusual looks and aristocratic comportment, combined with a compelling speaking voice, made her many fans, but she won an even greater following as a character actress. She found herself in demand not only as an actress but as a speech coach in Hollywood after 1929. By 1933 she was winning accolades as a 1933-style monster mother in *The Silver Cord*.

Gossipy, shrewd, negatively sophisticated ("I know men, I know women, I know human nature, and I have no illusions about anybody," she told an interviewer in 1935), Laura was one of the first to articulate the well-known axiom that if you want to know *others* well, just study *yourself*, or as she put it, "What you are, they are—what you want, they want. You're no better or worse a person than the one next to you!"

Laura helped immeasurably to make Gloria a success in *The Trespasser*. Gloria later recalled to me Laura's perfectionism, her insistence that, despite the awkward camera placements essential in early talkies, the dialogue could be written naturally and spoken naturally. Laura even took over the direction at times from Eddie Goulding, especially when she felt Gloria was being self-conscious and artificial. She helped to write the dialogue for the film also.

"Laura was like a mother to me," Gloria recalled. "But she was a wise and firm mother; tolerated no nonsense; made me work hard in that film" Laura did not care particularly for Joe Kennedy, felt he would inevitably hurt and leave Gloria, and resented his appearances on the *Trespasser* set "where he contributed nothing creative, just threw his weight around." Joe didn't like Laura much, either.

====

Mabel Normand (1894–1930)

Mabel began as an actress for Biograph as early as 1910 and, under Mack Sennett's direction, metamorphosed as a major star in 1915 along with her contemporary, friend, and co-star, Charlie Chaplin. Starting in slapstick under Sennett, she later revealed, in such films as *Mickey* (1918), a waiflike, effervescent vulnerability combined with a sparkling *joie de vivre* that made her beloved by film audiences nationwide. Mabel left her mentor Sennett and later worked for Goldwyn and other studios. By 1920 her drug habit had gained a secure hold on her, and she was to struggle with it, on a steadily downward progression, until her death in 1930 at thirty-five. She was married for a while to racy screen he-vamp Lew Cody, whom Jimmy Quirk, a close friend of both, dubbed in one of his *Photoplay* articles, "the Butterfly Man" and "the Little Clown." Saddened by her excesses and defeats, Jimmy wrote of her in a 1930 memorial article, "She has gone home now to the Great Heart that Understands All."

Mabel's downfall was accelerated greatly when she was linked with the murder of director William Desmond Taylor in 1922 (she was not a suspect but had been deeply involved with him). Then her chauffeur committed a murder—with Mabel's pistol. Mabel sought further escape in drugs. Pneumonia and tuberculosis were credited with her demise, but drugs and the failure of the will to live accelerated it.

In 1927 Lew Cody and Mickey Neilan had tried to get Joe Kennedy to give her a fresh chance at his studio, but he turned them—and her—down curtly. "She's a hopeless drug addict. She had no character and no reliability left in her, and I can't gamble good money on her," Joe said. Mickey and Lew never forgave Joe for that.

Mabel never was on Joe Kennedy's "romancing" list— she was too ill and too disoriented by the time he was riding high in Hollywood. But whatever she might have missed in that quarter, she obviously escaped a lot, too.

═══════════

John Lodge (1903–1985)

John was the grandson of the famed Yankee senator, Henry Cabot Lodge of Massachusetts, and the younger brother of the later Senator Henry Cabot Lodge Jr. He was a handsome, pleasant man who after graduating from Harvard had first elected for the law. Then the lure of acting proved too strong, and by 1933, at thirty, he was appearing with Katharine Hepburn in *Little Women* (1933) and as Marlene Dietrich's leading man in *The Scarlet Empress* (1934). After a WWII navy career, he went into politics, serving as a congressman, governor of Connecticut, and later an ambassador. He was Richard Nixon's vice presidential running mate in 1960.

The animosity between the Lodges and the Fitzgeralds was long-standing. The elder senator had beaten Honey Fitz for the Senate; later JFK was to even the score by ousting the younger Lodge from the Senate in 1952.

Joe Kennedy shared his father-in-law's hatred of the Lodges, who represented all the moneyed, privileged, and lineaged aristocracy of Boston that had snubbed him through his early life.

He enjoyed saying that Lodge had left acting after 1940 because he "couldn't act his way out of a paper bag." In 1939 when he was hobnobbing with Marlene Dietrich on the Riviera, Joe asked her "why a stick like that ever got to be your co-star in the Catherine the Great picture [*The Scarlet Empress*]?" As much to get his goat as to defend a fellow actor she respected and admired, Marlene retorted that as her lover in that film John had shown a great deal of fire and virility. Joe, who never thought of himself as handsome and who resented handsome men (unless they were his sons), always opined to Eddie Moore and others that John Lodge had ridden with the gravy train of his money and lineage and connections and that his "dabbling" in "facemaking" (as Joe called acting) had been plumb ridiculous. Yet Joe's own sons would have their own sleigh ride with money and connections in the course of time.

Phyllis Haver (1899–1960)

Phyllis Haver was a wild, sexy blond actress who won her principal fame in silent pictures playing gold diggers, ladies of the evening, and vamps with a past, preferably lurid. Mickey Neilan had said of her that maybe she wasn't the can't-say-no girl onscreen and off, but she certainly qualified as the maybe or if-I'm-in-the-mood type. Mickey had had an affair with her himself in 1921.

Phyllis had debuted in 1917 at age eighteen in a picture aptly (or maybe mistakenly) titled *The Bedroom Blunder*. She hailed from Douglas, Kansas, which, she later told *Photoplay's* Herb Howe, "I had the good sense to vacate at the earliest opportunity." She then went to Chicago, where she used her piano-playing skills to provide silent-film accompaniments in theaters. Then she broke into the movies as a Mack Sennett bathing beauty.

Soon she was appearing in leading parts in such films as *Love, Honor and Behave* (1920) and by 1923 was scorching the screen as *The Perfect Flapper* and furiously fanning *The Breath of Scandal* (1924). During this time she indulged in a series of wild affairs with Hollywood's most romantic leading men, some of them married.

Joe Kennedy had seen her on the screen and, considering her "pretty hot stuff," asked Jimmy Quirk to introduce them in 1926. The introduction led to dates which in turn led to an affair, but fickle Joe left her for Evelyn Brent in short order.

I talked with Phyllis in 1956; she had just gotten a divorce from a millionaire she had lassoed, then married in 1929. She had left the screen that year for him. "I was thirty then," she said, "and for my kind of role, thirty was getting on. I wanted to get out while I was ahead." Phyllis committed suicide in 1960.

───────────

Owen Moore (1886–1939)

The handsome Owen Moore, first of the male film stars—or among the first anyway—was the husband of Mary Pickford (the first of three, the others being Doug Fairbanks Sr. and Buddy Rogers). Entering films with Biograph in

1908 when he was twenty-two, Owen played in many of D. W. Griffith's early films and wound up as Mary Pickford's leading man; they were married in 1911. By 1920 Doug Sr. had taken over Mary's romantic life and hubby Owen was out in the cold; he was very bitter about Doug cuckolding him and threatened physical violence. It was all smoothed over when he was paid a sum of money.

Owen ricocheted through Hollywood of the 1920s, romancing many lovelies and trying one other marriage, to actress Kathryn Perry. But a ladies' man supreme was Owen, and he managed to get into several paternity and breach-of-promise messes while romancing major leading ladies in a series of films. Not much of an actor, Owen had his full measure of Irish charm (his brothers Matt and Tom were also actors—all were native Irishmen), and the critics usually described him as "personable" and "pleasing," damning his performances, if such they were, with faint praise.

Owen came up against Joe Kennedy in 1930; by then a ripe but still romantically serviceable forty-four, Owen was playing opposite Gloria Swanson in *What a Widow!* a forgettable comedy failure that was Gloria's second talkie but a sad comedown from the first, *The Trespasser*. *What a Widow!* had been Joe's idea, and a lousy one it was. When *What a Widow!* became a critical and popular flop, Owen was one of those Joe took it out on. He had come on the set during shooting and seen Owen handling Gloria's right breast during a shot (later excised). Controlling his rage at the time, he reportedly decked Owen at the premiere—after he had seen the audience's listless reaction.

Walter Byron (1907–1972)

Walter Byron was a handsome, charismatic Englishman who loved the ladies with an indiscriminate and driving passion than stamped him, as Adela Rogers St. Johns later put it, "as more of a Frenchman than an Englishman." No reserved Britisher was Walter. After stage work in England, he showed up in Hollywood in the late 1920s; reports of the time said that he'd had to leave England because a duke's wife had spilled the beans and His Grace was gunning for Walter.

Erich Von Stroheim took note of Walter in a bit role and soon had him co-starring with Gloria Swanson in the ill-fated Swanson-Kennedy venture, *Queen Kelly*, which ended halfway through shooting and never got a formal U.S. release.

Walter figured in the famous scene where Gloria throws him her panties (he is a prince on a high horse, she a girl of lowly origin). Walter runs the panties slowly in front of his nose—a Von Stroheim inspiration that inspired Gloria to call a shocked halt to the picture.

Joe Kennedy later admitted to Eddie Moore and others that he had thought the scene amusing and essentially harmless. (Joe never had a very subtle mind when it came to salacious screen innuendo.) But Joe's attitude toward Walter (if not the scene) changed when, after the picture had been scrapped and Von Stroheim sent on his way, he came upon Gloria "comforting" Walter, who was distraught because what he called his "one big chance" had been scrapped. The extent of Gloria's "comforting" of Walter is a matter of debate to this day. Gloria's good friend, the silent screen actress Lois Wilson, told me decades later that Gloria had confessed to a crush on handsome, dashing Walter. "Walter had a lost-little-boy element, too, and believe me he was no reserved Englishman—not at all!" Lois added. In any case, Joe put

MORE KENNEDY LOVERS, FRIENDS, AND ENEMIES 301

his foot down, Walter sought comfort elsewhere, and his prediction about *Queen Kelly* being his "one big chance" turned out to be right on target; his film career until his retirement in 1939 remained eminently forgettable. "No comment," he sharply barked when I brought up Gloria, Joe, and *Kelly* during an encounter in 1964. He was old, tired, and sad by then—none of the dashing Walter of 1928 could be discerned.

Jack Pickford (1896–1933)

The handsome, magnetic, and (for a while) dynamic and ambitious Jack Pickford was Mary Pickford's younger brother. He trailed after Mary, three years his senior, and Mary doted on him and their (also ill-fated) sister Lottie, fighting for them at every turn. Result: Jack grew up as not only a mama's boy (Mary's mother was a powerhouse of familial support) but as a sister's boy, too. Thanks to Mary, Jack became a Biograph actor at age fourteen. When she got her million-dollar contract at First National in 1917, she stipulated Jack was to be taken on too.

Jack went on to a fairly prominent career in the 1920s as a leading man, occasional star, and (several times) director. But as I said in my Norma Shearer biography, Jack always had "an aura of reckless scandal" about him and had a penchant for coming on so compulsively strong with feminine co-stars (such as Norma in the 1925 *Waking Up the Town*) that he frightened them away.

Jack's lovely wife, the actress Olive Thomas, had died mysteriously in Paris in 1920 while they were on a "love-trip" (a 1920 term). Drugs were suspected. The matter was never satisfactorily cleared up, and Jack's notoriety was a given after that. He tried marriage again, to Ziegfeld star

Marilyn Miller (1922–1927), but that, too, blew up in his face, as did a short-lived marriage to Mary Mulhern just before his death.

Jack never made a talkie—his voice was not regarded as up to par and the jaunty nonchalance he could summon in silents failed to show up in his abortive talking screen tests. Depressed, he sank into a miasma of drink and drugs and became the "kept boy" of several wealthy and influential older men when Mary cut off his funds. Gloria Swanson had tried to help him, for Mary's sake, and had fought Joe to get him into *What a Widow!* One of their few quarrels occurred when Joe called Jack "a hopeless loser" and accused Gloria of a romantic interest in him. Jack never got into *What a Widow!*

He finally died in 1933, used up, run-down, and only thirty-six. Syphilis and other venereal infections were suspected, as well as a drug overdose.

Tom Mix (1880–1940)

Tom Mix, the legendary cowboy star, was one of those luminaries of the screen who worked under Joe Kennedy when Joe headed FBO in the 1920s. Joe liked Tom, but was more enthralled with Fred Thomson, who with his horse Silver King, captivated Western audiences until his untimely death in 1928.

Fred made a great deal more money than Tom, simply because his films were more popular and his fans legion across the country. Joe met his match in Tom when it came to arguing about money, grosses, and Tom's salary. "He was one of the toughest negotiators when it came to the buck that I ever encountered," said a half-admiring, half-annoyed Joe to Eddie Moore in 1926. Tom knew his worth and dis-

combobulated Joe by declaring that the booking of his pictures was deliberately manipulated to favor Fred. (What
Fred Thomson thought about all this has not gone down on
the record.)

Tom portrayed himself as a tough hombre with a background and track record that had been exciting, adventurous,
and variegated. The son of an army officer, he was educated
at Virginia Military Institute, served in the Spanish-
American War, the Boer War ("but he wasn't *English!*" one
puzzled columnist said of this), and the Boxer Rebellion.
Then he was a Texas Ranger for a while.

Later truth reared its head: Tom was a laborer's son and
never got past the fourth grade. And although he served in
he military, he never saw action and was labeled, at twenty-
two in 1902, a deserter. (It seemed to be true, however, that
he was a Texas Ranger.)

In 1906 he joined a Wild West show and then landed in
films, becoming a Western star as early as 1911 (age thirty-
one). His Selig films gradually improved, and he was noted
for doing his own stunts, occasionally suffering injuries. Tom
then went on to Fox Films, then to FBO and salary arguments with Joe Kennedy. He and his famous horse Tony
later became circus stars, then worked for Universal. He
retired from films in 1935, at age fifty-five. Asked in later
years about Joe Kennedy, Tom Mix called him "a tight-assed,
money-crazy son of a bitch!"

Jesse L. Lasky (1880–1958)

Jesse Lasky, when I interviewed him in 1949, was an intelligent, cultured man of sixty-nine who was a rich fund of reminiscences about the early Hollywood in which he had
figured prominently, indeed, spectacularly. He told me that

his first encounter with Joe Kennedy had been a dinner introduction from Jimmy Quirk. The three had dined for hours, and Jesse remembered the vitality, the intelligence, the fierce intentness of Joe Kennedy's blue eyes. "Joe was in his mid thirties, I believe, then," Jesse remembered, "and I never knew a man more ambitious, more concentrated. It was almost frightening that degree of concentration he had, combined with his intensity of personality. Joe didn't just digest ideas—he ground them into pieces, reassembled them, formulating them to suit his own concepts."

Jimmy had felt that Joe, who was anxious to know all aspects of the movie business, would profit from "assisting" Jesse and learning from him. "But Joe was never anyone's 'assistant,'" Jesse recalled. "He was an observer, a notetaker, and how he sopped up information, all kinds—it was a caution just watching him operate!"

Joe turned often to Jesse for advice during the mid 1920s when he was trying to master the film business. He would ask Jesse what stars to keep at FBO, what stars to ease out; he would ask him about costs, about overruns, about labor problems, about differing studio "styles"—anything and everything.

Jesse said something about Joe Kennedy during my several meetings with him that would always stay in my mind. "He is man of egomaniacal ambition, but somehow I sense seeds of self-destruction in him. I suspect he will come to a sad end, somehow." Jesse Lasky died at seventy-eight in 1958, three years before Joe Kennedy was felled by a stroke, spending the next eight years in a helpless, near-vegetative state. After Joe's death I thought a number of times of Jesse Lasky's almost mystic prediction concerning his eventual ending.

But in the 1920s Joe was operating at full strength, and Jesse lavished all the advice and help he could.

Jesse Lasky Sr. began in journalism, then went into vaudeville. In 1913 he and his brother-in-law, Samuel Goldfish (later Goldwyn), and their friend and associate, Cecil B. De Mille, formed the Jesse L. Lasky Feature Play Company (Jesse was president). Its first big hit was *The Squaw Man*, the first epic Western (1914). In 1916 they merged with Adolph Zukor to form Famous Players-Lasky, precursor of Paramount Films. In the 1930s Jesse became an independent producer, then for a while tied up with Mary Pickford in Pickford-Lasky Productions. Later severe financial problems forced his retirement. He then wrote an autobiography called *I Blow My Horn*.

"My father was a *real*, a *great* pioneer," his hero-worshipping son Jesse Jr. told me in 1960. "He was philosophical about life, took the good with the bad. Even when those financial and corporate problems hit him later, he took it in a balanced way."

"I've had a great life; I have no right to kick," he had told his son.

═══════════

Adela Rogers St. Johns (1893–1988) and Helen Ferguson (1901–1977)

Two ladies I knew well in my years as fan-mag editor and freelance writer on the Hollywood scene were Helen Ferguson and Adela Rogers St. Johns. Helen had been a prominent silent film actress and had been married to, and widowed by, the actor William Russell, a Hollywood fixture who died in 1929. Later she became a well-known publicist. During my visits to and residence in Hollywood, she was the most hospitable of friends, and we would sit long into the night talking about the old days.

She told me that Joe Kennedy had met her at a party around 1928 and, without even inquiring if she were married, had asked her to go home to his mansion with him.

"Gloria must have been busy that night or something," Helen remembered. "I said no. I knew his reputation— Evelyn Brent had told me horror stories about him—but I later made the big mistake of mentioning it to my husband. He got very angry, called up Joe, threatened to punch him in the nose if he came near me again." Helen was a friend and admirer of handsome Robert Stack and told me she had done what she could to further his career—and even had been secretly in love with him, in the mid 1940s. But the age difference was too great, and Bob's allegiance was elsewhere: "Bob never knew how I felt." She added, "He was one of the nicest people I ever knew—Rosemarie [his wife of many years] was lucky to land him!"

Adela St. Johns, daughter of the famed criminal lawyer Earl Rogers (on whom Lionel Barrymore modeled his Oscar-winning role in *A Free Soul*, for which Adela wrote the screenplay) was a rich source of much Hollywood lore for me. She had gone to work as a writer for my uncle's *Photoplay* in 1917 and knew not only where all the bodies were buried but who had broken his or her heart over whom. She told me that Miriam Hopkins, who later helped rescue the widowed May Allison from Joe Kennedy, held Joe in deep contempt. ("Maybe because Joe never made a pass at her," Adela laughed.)

====================

Lee Remick (1935–1991)

One Hollywood actress on Bobby Kennedy's extremely short list of movieland conquests was Lee Remick. Lee began her career as a dancer, then acted on the stage and television before debuting rather conspicuously as the pert drum marjorette in the Elia Kazan film, *A Face in the Crowd* (1957), in which, incidentally, Mickey Neilan made a last-hurrah acting appearance as a senator (he died a year later).

Lee's role led to a number of starring roles in such note-worthy films as *Anatomy of a Murder* and *Days of Wine and Roses*. Meanwhile Lee was working her way through two marriages, to director-producer Bill Colleran (1957–68) and British director Kip Gowens. Later she did films in England, then found new prominence in television movies. She died of cancer at fifty-five.

Bobby Kennedy reportedly met her at a party in Washington in 1961 and was immediately smitten. *He* was married and *she* was married, but that didn't stop Bobby. Possibly because he was being inundated with cover-up operations designed to protect JFK from any open scandal brought about by *his* multifarious amours, Bobby might have caught the "adultery infection," as Peter Lawford later termed it.

When Bobby next went to Hollywood, he asked Peter to facilitate an introduction, and the story goes (corroborated by several sources) that when Bill Colleran was out on location shooting, Lee and Bobby "made it" at a secluded place Peter found for them in Malibu.

In 1961 Bobby Kennedy was thirty-six, and Lee Remick was twenty-six, approaching the height of her acting career. Bobby was by then his brother's newly installed attorney general. Writer Jerry Asher, a good friend of Lee's, was one of her more intimate confidants, and he opined later to me that it was a matter of power (Bobby) meeting pulchritude (Lee). Both were attracted to the other for different reasons; Bobby's authority and take-charge charisma stimulated Lee, who for all her beauty tended to be withdrawn and oddly deficient in self-confidence, as she once told me in an interview. The liaison was short—both knew it was wise to "get out early." (Bobby was also rumored to have a "crush" on Andy Williams's onetime wife, the lovely Claudine Longet, but that has been kept pretty much *sub rosa*, so it must be passed over.)

Lee liked to spread herself around. She was bored with her marriage to Bill Colleran, and motherhood fulfilled her only to a point (she had two children with Colleran).

Adulteries, especially with men who, like herself, were married, seemed to turn Lee on. "I never had much self-esteem," she told me once. "I did everything I could to shore it up—everything." She had appeared in a television play with Peter Lawford, who had acted as go-between for Bobby with her, and soon *they* were involved in a heavy affair. What Colleran thought, what Pat Lawford thought, these considerations mattered little to Lee.

They even appeared publicly together. Peter rationalized this by saying they were acting together at the time and had script matters to discuss, but ever-nosy columnist Hedda Hopper knew better and said so in one of her columnar blind items: "The big news in Hollywood is a romance that can't be put into print." After interpolating that she didn't really like blind items, she continued: "I guarantee that if this one hits the papers it will curl hair from Washington to Santa Monica."

Lee even had the "gall," as Pat put it, to show up at a party she and Peter threw. Pat, of course, knew all about Lee's flings, first with her brother, then with her husband. The marriage of Pat and Peter being a "front" and "alliance of convenience" (as Pat put it) by that late stage, she emulated her mother and smiled offhandedly (if a little grimly) as she greeted Lee and Bill Colleran.

Bill Colleran reportedly had gotten fed up with Lee's extramarital "romantic experiments" (as Jerry Asher termed them), and her obsession with matters Kennedy really exasperated him. Neighbors reported that the screaming matches between Lee and Bill could be heard all over their neighborhood. "Two little children are the real victims in a marriage breaking up rapidly because the wife is man-mad and out of control," said one column item in 1962.

Later Lee promised to behave herself (she didn't), and she and Bill stumbled on "in a half-ass way," as Jerry Asher put it, for another five or six years. Then Bill threw in the towel, with one friend commenting: "I'm surprised he waited so long."

Angie Dickinson (1931–)

Jack Kennedy's affair with Angie Dickinson—if that is what it was—was a constant gossip staple in his lifetime and ever since. Angie was always very close-mouthed about it—not because these wasn't anything to say but because she had an inherent sense of dignity and privacy. Her sexy and flamboyant film image belied the personality of the woman I interviewed during the 1960s. She was that rarity among the up-and-coming female star contingent—a genuine *lady*.

Raymond Strait and others have claimed that Angie and Jack rendezvoused in a Palm Springs cottage shortly before he was inaugurated. Angie had been on hand during a fundraising dinner hosted by Frank Sinatra during the 1960 Democratic convention. One story has Sinatra doing the actual introduction honors between her and Jack. Another has it that Peter Lawford was doing his usual pimp bit. Red Fay, the undersecretary of the navy, a good friend, escorted her to the 1961 inaugural celebrations. Raymond Strait numbers Angie among the women Jack saw a lot of during 1962—listing her with Jayne Mansfield, Marilyn Monroe, and such non-Hollywoodians as Mary Pinchot Meyer and Judy Campbell.

Raymond Strait has been the most outspoken writer concerning Angie and JFK. He feels they did have an involvement but admits that it was conducted (whether or not it was directly sexual) with a great deal of restraint, decency, and dignity—qualities Angie has always prized.

According to writer Wesley Hagood, "Angie has never directly confirmed or denied whether her relationship with Jack was of an intimate sexual nature. She once said, 'I have nothing to hide about my relationship with the Kennedys,' adding, 'people keep throwing up the rumor, trying to make something more of it than it was.'"

But Hagood notes that Angie also hinted coyly at the extent of the relationship by making several suggestive remarks with double entendres like "he's the only presidential candidate who has ever turned me on" and "he was wonderful. . . . It would be bad manners to say more."

When Angie Dickinson and Jack Kennedy first met in 1960, she was twenty-nine and he was forty-three. Born Angeline Brown in the small community of Kulm, North Dakota, she matriculated at such colleges as Immaculate Heart and Glendale, but grew impatient with formal education and pedestrian associations. From early on, Angie had her heart set on a more glamorous, exciting life, and soon she was winning beauty contests.

A scout for one of the Hollywood studios saw her in one, and beginning in 1954, age twenty-three (a late starter for a Hollywood beauty), she played bits and small roles in a host of films. In a later interview with me, she characterized her beginnings as "the slow-but-sure kind." In 1959 director Howard Hawks gave Angie her big break (at age twenty-eight) in the film *Rio Bravo*. *The Bramble Bush* and Frank Sinatra's *Oceans 11* gave her added boosts, and when I interviewed her on the set of *The Sins of Rachel Cade* in 1960 (she was pushing thirty), she seemed to have finally arrived at stardom. She was happy and confident at the time and said she had always worked hard, had tried to keep a level head, and "kept my mistakes with men to as much of a limit as anyone human can."

Her acting name came from her earlier marriage to football star Gene Dickinson—she told me Dickinson sounded more theatrical than Brown, so she kept it. From 1965 to 1980 she was married to composer Burt Bacharach. In recent years she has moved into a dignified and self-contained, mature period (she is now sixty-five) and has graced recent films as a respected character actress. She also had quite a run on television, starring in the 1974–1978 *Police Woman* series. There is a possibly apocryphal story that she is in possession of an autographed picture of Jack Kennedy with the inscription: "To the only woman I've ever loved."

Angie in recent years has displayed a penchant for dating men much younger than herself, and recently she was linked with John Barrowman, who played a John-John-type character in *Central Park West*. "Angie is a nice person," a friend says. "What she does—and did—is done with *dignity*."

Peggy Cummins (1925–)

During his 1946 Hollywood visit, Jack Kennedy pursued the pretty Welsh actress, Peggy Cummins, then twenty, who had signed with Twentieth Century-Fox and was to figure prominently in such films as *The Late George Apley* and *Moss Rose* (both 1947 releases).

Peggy had gone on the British stage at age twelve, then graduated into teenage and ingenue roles in such British films as *Dr. O'Dowd* and *Her Man Gilbey*. After a number of other films, Peggy retired from the screen in 1961.

On August 18, 1946, Sheila Graham's column noted: "Peggy Cummins and Jack Kennedy are a surprise twosome around town." Jack's friends felt Peggy was just another pretty actress whom Jack found enticing as long as she remained unattainable. Once the conquest was successful, the interest would wane—sometimes instantaneously.

But the problem here was that Peggy was a refined Brit, intelligent, cultured, well-educated. She wasn't any man's prey, and cheap bed-downs were not her style. Peggy, as Delight Evans later recalled, was out for serious involvements, engagements (preferably lengthy), crowned with a lavish wedding ceremony and all the lavish appurtenances thereof. She had Jack Kennedy's number early in the game, and she wasn't buying in, according to Delight.

Nigel Hamilton later interviewed Betty Spalding, who knew both Jack and Peggy well in 1946. According to Betty: "As Jack saw it [Peggy] was just a girl to date. . . . Jack was quite thin and sickly at that time and he got out of Boston deliberately, because he didn't want to be sucked into paying off a lot of election debts and be bound by it. So he ducked out [to Hollywood] for his jollies and sun and rest."

Betty remembered also that Jack "didn't have any manners in the sense of letting women go through the door first or opening doors for them or standing up when older women came into the room."

She added: "He was nice to people, but heedless of people, heedless about his clothes, and heedless about money." Betty remembered that Jack never had any money with him and that he was very tight, indeed quite parsimonious."

(Red Fay and other friends recalled Jack's fears that people were after his money, or rather his family's money. So he affected a jaunty, bohemian sloppiness.)

There is no question but that the staid, decent, sensible Peggy Cummins was very hurt by Jack's attitude and approach in general. She certainly did not become one of his easy lays or quick conquests, and to his chagrin, they never were intimate.

Delight Evans felt that Peggy may have been in love with Jack at the time, though without illusions about him. "There was this little-boy insouciance about him, his lack of self-consciousness, his indifference to what impression he was making on anyone or everyone," Delight recalled, echoing what Gene Tierney later remembered about him. "Peggy knew he was heading for Congress, that he had a much-ballyhooed war career and had even written a book, which Peggy had gone to the trouble of looking up and reading."

Peggy seems to have been hurt that Jack didn't consider her marriage material, not realizing at the time that marriage was the furthest thing from Jack's mind. He was not well, was plagued with back problems. At twenty-nine (to Peggy's twenty) he was out for a good time, escape—surcease from thoughts about possible early mortality, looming political responsibilities as a freshman congressman for his working-class Boston constituents, and the ever-irritating need to please his ambitious father. In 1946 Jack was *not* marriage fodder.

===

Sonja Henie (1910–1969)

In 1946 Sonja Henie was thirty-six years old, Jack Kennedy twenty-nine. Red Fay was the first to reveal that Sonja and Jack were involved that year. According to Red, when Jack visited him and his family in Woodside, California, in 1946 on sabbatical from his Hollywood woman chasing, he bragged considerably about what a great lay Sonja was and

about how her muscles, well-developed from her ice skating, were so "sexily adaptable," as Jack put it, to various
sexual positions.

Red Fay remembered Jack's careless, cavalier attitude
throughout his visit to Woodside. He left a party to go to a
movie, leaving guests stranded and feeling put down. He also
borrowed money from Red, who couldn't afford to lend it,
and Red had to write him several times to get it back.

Red, Henry James, and other friends felt that Jack was
changing, and it wasn't just the politics influencing him. "He
might have felt he wouldn't live long," Red Fay recalled later.
"All that back trouble and general ill-health; maybe he was
just trying to get-it-all-baby while the getting was good."

As for Sonja, by 1946, she had seen it all and was ahead
of the game in her knowledge of men. Before she was
through (she died in 1969 at a relatively early fifty-nine), she
had ploughed through three marriages.

Born in Oslo, Norway, in 1910, Sonja had begun dancing at age four. Eight years old in 1918, she had developed a
passion for ice skating that took her on to the Skating
Championship of Norway in 1924 at age fourteen. By 1925
Sonja Henie was the ice skating champion of the world. She
triumphed in a succession of Winter Olympic Games, setting new records and winning a plethora of gold medals, her
1936 feats in particular winning world notice.

At age seventeen in 1927, Sonja had done one Nor-
wegian film (*Svy Dager for Elisabeth*), and after touring the
world with a succession of ice shows that brought her status
as an international celebrity, she accepted a Twentieth
Century-Fox contract and debuted in 1937 as an instant
Hollywood star in two smash box-office movies, *One in a
Million* and *Thin Ice*. Her movies were always thin, slick
romantic trifles usually built around her skating prowess.

The highlights of the films usually involved skating exhibitions and flashy climaxes with Sonja whirling round and round while surrounded by adoring "skate boys" and hysterically acclaimed by large, responsive audiences.

By the time of *Sun Valley Serenade* (1941) and *Iceland* (1942) Sonja's vogue was on the downswing with movie audiences, but she successfully kept her hand in with her Hollywood Ice Review Extravaganzas at Madison Square Garden in New York. She also continued to make highly successful coast-to-coast tours. In 1960 she retired altogether (she was then a ripe fifty); her 1969 death was due to leukemia.

In 1946 she was "resting" between pictures, the 1945 *It's a Pleasure*'s grosses having proved disappointing. Sonja in general was disappointed—disappointed with marriage, disillusioned by love, and increasingly fed up with her career. Margaret Ettinger, the Hollywood public relations exec and cousin of Louella Parsons, who knew Sonja well, said that by 1946 Sonja (at thirty-six) was worried about the future and resentful of the extra work needed to get her maturing muscles to perform with youthful flexibility. "The spontaneity was gone, the agility was not what it had been," according to Margaret. "And she was worried about her looks, claiming that her squarish Scandinavian features would not age well."

Jack Kennedy, twenty-nine, frail, sexually hot-to-trot, had met her at a party, and a mutual spark was set off. For Jack, it was a lark to sleep with a celebrity of Henie's caliber. He knew too she wanted no ties and would not go serious on him; she found him amusing, boyishly ardent and moreover was an admirer of his father, Joe Kennedy, whom she had met in New York. Margaret said there had even been rumors that Sonja and Old Joe had had a brief fling. Perhaps Old Joe had recommended her to Jack. In any event the encounter (*affair* would be too dignified a word) was short.

Joan Fontaine (1917–)

Joan Fontaine in her autobiography, *No Bed of Roses*, told with an ill-disguised amusement bordering on contempt how Joe Kennedy propositioned her at a dinner party she threw in the early 1950s. After dinner he had sought a private audience with her and informed her that he could "rescue" her career and manage her affairs as he had done with Gloria Swanson twenty-odd years before. He went on to say that the affair would have to be discreet and he could never marry her. Joan put him off as tactfully and painlessly as she could, but according to friends who knew her well at the time, she found the entire encounter and proposition a colossal horse-laugh and dismissed it as of no consequence.

Some ten years later she found herself dining with President John F. Kennedy and mischievously decided to tell him of the proposal his father had made to her ten years before. She recalled JFK's amusement when he heard the story and his follow-up remark—that he hoped *he* would be as enterprising romantically as his father when *he* got to be that age. Joe Kennedy had been about sixty-four when he had made his pitch to Joan, and son John was forty-five when Joan told him about it. Although he never came close to the sixty-four his father reached, after JFK's untimely demise at forty-six one of Joan's many husbands, Collier Young, remarked that Jack had covered as much woman-territory as Joe had by sixty-four—he hadn't missed all *that* much.

Joan Fontaine had gotten out from under the burden of being Olivia de Havilland's one-year-younger sister by 1940 when she became a star in *Rebecca* opposite Laurence Olivier.

Before *Rebecca* she had struggled up over a five-year period, through a slew of insignificant parts. She won an Oscar in 1941 for *Suspicion* opposite Cary Grant, and a host of quality pictures followed, most notably *The Constant Nymph* (1943) and *Letter from an Unknown Woman* (1948), which made her a star to reckon with.

It was true that by the time Joe Kennedy got at her around 1952 her career had reached the same crossroads that Gloria Swanson's had in 1927 (the year *she* met Joe) and such pictures as *Something to Live For* had not achieved the box-office success hoped for.

The middle and late 1950s saw a gradual decline in Joan Fontaine's career, with the pictures getting more shallow and throwaway and the releases more and more infrequent. By the mid 1960s, after her last film, *The Devil's Own*, was released, Joan moved to New York. She had something of a stage career, and when I met her in 1954, she was starring with Tony Perkins in *Tea and Sympathy* (they had taken over from Deborah Kerr and John Kerr who later starred in the 1956 movie version). By then already a veteran of a series of failed marriages and the "co-star" in a running feud with sister Olivia de Havilland, Joan at thirty-six seemed to me intelligent, cultured, and wise indeed toward men, whether in friendship, business, or romance.

She always brushed off with contemptuous witticisms the encounters with the Kennedys that recurred throughout her life and career. Friends felt that Joan did not think Old Joe or his sons were really in touch with reality where women were concerned and that they considered them only objects of conquest or pursuit, never as sources of affection, consolation, or sincerity.

The Joan Fontaine I knew in the 1950s and 1960s always seemed to me (especially after she based herself in New

York) to be thoroughly realistic, disillusioned, and even a little tired. (Had Joe Kennedy in 1952 really known the woman
he was so frivolously addressing he probably would have run
a mile in the opposite direction; no Kennedy patsy-candidate
was Joan.)

Tony Perkins always spoke of Joan with love and
respect; he recalled his *Tea and Sympathy* sojourn with her
as instructive and inspiring. "She could have had a major
stage career—she wasn't just a movie actress!" he said to
me. Her former husband Bill Dozier said to me: "She'd
probably have been far happier had she never known marriage or motherhood. She would have been supremely content as a loner." Now approaching eighty, Joan lives *alone* in
Carmel, California.

June Allyson (1917–)

June Allyson is today best known as "the Queen of Leak"—
famous for her television advertisements for Depend
Undergarments. But fifty years ago she was one of Hollywood's brightest young stars and the object of Jack
Kennedy's romantic pursuit. Jack Kennedy seems to have
romanced June at roughly the same time as Gene Tierney,
and it appears that in 1946—the year Jack was really hitting
on Hollywood gals—neither knew about the other's involvement with the handsome twenty-nine-year-old "son of the
ambassador," soon to be a congressman.

Author James Spada, in *Peter Lawford: The Man Who
Kept the Secrets*, quotes Jack's friend Chuck Spaulding on
Jack's 1940's attitude toward Hollywood women: "[Jack] was
fascinated by how sexual dynamism in Hollywood translated
into power—and vice versa," Spada stated. As Spaulding analyzed it: "'Charisma' wasn't a catchword yet, but Jack was
very interested in that binding magnetism these screen per-

sonalities had. What exactly was *it*? ["It" was a term invented by novelist Elinor Glyn in the 1920s to explain the come-hither magnetism of stars like Clara Bow.] How did you go about acquiring it? Did it have an impact on your private life? How did you make it work for you? He wouldn't let go of the subject."

Peter Lawford had first fallen in love with June when he did a picture with her in 1946 called *Two Sisters from Boston*. June, then married to Dick Powell, had not encouraged Peter, and it appears that his original infatuation turned to indifference, then hatred. "Peter really developed a strong dislike for June," Jerry Asher remembered. "I don't think she let him down lightly—or even tactfully. But then Peter should have known better. After all, June was married to Dick Powell at the time!"

June in her autobiography deals rather mildly with Peter: "[I] was often over at Peter Lawford's house," she wrote. "I never was as close to him as I was to Van [Johnson]. But I grew very fond of him in a mildly romantic way. We had a lot of fun. I loved his devil-may-care attitude and his British accent fascinated me."

Several writers have placed June Allyson's involvement with Jack Kennedy in the early 1940s, but as June didn't come to Hollywood until 1943 after a successful career in stage musicals, and since Jack was in the service at that time, 1946 seems to be the correct date for the coming together of the pair.

In her autobiography, June is highly circumspect about her relationship with Jack Kennedy, probably because she kept in mind that in 1945 she had become the wife of Dick Powell. "I didn't know his father was an ambassador," she recalled, "and I certainly didn't know I was being pursued by a future president of the United States." As she remembered it, "[Jack and I] laughed a lot. He reminded me of Peter Lawford—both had the same charm and fun-loving ways."

June made her fame as the sweet, wholesome girl-next-door. Later in her career she specialized in supportive wife roles, her spouse usually being upwardly mobile and in need of womanly sustenance and morale boosting. She had been born Ella Geisman in the Bronx in 1917 and was a good twenty-six when she came to Hollywood—late for a burgeoning screen personality. She had begun as a Broadway showgirl in the mid 1930s and attained prominence in the 1941 Broadway musical *Best Foot Forward*. After her screen career ended, she did a lot of television, stage, and commercial work.

It had never been clear just how far her relationship with Jack Kennedy went. If she put him in the same category as the spurned Peter Lawford, she had been, straight through the encounter, dismissing him as "charming" and "fun-loving." It is unlikely that in 1996, the now seventy-nine-year-old Queen of Leak will spill any beans on Jack, if there are any beans to be spilled at all.

TWENTY-ONE

Maria and Her Body Boy

Maria Shriver is the daughter of Rose and Joe's fifth child, Eunice (born in 1921) who married lawyer R. Sargent Shriver. Shriver, the first director of the Peace Corps, was George McGovern's running mate in the 1972 presidential election. Maria's parents founded the Special Olympics in 1968 and were active in many worthy causes. Born in 1955, Maria is the only girl in a family of boys.

Eunice Shriver has always been regarded as the strongest, most enterprising, and most together of the Kennedy women. Maria remembers adopting at an early age her mother's practical, resilient approach to life's problems.

She has made a distinguished career for herself as a television journalist, her interviews with other famous people being succinct, highly disciplined, and honed to get to the heart of matters. Now the mother of several children by her husband, Body Boy turned major movie star, Arnold Schwarzenegger, she has successfully combined homemaking with career duties. *Cutting Edge with Maria Shriver* was one of her best television shows, and along the way she has also cohosted *Sunday Today* and *Main Street*, a monthly news show for the young. She enjoys her way of life and once told an interviewer, "I've heard from so many women who said, 'Thank God, I can work to a certain point and still have the option down the road of having a family.'"

Brought up to believe—and with four brothers setting a pace and style—that she can do anything a man can do, Maria has credited her mother for inspiring her with discipline and drive. Recalling her mother, she has said, "My mother is as tough as nails—a great mother and a great woman, very independent. She's constantly pushing and challenging herself and has told me that much has been given to me and therefore I should do something with it!"

Recalling that before becoming involved with Arnold Schwarzenegger, she had only two boyfriends, one in high school and one in college, and that the family watched her "like a hawk," she took her time in tying the knot with Arnold—nine years in fact. They met in 1977 and were not married until 1986 when Maria was thirty. She remembers that she felt she had to do something—and do it really well—on her own. She and her brothers were trained and conditioned to excel. She felt she had to be right with *herself* before she could allow anyone else to "buy into" her, as she put it, especially when it came to marriage.

Many have wondered what diminutive (physically) and fastidious Maria found in muscle-builder, self-made Arnold, who came from a humble Austrian background to rise through his business interests into movie fame. Maria likes to remind one and all that she admired—and admires— Arnold not only for his humor, balance, and humility but for his sound business sense and disciplined careerism that turned him, in time, into one of Hollywood's biggest money-making stars.

Maria has never been fazed by his staunch Republican politics. "Women don't like men who are too tame," she has said. "I like a man who is supportive and responsible but who goes his own way in matters in which he strongly believes." Friends feel that Arnold's firm character won Maria for him. "She always wanted a man on whom she could rely but who was an entity in his own right and followed his own course," says one.

Maria and Arnold had a major wedding in Hyannis Port that was given top media coverage. She recalls planning it for close to a year in advance. It was well attended by family and the bride's and groom's many friends. Despite a broken toe sustained in an accident just before the wedding, Maria carried on gamely, switching to sneakers when the dancing began.

For years Arnold and Maria have lived in a Mediterranean-style house in Pacific Palisades, with pool and tennis courts. They like to spend the holidays in Aspen, Colorado, where they ski.

To be sure, there have been some ironic twists on the Arnold Schwarzenegger poor-boy-to-superstar story. A while back when Republican politicians sharply criticized Hollywood's violent, explosive movies, they deliberately avoided mentioning Schwarzenegger's cut-slash, blow-up, maim-bash movies that while low in taste and culture reap large box-office grosses. The violence in the Schwarzenegger movies certainly does not add to the cultural uplifting of American youth, the assertion goes.

Arnold's defenders claim that he is only being practical and following the current moneymaking trend in American movies because he knows perfectly well that if he went in for subdued, children-oriented fare unduly, he wouldn't have an audience. To his credit, Arnold has tried playful, gimmicky, nonviolent movie fare, but they have not reaped the profits of "that other stuff." Others who know Arnold well feel that the profit motive is deeply imbued in him after his humble beginnings in Austria. "He feels money—lots of it—not only makes a gracious life possible but ensures security for the children he and Maria have brought into the world and allows them a choice range of professions and callings."

One thing is certain: Arnold and Maria will instill in their children, as they mature, their own values—values that include hard work, self-realization, firm goals, and the discipline to give those goals fruition. And they will make their kids realize what they have long known from their own experience: that there is no satisfaction like the rewards from honest trying, honest striving to realize one's best potential.

One writer has said of them that they are a strong mutual admiration society, adding, "Although Arnold's public image is that of a movie jock, friends know him as an intelligent, civilized man with a delightful sense of humor, who earned a handsome salary in real estate long before he struck it rich in the movies." Maria is quoted thus: "Arnold is very warm and family-oriented, but he combines that with a great sense of drive. He is also very goal-oriented, so he accepts that in me."

She sees herself as "a woman, Maria Shriver: married, working, blessed with a wonderful family, with parents I love."

One writer tartly wrote of watching Maria Shriver talking with Jane Fonda at a New York party in 1993: "Those two girls would have wound up behind a five-and-ten counter if one weren't a Kennedy and the other a Fonda. They love to talk about how hard they worked, but some people struggle all their lives to arrive at the place those two privileged ladies were born into!"

Maria's—and self-made Arnold's—attitude is that Maria could easily have coasted along on her share of a family trust and made no effort to have a contributing, fulfilled life. Would the public have admired her more had she done *that*?

Arnold for years was accused of deliberately setting his sights on a well-connected, moneyed, and privileged wife to enhance his own upward mobility, which all agree has a special level of intensity. "Think of all the women he could have fallen in love with," one commentator noted, "and he goes for a *Kennedy!*" But the more likely scenario is that both recognized in the other solid qualities of character and motivation—and like attracted like.

As to criticisms of Arnold's politics—right slanted as he is—his defenders point out that if he had really wanted to buy into Kennedy power and privilege by osmosis wouldn't he have switched from Republican to Democrat, as undoubtedly his in-laws would have preferred. Yet he didn't. Arnold is obviously his own man.

There have been other spins on "perfect" Maria Shriver Schwarzenegger and her "perfect" life and her "perfect" marriage.

Barbara Gibson, Rose Kennedy's longtime secretary, in talking about "the President's bedroom," the best guest room in the Kennedys' Palm Beach house (named after, but never used by, JFK) recalled: "It became the ideal family trysting place." Gibson said she "laughed when Maria Shriver, whose libido was as healthy as any of the other family members, appeared on the Arsenio Hall Show and talked about her marriage to Arnold Schwarzenegger. She was working in television network news and apparently felt the need to maintain the image of the demure newlywed. She essentially claimed that she had never had the relationships of her famous uncles because of her strict Catholic upbringing and her intense work schedule, implying that she was an innocent virgin when she married Arnold." *However*, Gibson remembered, she came into the dining room one morning and found Maria at the breakfast table with a male companion from the previous evening. "The maid was serving them . . . and later told me that Maria's actions were not unusual, especially when she knew that there was no risk of her grandmother catching her." Gibson added: "The maid later joked about Maria's affairs during those nights in the President's bedroom, 'She'll never die wondering.'"

Many feel that Maria has remained surprisingly level-headed considering that the vaunted "perfect marriage" of her parents, Eunice Kennedy and Sargent Shriver, was anything but, with personal problems between them becoming so acute that they not only maintained separate sleeping quarters in their house but distanced themselves even further in their bedroom arrangements when they visited or traveled. A number of people have even compared the Shrivers' marriage to that of sister Jean Kennedy and Steve Smith. According to a family insider, "Jean took a lot of shit from Steve—he was abusive, dictatorial, unfaithful, cold, distant, you name it." Jean, now sixty-eight and ambassador to Ireland, is said to be far happier on her own, and Steve's death of cancer some years ago has, a friend said, "allowed her to be her own woman, living her own life. She always covered up for Steve, before and after his death, but the truth was she was too easy, too submissive, and he walked all over her. Now, she is free. *That* death came as a blessing for her!"

Although Maria is one-fifth (roughly) the size and weight of her husband, insiders say she stands up to him and holds her own fifty-fifty in the marriage. Another friend says of Maria: "She does not use the Kennedy connection in her marriage—she's dignified and independent." (But since everyone knows who she is anyway, why would she have to underline it?)

Maria maintains that Arnold's public image is on a far greater scale than her own, but she is more watched and commented upon than she may think. In many ways, she is a more interesting personality (at least privately) than Arnold, who puts whatever color, force, and dynamism he is credited with into his violent films.

Maria also had a more sophisticated and geographically wide-ranging early life than her cousins, even John and Caroline. After all, her father was ambassador to France, Peace Corps director and a vice presidential candidate, and while Sarge is a serious reader and more cultivated and intellectual than Eunice ("the hardheaded, practical one," as Maria has called her), there is no denying that her father's wide-ranging cultural interests vastly enhanced Maria's inner schematics. Also, being the only girl among her brothers, she acquired early an understanding of what makes men tick. This is credited with the success of her own ten-year marriage. Maria knows men—too well—and can not only beat them at their own game but has a preternatural understanding of their wants and needs including a gift for providing Arnold with what he needs before he realizes he needs it.

As one writer has commented, prior to her marriage, Maria was all over the lot, living on a kibbutz in Israel, meeting all kinds of people from all areas of the world when her dad was in the Peace Corps. She also took on many of her father's attitudes, including his hatred of bigotry in any form. His broad-mindedness and universal acceptance of people made even the leading Kennedys look provincial.

Sargent Shriver, during his relatively brief flirtations with politics, also took positions in which he firmly believed, scorning the Kennedys' pragmatic and limited "win for the sake of winning" ideas. He never depended on Kennedy money; he paddled his own canoe, even throwing in his lot with people the Kennedys didn't approve of. "It's *my* life," Sarge would say; "I have a family to raise and I use my own judgment as to what is best for all of us."

These attitudes proved a good influence on Maria. Maria, however, does have a tendency to rationalize. She continually claims that she got into television because of her own unaided efforts, which is arrant nonsense. Everyone knew who she was, everyone wanted to help—not out of concern for her, but to get a payback sometime from her father, uncles, or cousins and the paybacks came.

Maria has never been a very impressive figure on television. She is a lovely woman physically, but the force, the precision, and the sharpness of personality that distinguishes most women interviewers and commentators on television has always eluded Maria. She seems nice, sensible, composed— and slightly colorless. "But that's Maria Shriver—you know, the Kennedy niece" is a recurring reference to her that will always outshine the exploits of more talented colleagues.

To be fair to Maria, she slimmed down, got a voice coach, studied makeup techniques. And she was hard-working. Through working for a Special Olympics special for WTBS, she advanced by the early 1980s to a post as national correspondent on *PM Magazine*. The contacts along the way helped, including Tom Brokaw, and she went on to be a West Coast reporter for *CBS Morning News*.

Maria likes to talk today about the "viciously sexist" conditions she encountered early in her career, when women were forced to take second place to men when it came to salaries, promotions, and job openings. But one wonders what such discrimination meant in Maria's case, especially with all those strong contacts—now, as Mrs. Arnold Schwarzenegger, she is in doubly solid.

Maria makes a friendly, strong, if not charismatically compelling presence when she does interviews on television—but she projects nothing that two hundred other women from the same background and with the same training could not.

Maria, when she reached coanchor positions on television, was hailed as a heroine for her "discipline" and "willingness to work thirteen-hour days," but as one journalist wrote, "While she deserves every credit for making the most of what she has gotten, there are others who would have worked just as hard if they had gotten the lift-up of her contacts and privileged background. So let's not make her Joan of Arc, okay?"

The Maria-Body Boy thing began in 1977, when her brother Bobby introduced her to Arnold. She was twenty-one; he was thirty. His *Pumping Iron* had made a big splash that year, and his audiences, many women and many more gays, were working him up, through collective hysteria and body-worshipping clubs, into a cult symbol.

Pumping Iron told the story of two body builders preparing, through Sturm-und-Drang schedules and exercise routines, for the Mr. Olympia contest. Few of its admirers cared about the plot; it was the sight of those men glorying in their bodies and pushing themselves to the outer limits that fired up the collective unconscious of the audience, which the film captured resoundingly.

All agree that Arnold and Maria did not fall into the proverbial love-at-first-sight category so popular in such tales of how famous lovers first met.

The meeting (there are other sites given) most likely took place at the Robert Francis Kennedy Tennis Tournament in New York. It took Maria several years to warm up to Body Boy supreme. She had heard stories of homosexual proclivities and the narcissistic obsessions of men who lived by their bodies, and she wanted to separate the wheat from the chaff, as she examined Arnold's private life. There had been cracks made about the male sponsors and patrons Arnold had picked up along the way, implying that some of the older patrons had a homosexual interest in him. Arnold earlier in his career was eternally trying to field—with his then-imperfect knowledge of English—interviewers who were obsessed with determining his true sexual orientation. When his skimpily clad body appeared with increasing frequency in gay publications, the embarrassing rumors grew.

But Maria learned that Arnold was promiscuous with women. Given the homosexual ambience of his profession, she found that *reassuring*, having long since bought into the attitude of the women in her family concerning the sex life of their men: *men are like that*. She often pondered that irony: that she didn't like Arnold's womanizing but was at the same time comforted and reassured by it—a contrapuntal emotion indeed for a woman falling in love to entertain.

One writer theorized that over the next few years, from the initial meeting in 1977 until the marriage in 1986, Maria came increasingly to feel that Arnold would protect, sustain, and aid her in her increasing need to gain independence from the Kennedy mystique. Maria had to weather cruel japes from some of the Kennedy males, including her brothers, about the Austrian accent Arnold has never been able to shake, and when a picture book about Arnold appeared, stressing his body-building and model period, the grotesquely swollen muscles and ugly outstanding veins that his weight lifting and physical exercises engendered were ridiculed by Kennedy friends—and some Kennedy family.

Maria passionately defended Arnold; according to one friend she went further than that, questioning the manhood of some of the young Kennedy males, telling them they were jealous of Arnold, ridiculing them as boys still hooked on masturbation. Abashed, humiliated, fearful of her and Arnold, the ridiculers gradually shut up, and by the time thirty-one-year-old Maria and thirty-nine-year-old Arnold tied the knot, the cracks were verboten and the good wishes in high style—at least in Kennedyland.

Arnold is as tough and shrewdly functional as his wife— more so, given that he is a self-made man who came up from nothing in far-off Austria and she was—well, given some heavy lifts along the way.

Born in Graz, Austria, on July 30, 1947, at fifteen Arnold rebelled against his stern policeman father who wanted him to be a soccer player and went all-out for body building, which the elder Schwarzenegger reportedly considered "degenerate," "shameful," and "an embarrassment" to his family.

By twenty-one, in 1968, Arnold had arrived in America, trailing some body titles, including Junior Mr. Europe. Known (thanks to a New York publicist's brainstorm) as the Austrian Oak, he pushed and shoved and exercised and browbeat and bullied his way to such titles as Mr. Universe (he was a five-time winner), Mr. Olympia (he made it seven times out on that one), and Mr. World. In 1980, at age thirty-three, Arnold decided it was time to get out while the getting out was good (thirty-three in pumping iron circles was "getting on").

Intensely ambitious and highly self-disciplined, Arnold displayed a formidable business sense, starting a mail-order firm, going into real estate, and investing various sections of his pumping-iron purse winnings in real estate while picking up college credits in business and economics from the University of Wisconsin. Before he was thirty, Arnold Schwarzenegger had already become a millionaire.

Arnold had appeared in his first film when he was twenty-three, *New Hercules in New York*, in 1970. *The Long Goodbye* had come in 1973. He had tried to "Americanize" his image by calling himself Arnold Strong in this period, but the Austrian accent, which some thought "funny and tinny," and his less-than-brilliant acting talents made only a limited impression among serious critics.

In 1982 Arnold, then thirty-five, broke through to movie big time with *Conan the Barbarian*, which, along with its 1984 sequel, *Conan the Destroyer*, proved a box-office bonanza. The science-fiction opus, *The Terminator* (1984), catapulted Arnold the Persistent into superstar status. He had long since ceased to be a laughing matter, especially in Hollywood circles where super box-office returns automatically earned super respect and admiration.

One critic nailed down the mystique he was projecting thus: "Curiously, Schwarzenegger's limited acting range, his deadpan expression and thick-accented delivery of American slang phrases proved assets rather than liabilities in his rise to top popularity, providing his toughest characterizations with a touch of humorous ease."

Soon Arnold was being hailed all across the country as the Cinderella boy from humble small-town Austrian beginnings whose rise to top fame and fortune "embodies the realization of the American dream."

Arnold attained American citizenship in 1983. He elected for the Republican Party. As one friend and admirer put it, Schwarzenegger thought Republicans did more for big business and the trickle-down economic principles he favored; after all Body Boy was himself big business.

Shortly before the Schwarzenegger-Shriver wedding, his close friendship with Kurt Waldheim, the secretary-general of the United Nations who later became president of Austria, was revealed by unfriendly sources tied to the Democrats, who stressed that Waldheim had had close Nazi connections and indeed had been one. Unfazed, Arnold declared his continuing friendship with and support for Waldheim and let the chips fall where they might. Whatever Arnold may have thought of Waldheim's former Nazi ties, he refused to be disloyal to someone he considered a friend. As the granddaughter of a former ambassador to Great Britain who in the 1940s had been accused of appeasing the Nazis, Maria tended to think Arnold's stand individualistic and courageous. Also, as a Republican, multimillionaire businessman, Catholic (*this* pleased the Kennedys), and movie superstar, Arnold Schwarzenegger in 1986 could hardly be accused of being either communist *or* fascist. "To his business associates and admirers, Arnold at that time was as All-American as you could get," as one friend put it.

Arnold later thoroughly established his credentials in Republican politics, winding up as President George Bush's chairman of the Council on Physical Fitness in 1990.

Later Arnold took on movie direction (a cable television remake of the Barbara Stanwyck comedy of 1945, *Christmas in Connecticut*). His films to date have been big box office, with the exception of the only tepidly-received *Last Action Hero* in 1993 and his ill-advised excursions into such cutesy-poo fare as *Twins* and *Kindergarten Cop*. It is obvious, as Arnold moves up to age fifty (1998), that his admirers prefer his violent, wild, exciting films to any divergences.

"In that action stuff, he is just right; in the comedy-characterization, light-touch stuff he is out of his element," critic William Schoell said in *Quirk's Reviews* in 1994.

With several children in their family nest now (the first was born in 1989), the Schwarzeneggers seem to balance responsible parenthood nicely with their busy respective careers. Maria has declared that the kids give her the thorough rounding her life requires, but that the career, too, is a galvanizing life-force for her. She believes, she says, that marriage, motherhood, and a career can be ably balanced with timing, discipline, and common sense. Observers have added that it helps to have millions of dollars with which to hire the best possible care for the kids, and aides who take off their hands the attritional trivia that poorer folk have to cope with.

Many commentators, gossips (professional and private), Kennedy and Schwarzenegger watchers, and the public at large have wondered if their ten-year marriage will last. Arnold, who led a promiscuous life before his marriage and still has an appreciation for feminine charms, may find himself tempted to stray. Maria, with her busy career and interests and her kids to watch over, seems to be following the usual party line of Kennedy wives from time immemorial: if Arnold strays I don't want to know about it; that's how men are.

Maria has no martyr complex like old Rose and she certainly isn't an escapist like Joan, the unfortunate first wife of Teddy Kennedy. She has a thorough understanding of the roving male and the motherly, nurturing female, and she doesn't think this division of sexual roles old-fashioned—rather, timelessly sensible.

One friend of the Schwarzeneggers has said of Arnold and Maria: "They have a good friendship. They understand each other. And they love their kids. These factors *should* keep them together."

TWENTY-TWO

The Trials of John-John

J ohn Kennedy Jr.'s heart has always been in acting. In acting he could escape into another world. In acting he could use the full powers of his creative imagination. In acting he could be his own man, follow his own instincts, his own designs for his life.

And he has always been frustrated in his acting aims, always prevented from doing his own thing, stepping to his own drummer. For this his mother, Jackie Kennedy Onassis, was to blame. She blindly tried to guide her son by her own conception of the type of person he should be, by her own ideas of the future he should have.

When in his early twenties John told her he wanted to be an actor, she threatened to disinherit him. She told him acting would force him into the public eye in a superficial way and that the company he would keep as an actor would be drug-oriented, superficial, immature, sexually cavalier-ish—and worse. John must have laughed bitterly to himself when she got other Kennedy family members to join her in impressing on him that acting as a pursuit would be bad for the family image. The family image? After the horrors of Chappaquiddick, it would appear that the family image had been set in the public mind for all time. A talented young actor in the family, sincerely dedicated to his craft, as John aspired to be, would, to any sensible, objective person, have constituted an *improvement* on the family image.

But it was not to be. Jackie informed John's sympathetic uncle-by-marriage, Peter Lawford, that he was not to continue encouraging John to act; Peter sympathized deeply with John, but he knew that Jackie's rage could harm him. And after all, hadn't he and his Rat Pack buddies caroused all over Hollywood, treating the institution of marriage lightly, reveling in the naughty-boy trendiness of the flagrant infidelities that their wives, in Jackie's view (she had been among them after all), had borne with what she felt was "admirable restraint."

Jackie liked Peter Lawford personally. She sympathized with the mess he had made of his life, the drug and alcohol problems and other misfortunes that his immature, self-indulgent "actor's lifestyle" (as Jackie's contemptuous term for it was) had brought on him. But she was not letting Peter influence young John's life in any way, shape, or form. And there was another reason: Jackie had never really forgiven Peter for acting as go-between for JFK and Hollywood women. She didn't care for Frank Sinatra, either, or Dean Martin; she couldn't see her boy hobnobbing with such people if and when he pursued a Hollywood career.

Jackie had always guarded John's and Caroline's environment and social lives. She thought the children of Ethel Kennedy undisciplined, rowdy, and self-indulgent. She deplored the drug scandals they brought on the family and their emphasis on what she regarded as "silly, rowdy" athleticism (their touch football pursuits won her ultimate disdain).

So John and Caroline were kept away from their cousins as much as possible. John was told he had to be circumspect, sensible—he was after all the son of a president of the United States. The family dignity, third-generation style, rested on his young shoulders. When Peter's son Chris Lawford got involved in drug scandals, along with Bobby Kennedy Jr. and David Kennedy, who paid with his life for his loose lifestyle, Jackie held them up to John as examples *not* to follow.

When she heard that Lem Billings, too, was involved (at a relatively advanced age) in Bobby, Chris, and David's drug escapades, she lost no time informing John that Lem should be given a wide berth. Although Jackie had always known that Lem was gay, it never seemed to be an issue until the story got around, with the help of David Kennedy, that Lem had several thick photo albums of John in skimpy trunks jogging along beaches and running in Central Park. At this point, Jackie really lowered the boom. Lem was out in the cold, thoroughly and conclusively.

The Lem business then focused Jackie on another horrible (to her) possibility: that her son, whom some of his cousins called a mama's boy because she ran his life and kept him away from them, might be gay. Horror of horrors! There would have to be remedies for *that*. Jackie's answer was to send John out, in his late teens, on overnight nature jaunts in the wild. Traveling in South America and elsewhere was another "manly" pursuit to prove his burgeoning manhood. She also reportedly had detectives spotting his every move, his every date.

She checked carefully on every girl he got involved with. If they came from nice, preferably well-heeled families and seemed like potential homemakers or followed nonglamorous career aims (like editing, for instance, which had been *her* choice of occupation), she let things work out.

But if they were actresses, would-be actresses, or in any way involved with the performing arts, Jackie immediately registered cold disapproval.

Lem Billings felt that John bore all this feminine supervision patiently. "He loved his mother, sympathized with all she had gone through, wanted to please her" was Lem's evaluation. Steve Smith expressed his respect for John's "desire to give his mother peace and happiness," adding, "I think his every action in those earlier years was predicated on the possible effect on *her* feelings."

What's sad is that John was talented—is talented—as an actor. Those who saw him in 1985 (age twenty-five) at the Irish Arts Theater in the Brian Friel play, *Winners*, raved about his "dimensional," "vibrant," "deeply empathizing," and "strongly sensitive" performance as a young Irish Catholic man who gets his girlfriend pregnant, with tragic consequences (they both die in the end). John at the time was dating the actress Christina Haag, who appeared with him in the play. Christina was a nice girl from a nice family with a profile that she kept, by her own choice, low. She could never had been characterized as a publicity seeker or someone out to cash in on or gain spurious notoriety from her association with John, yet despite these merits she was suspect to Jackie because she wanted to *act*.

At Brown John had made his interest in acting manifest, and his classmates had applauded his workmanlike, creditable performances in such plays as *In the Boom Boom Room*, *Volpone*, and *Short Eyes*.

In a 1982 performance of *Playboy of the Western World*, the J. M. Synge masterpiece, the director Don Wilmeth said, "[John] did a fine job." The play was put on at Brown's Fauce House Theater. Chris Harty, who appeared with John in the Brown University Production Workshop's *In the Boom Boom*

Room, thought him "very good." (In this John was a street bum involved with a go-go dancer.)

Of this play the *Brown Daily Herald* critic wrote: "Kennedy's performance was really the high point of the evening," adding, "it is not easy to take a stereotypical part like that of macho boyfriend and to play it convincingly— without hardly ever succumbing to the characteristic Pacino-type movements and speech patterns so many actors feel obliged to take on." Caroline was in the audience for that play. Her mother was not. She hated the whole idea, and not only by her absences but also by her sharp words on the phone and in person, she let John know that the whole idea of following acting as a serious career horrified and repelled her.

Chris Harty, who also played John's father in *Playboy of the Western World*, said, "I think John was drawn to acting for the usual conscious and subconscious reasons. But he may have had less of a conscious reason than most people. After all, he didn't need to get more famous or better looking. He acted because he was a good actor."

Fellow cast members supported John in his acting ambitions. John sought to meet actors wherever he could. He loved their company, loved to discuss their approach to their craft with them. His interest in acting continued for several years after leaving Brown.

His sympathetic sister Caroline tended to feel that John should follow his own instincts. But Jackie tried to throw cold water on the Irish Arts venture of 1985, which ran six performances. Not only did she not attend, she prevented reviewers' attendance likewise. According to Barbara Gibson: "I never did learn whether this was because she was afraid her son would be hurt or if she feared he would be encouraged. Whatever the case, with John's looks, interests, and abilities, had Jackie not been so hostile to the entertainment world, John [would now] be earning his living on the stage and in films."

Probably to deflect his mother's wrath, John kept his own counsel about his secret aims, desires, and hopes, telling the press: "This is not a professional acting debut. It's just a hobby."

This was not quite the end of John's acting attempts. Randy Poster, a pal from the Brown days, produced a movie in 1988 in which John's girlfriend Christina Haag was cast. The film, *A Matter of Degree*, showcased John in a brief role as a "guitar-playing Romeo." The film was shown later in Europe but (Jackie's long hand being what it was) never in America.

Jackie was determined to make John a "substantial citizen." A series of what one sympathetic pal of John's called "nothing made" jobs, designed to give John a taste from above of real life, led from law school to his three years as an assistant district attorney. Before passing the bar, John failed three times, with one paper jeering "The Hunk Flunks" when news of one of his failed attempts got out.

"John's heart was *never* in law," one friend says today. "Calling him dumb, self-indulgent, and lazy—and all those other crappy adjectives—it was so unfair! John is highly intelligent and if he is *interested* in something he attacks it full force, masters it. Considering that he was psychologically resisting a dry, dull, boring pursuit like law, it's a wonder he every got by in it at all. John is an artist. Law is for eager-beaver, money-chasing clunks."

As an assistant district attorney in New York, John did his work, caused no problems, but didn't particularly shine, either. "He was out to please Jackie, to come on substantial," said another friend. But there came a time, after a few years of being—and acting out—something that he was not, when John finally rebelled. He quit, and for a time became a "gentleman of leisure," or as one paper unkindly dubbed him, "the country's most glamorous hedonist."

Then, in May 1994, Jackie died.

John at last was free to be his own man. With millions of dollars safely in the kitty, he didn't need to live by any rules other than his own. But he was in his mid thirties—rather late to begin a serious acting career. "He would have had to work hard to make up the lost time his mother had inflicted on him," a friend said, "but there is a premium on youth in the acting line—and in five years John would have been forty!" She added: "And that is late for a glamor boy, especially one who hasn't been allowed to acquire the background."

So John cast around for something else to do. The result was his magazine, *George*, which debuted in September 1995. It is significant that the first two covers, both featuring people in Washington-style wigs (he named the magazine for George Washington), highlighted performers—supermodel Cindy Crawford on the first, actor Robert De Niro on the second. No one could be completely sure what John was aiming at here. John Masterton, as editor at *Media Industry Newsletter*, described John's involvement with the mag as "a catalyst" and that he "made the sales calls easy for everyone." During the gestation of *George*, everyone seemed to want to get on the JFK Jr. bandwagon, and the advertising sales went phenomenally well, at least for the first two issues. Then, in early 1996, it began to appear that the novelty of John Kennedy, editor-in-chief of *George*, was dissipating.

According to John Masterton, "As long as [John] is there, the magazine will have some cachet." He added, "[John] is intelligent, but we don't know how he'll do as editor of a major magazine." (In January 1996 John fired editor Eric Etheridge and had taken over full editorial duties himself, his title previously having been editor-in-chief.)

Masterton also felt that *George* was "trying to be like *Vanity Fair* with a fuzzy, political direction," adding that he, for one, was *not* sold on the premise.

Hachette Filipacchi Magazines, which had bankrolled *George* to the tune of $25 million, seemed determined to press on despite the decline in ad sales with the third issue. "They are shrewd enough to know that John's name will keep up its momentum indefinitely," said a publishing source.

George is certainly a strange product. John had insisted originally that it was designed to humanize the political scene by highlighting personalities from that world entertainingly and that it would be nonpartisan and neither liberal nor conservative. Careful perusal of the first two issues reveals, however, that it seems to be veering more toward a general, entertainment-type magazine. John's interview in the first issue was with George Wallace; for the second, he zeroed in on Warren Beatty. Madonna even wrote a column for issue one, cracking about the armed forces coming out of the closet *en masse* and discussing her qualifications (only a joke) for the presidency.

As Masterton and others have noted, *George* is still trying to find itself. Perhaps it only appears that way. For the underlying truth is that John Kennedy Jr. is slowly, surely inching his way back to his original true love, show business. Yes, he is smart enough to realize that age thirty-five is late to inaugurate a major acting career in a youth-obsessed pursuit.

But Jackie isn't standing over him any more. "Deep down, John resents Jackie's having interfered with his acting ambitions; he resents her self-centered, self-defensive, almost paranoid fears about the entertainment world," one friend said. "And why was Jackie coming on so moralistic in the first place? Wasn't she living openly with a married man, Maurice Tempelsman, in her Fifth Avenue place while his wife seethed elsewhere in the same city? Didn't she blatantly and obviously marry an ugly old man, Aristotle Onassis, for money and security? Who was she to lecture anybody?"

John had had to stand by while Jackie did exactly as she pleased. She took up editing for a major publishing company. "It was no doubt Jackie's way of being (she thought) 'creative.' It was a hobby, a dilettante thing, really no more mature than her wangling a job in early youth through connections as a reporter-photographer for a Washington newspaper, though she was supremely talent-less in that pursuit, too."

Jackie laughed at her sister Lee's acting pretensions. The untalented Lee Bouvier, as Bob Stack and others attested, had made a mess of her undeserved role on television as *Laura* back in 1968, and Jackie never forgot it, teasing her about it mercilessly. One friend said, "I really think Lee married the film director Herbert Ross to get back into a creative line by osmosis; maybe she was hoping some of Herbert's directing talent would rub off on her—along the lines of if you can't be talented, then *marry* talent!"

Jackie, in the years following Lee's acting attempts, enjoyed rubbing into John what happened when someone famous tried artistic pursuits for which she had no talent. One supporter and friend of John's commented on this: "But there was a difference; Lee had no acting talent; John *does*!"

Will *George* move John further and further toward the show-business milieu he has always longed to be a part of? And will he let *George* sink if he thinks it has served its purpose as a bridge to the world his mother deprived him of?

There was considerable comment when John made a cameo appearance in a *Murphy Brown* segment in 1995—was *this* a belated step toward performing? While his appearance—a comedy jape aimed at publicizing the advent of *George* (which, naturally, got prominently displayed)—was sneered at in some quarters, it seems to have heartened John and hyped up his adrenaline. One commentator snidely commented, "Maybe John was wise to move on from acting—he is handsome but his voice is rather flat and light and he doesn't come on with the sex-charisma one expects," which evades the fact that it was a mere walk-on bit designed to promote *George* and hardly offers any challenge or any indication whatever of how John might rise to the occasion of a strong dramatic part or something expressly written to showcase his thespian abilities.

Of the charisma there can be no question; since the 1980s John has been featured as "the Sexiest Man Alive" and one of the sexiest hundred people in the world. Photos of him in a brief swim wraparound have been at a premium for years; his well-developed body with perfect pecs and strong legs have figured in an exhaustive series of tabloid and magazine layouts.

John has always demonstrated a characteristic actors' trait: narcissism. He loved to tease men he felt were homosexually oriented by parading around nude at athletic clubs. A tabloid reportedly got a picture—front view—of John urinating beside a bush, and he saw the photographer and merely laughed, making no attempt to procure or smash the camera. "John's in love with himself—sure," says a friend.

"How in hell could he not be? All he has to do is strip and look in the mirror or glory in himself dolled up in a tux."

David Kennedy has always been regarded in certain circles as the only potentially creative and artistically sensitive of Bobby's sons, but the macho insensitivities of his touch-football-crazy siblings downed any individualist tendencies David had—writing was one of his original enthusiasms—and so for twelve years he has lain in the cemetery with grandfather Joe, joined in 1995 by grandmother Rose. "An old man of eighty-one, an old woman of a hundred and four, and a young guy of twenty-nine—what a strange threesome in that lot!" a commentator has noted.

Some feel that Jackie Kennedy should have gone to her grave grateful that John didn't go the way of David, considering the raffishness of his relatives and the fact that in his teen years, one of the futile acts of rebellion John adopted was experimenting with drugs (fast driving was another—he picked up numerous fines).

To John's credit, he never did more than experiment, and drugs have not been associated with him in any way since that time, or not publicly anyway.

Another clue to John's long-standing desire to "go Hollywood" has been his romantic involvements with such feminine Hollywood lights as Daryl Hannah and Madonna. Daryl was a vulnerable, sensitive young lady, product of a divorce and her mother's remarriage to a rich Chicagoan; she had lived for nine years with Jackson Browne, a rock star who had physically abused her. When she turned to John in the aftermath of that experience, he had come on to her as prince on the white charger, knight-protector. Certainly he was very solicitous of her in the year that followed, and soon they were intimate. They had met at Lee Radziwill's wedding to Herb Ross, and the spark seems to have been struck immediately.

Barbara Gibson seems to have held Daryl Hannah in high regard. While she and John were intimates, Barbara said of her: "[Daryl] is not a Hollywood bimbo. She is not a high-profile celebrity. She is known only for long-term committed relationships."

Daryl and John had a strong relationship for a number of years. Jackie, of course, had reservations about her because she was an actress; financially, there were no grounds for suspicion because Daryl came from a wealthy Chicago family and would inherit millions. But should John ever have entered politics, Jackie kept reminding him, Daryl as Mrs. John Kennedy Jr. would have been a liability—she had lived with Browne out of wedlock. When John reportedly reminded his mother that Ronald Reagan was divorced from one actress and married to another, Jackie's rejoinder was that Ronnie was not a Catholic so public acceptance came more readily.

There seem to be a number of theories as to why John and Daryl ceased to be an item shortly after Jackie's death. Friends feel that the interest on both sides (particularly John's) had evaporated, and when push came to shove, John did not want to commit himself legally. Daryl has had little or nothing to say about the parting, but friends suspect that she was more than a little disappointed. "But then John never stays with any girlfriend *too* long!" one friend comments, "a few years at most. And Daryl did have a long run!" Daryl keeps continually busy with films, and though she isn't a top liner, she gets into major films with well-received critical receptions for her performances. "So obviously she isn't brooding unduly over John," as one friend puts it. "Daryl likes a lengthy, serious involvement; she isn't easy and she doesn't play around just to get her name in the paper. Daryl is a nice person—too bad, she'd have made John a good wife."

When John got involved briefly with Madonna, the consensus of opinions was that Madonna was too racy for him, and too freaky. John had taken Madonna to visit Jackie before her death, and Jackie was horrified by the pairing, especially because stories were rampant that Marilyn Monroe had been Madonna's idol. There is considerable pro-and-con debate as to whether John and Madonna ever were intimate; those who claim they were say Madonna found him too straight arrow and missionary-position predictable for her; she liked her sex more freaky and kinky.

John at the moment seems to have settled neatly into his Soho (Manhattan) digs with girlfriend Carolyn Bessette, a former Calvin Klein exec with no love for the spotlight. There have been stories that John will marry Carolyn. But a man pushing thirty-six who has evaded that kind of commitment to date will not be the subject of bets that he is about to break the mold of bachelorhood.

"John has a lot in common with Princess Di," says another friend. "They both like attention—lots of it!"

Writer Gregory Speck, who has socialized with John Kennedy Jr. at various New York parties, found John to be "shy and sweet, but fundamentally distrustful of anyone connected with the press." Speck adds, "Like all celebrities, John finds fame to be a double-edged sword; on the one hand it is human nature to want appreciation, recognition and affection, but on the other hand, fame magnetizes so much that is negative that the benefits must often seem to be outweighed by the costs."

Julia Roberts was another of John's encounters. They became acquainted in 1990 after a meeting at the Four Seasons Hotel in Los Angeles. What followed was a wild, sexy weekend. Julia was as fascinated by John—and as curious about him—as he was about her. This time, however,

Julia was the one who dumped him—either because she found him a dull lover or because she felt she had better do the dropping before she found herself dropped.

John really worked up steam over her while the affair was red-hot (red-hot for *him*, rather), sending her many presents and even trying to flatter her by compiling a book of photographs featuring Julia in a series of on and offscreen shots. "But Julia had other things on her mind," a friend said. "Her career, her next film role, her fan letters, sessions with her lawyer, her agent, her taxman, you name them. And there were other men—lots of them—making demands on her attention." John sent her letters, which she (honorably) returned; his phone calls went unanswered. Soon he was on to other diversions.

Melanie Griffith and John crossed paths in 1994 at East Hampton. At the time Melanie and Don Johnson had separated, and she found herself a summer neighbor of John's.

This time, Melanie was the pursuer and John the pursued. Failing to get anywhere with notes and phone calls, Melanie reportedly adopted more drastic measures. John came in from swimming in the ocean and found Melanie in his bedroom, blocking the way to his bathroom and shower and wearing nothing but a skimpy towel that stopped at the very top of her thighs but began teasingly down her breasts. John gave her a brief fling—as curious as any man—but tired of her quickly. "Stop popping up unexpectedly—let me take the initiative" was the substance of his advice to her. Then he suggested she call his new private number, but gave her a wrong number. Melanie took the hint and withdrew.

Just as that other John Kennedy in long-ago 1940 found Hollywood the magnetic mecca and drank his fill of its delights, so the current John Kennedy demonstrates, both personally and careerwise, La-La Land's subconscious appeal to his hopes and dreams. Though geographically a New Yorker—and what appears to be a confirmed one—John the second cannot help but look westward in his imagination to that magic city where his grandfather Joe loved Gloria and Nancy and Connie; aspired to Greta and Norma and Joan; dithered with, then dumped, Evelyn and Phyllis and so many others; and mourned a male hero, Fred Thomson.

Hollywood, where his father, John the first, came half-cynically, half-excitedly, to emulate Joe the lover of many women, with Gene Tierney, Sonja Henie, Angie Dickinson, Jayne Mansfield, and that siren of all sirens, Marilyn Monroe.

Will John the second, with the Daryls and Melanies and Madonnas and Julias already in his past, one day follow the ancestral mystic trail to Hollywood?

At thirty-five, John the second, no longer John-John, no longer (no, not really) John Kennedy *Junior*, has the time, decades of it, to search for his own truth.

Epilogue

And so, there they are—the seed of Joe and Rose entering the eighth decade of the collective family flirtation with seductive, treacherous, unpredictable Hollywood—the land of often tragic, rarely upbeat endings.

Will Arnold and Maria survive as marrieds—and will their kids, in turn, be lured by Hollywood? Will self-destructive Peter's sad, fundamentally decent but consistently unlucky Chris, now forty-one, tackle his and his dad's thespian heritage with renewed determination, despite his present hiatus? Will John-John, pushing thirty-six, his own man now, move on from lawyer to editor to the profession his heart has longed for from the very beginning, a profession—an art for those who practice it with appropriate reverence and an endowment of sufficient native talent—that sets a ruthless premium on youth?

Are the shades of self-destructive, wayward Marilyn and the long-ago lover of Glorious Gloria looking on at all this? Is the ghost of Gloria still hurting, bitter, and lost, and do she and Joe still haunt the Hollywood mansion where once in the hey-hey-gone-to-hell 1920s, they defied convention? Do Peter's ashes stir from the seas where once they were scattered and concentrate briefly to mourn the decline of youth and beauty and idealism and hope? Does Frankie Boy of the magnetic, insinuative, irresistible voice mull over, in his eighties, the loved and lost?

Will the new generations, sons and daughters, grand-children and in-law offspring read of the mistakes of the past and contemplate the principal actors, marred by age or silent long since in their graves?

Is the shade of Jimmy Quirk doing penance for his fatal, fateful act—facilitating the meeting of Gloria and Joe? Are Nancy Carroll and Connie Bennett and Evelyn Brent and Marlene Dietrich and May Allison and Greta Garbo in their celestial kaffeeklatsch rehashing the wasted emotions and betrayals and false alarms and foolish feintings? And does the shade of Rose Kennedy—rich in 104 years of living—come to join them, shrugging her shoulders and intoning: men are like that, like it or not?

All the vital, life-loving people who dominated that Hollywood scene of the roaring, ribald, mesmeric, irre-sistible 1920s are now souls silent in the wind—silence is the keynote now.

And the third and fourth generation survivors—are they not silent too? Silent wondering what the future will bring. Silent wondering if the more malign fates will cruel-ly and insistently repeat themselves? Silent but quietly hopeful, too, in some cases—hopeful that some vestiges of peace and valor and hope and positivism will emerge from all the sadness and negation of the past and assert them-selves before it is too late.

Kennedys—and Fitzgeralds and Connerys and Quirks—ventured forth from unhappy Ireland in those now legendary, formidably distant 1840s. They went to a land where hope was to be garnered and the future to be seized, and there they met their variegated fates. And eighty years later some pioneered a journey to Hollywood. They, too, hoped to garner love and joy and glamor and all the beauty and excitement that satan had set before the lord in the time of temptation. And the reality that came upon them they still whisper about in ghostly tones, and many of them mourn, and hopefully some find in their hearts the peace of forgiveness.

There is an Irish Catholic legend of a mystic kind, about the spirits of the dead meeting and communing in the Other Place, described by Shakespeare as that bourne from which no traveler returns. My maternal aunt, Mary Connery Gorham, used to put a humorous Irish spin on the Land Beyond: she'd joke that after the entire Connery family had made it to the family lot in St. Mary's Cemetery in Lynn, Massachusetts, a visitor could put his ear to the ground and hear them all rehashing their ancient quarrels. One wonders whether Joe and Rose, in their lot, are rehashing what is better left alone, and whether young David, the grandson lost to drugs at twenty-nine, is mourning the tragedy of a life unlived and unfulfilled.

Hopefully there is another mystic visitor to Joe Kennedy's grave—one departed this life for some sixty-seven years now. I want to feel that decent, good Fred Thomson's shade comes visiting and that he whispers comfortingly to the spiritually beleaguered friend who in life loved him above all other men: "It's all right, Joe. It's all right now, guy."

Notes

1. The Root Source

Sources:
Author's personal memories.
Lawrence J. Connery to author.
John F. Fitzgerald to author.
Walter Howey to author.
Myles McSweeney to author.
The Founding Father (for all
    books, see bibliography).
John Kennedy to author.
Lem Billings to author.
Joe Kane to author.
The Kennedy Family.
John Kennedy: A Political Profile.
The Fitzgeralds and The Kennedys.

2. The Boston Beginnings

Family memories of author.
Andrew L. Quirk to author.
Lawrence J. Connery to author.
Mary Connery Gorham to
    author.
The Fitzgeralds and The Kennedys.
The Founding Father.
John F. Fitzgerald to author.
Walter Howey to author.

Articles on Connery family in
    Lynn *Item* and Lynn *Post.*
The Kennedy Family.
JFK: Reckless Youth.
*The Kennedys: Dynasty and
    Disaster.*

3. Mentor Jimmy Quirk and Hollywood

Author's personal memories.
Kathryn Dougherty to author.
Jean Quirk Sullivan to author.
"Quirk of *Photoplay*," *Films in
    Review*, March 1955.
"Jimmy Quirk: Hollywood's
    Father Confessor," *TV-Radio-
    Movie Guide*, Dec. 1966–Jan.
    1967.
Adela St. Johns to author.
Hedda Hopper to author.
Billy Grady to author.
Photoplay Anthology.
*Norma: The Story of Norma
    Shearer.*
Marshall Neilan to author.
Joseph P. Kennedy to author.

John F. Fitzgerald to author.
Jesse Lasky to author.
Will Hays to author.
Adolph Zukor to author.

4. Enter Gloria
Films of Gloria Swanson.
Gloria Swanson to author.
Marshall Neilan to author.
Kathryn Dougherty to author.
Robert Francis Kennedy.
Jack discovering Gloria and Joe
    making love on sailboat:
    Kathryn Dougherty to
    author; Lem Billings to
    author; George Cukor to
    author; Adela St. Johns to
    author; *Good Ted/Bad Ted.*

5. Nancy, Connie, Greta—and Joan
Nancy Carroll to author.
Joan Bennett to author.
Joan Crawford to author.
May Allison to author.
Adela St. Johns to author.
Ruth Waterbury to author.
Jerry Asher to author.
Hedda Hopper to author.
Harriet Parsons to author.

6. Fred Thomson: Joe Kennedy's Only Hero
Frances Marion to author.
Off With Their Heads.
Kathryn Dougherty to author.
Rose Kennedy to author.

Hedda Hopper to author.
Mike Connolly to author.
George Cukor to author.

7. Joe in the 1930s
Claudette Colbert to author.
Marlene Dietrich to author.
Robert Francis Kennedy
A Hero for Our Times.
Sins of the Father.
Seeds of Destruction.
The Fitzgeralds and The Kennedys.
The Founding Father.
John F. Kennedy.
Kathryn Dougherty to author.
William Powell to author.
Films of William Powell.
Fred MacMurray to author.
Adela Rogers St. Johns to
    author.
Hedda Hopper to author.

8. Marlene
Marlene Dietrich to author.
Blue Angel.
Marlene.
Lem Billings to author.
Ruth Waterbury to author.
Jerry Asher to author.

9. Lem the Adoring, Eddie the Faithful
Lem Billings to author.
Steve Smith to author.
Seeds of Destruction.
The Kennedys.
The Kennedy Men.

JFK: Reckless Youth.
The Other Mrs. Kennedy.
Swanson on Swanson.
Nancy Carroll to author.

10. Jack Goes Hollywood
Robert Stack to author.
Gene Tierney to author.
Straight Shooting.
Self-Portrait.
Hedda Hopper to author.
Harriet Parsons to author.
Jerry Asher to author.
JFK: Reckless Youth.
The Kennedy Men.
George Cukor to author.
Cary Grant to author.
Lem Billings to author.
Steve Smith to author.

11. The Poignant Gene Tierney
Self-Portrait
Gene Tierney to author.
Vincent Price to author.
Clifton Webb to author.
Tyrone Power to author.
JFK: Reckless Youth.
Robert Stack to author.
Helen Ferguson to author.
Hedda Hopper to author.
Harriet Parsons to author.
Perry Lieber to author.
Jim Reid to author.
Author's personal memories.

12. Peter Lawford: Friday's Child
Author's personal memories.
Peter Lawford to author.
Eddie Mannix to author.
Billy Grady to author.
Peter Lawford: The Man Who Kept the Secrets.
The Peter Lawford Story.

13. Peter and Lana and Ava— and Bob
Peter Lawford to author.
Author's interviews with subjects.
Marilyn Monroe.
Marilyn: The Last Take.
Peter Lawford: The Man Who Kept the Secrets.
The Peter Lawford Story.
Eddie Mannix to author.
Jerry Asher to author.
Seeds of Destruction.
The Kennedy Men.
The Other Mrs. Kennedy.
A Woman Named Jackie.
John F. Kennedy.
Numerous biographies on Lana Turner, Ava Gardner, Bob Walker, etc.

14. Chris Lawford's Lonely Journey
Peter Lawford to author.
Lem Billings to author.
David Kennedy to author.
The Kennedy Men.

*The Kennedys: The Third
    Generation.*
Sins of the Father.
George Cukor to author.
Jerry Asher to author.

15. Frank and the Kennedys
Lem Billings to author.
Joan Crawford to author.
Nancy Sinatra to author.
His Way.
Films of Warren Beatty.
Robert Francis Kennedy.
A Woman Named Jackie.
Hedda Hopper to author.
Helen Ferguson to author.
Billy Grady to author.
Eddie Mannix to author.
Marilyn Monroe to author.
Jayne Mansfield to author.

16. Marilyn
Hollywood Royalty.
Marilyn Monroe to author.
Jerry Asher to author.
Helen Ferguson to author.
Mike Connolly to author.
Dean Martin to author.
Robert Stack to author.
Straight Shooting.
Hedda Hopper to author.
Harriet Parsons to author.
The Marilyn Scandal.
Jayne Mansfield to author.
Marilyn's Men.
Marilyn Monroe.

Perry Lieber to author.
Sonia Wolfson to author.
Barbara Barondess MacLean to
    author.
Don Murray to author.
Yves Montand to author.
Laurence Olivier to author.

17. Clowning Around with Jayne
Jayne Mansfield to author.
Sonia Wolfson to author.
Perry Lieber to author.
Adela Rogers St. Johns to
    author.
Jerry Asher to author.
Hedda Hopper to author.
Author's personal memories.
*Fallen Angels: The Lives and
    Untimely Deaths of 14
    Hollywood Beauties.*

18. The Kennedys on Camera
Appearances in movies, televi-
    sion, etc. mentioned in text.
John Kennedy Jr.'s interview
    with Warren Beatty in *George.*
"Man Who Plays the President,"
    (on Cliff Robertson),
    Movieland Magazine, 1963.
Films of Warren Beatty.
Films of Paul Newman.
Robert Francis Kennedy.
JFK: Reckless Youth.
Seeds of Destruction.

19. Jackie, the Fan Mags, and Me

Robert Francis Kennedy.
Photoplay Anthology.
"Why Don't They Leave Jackie Alone?" *Screen Stars Magazine*, 1965.
Steve Smith to author.
Robert Kennedy to author.
Edwin Guthman to author.
Richard Drayne to author.
Author's personal memories.

20. More Kennedy Lovers, Friends, Enemies

June Allyson to author.
Angie Dickinson to author.
Mickey Neilan to author.
Kathryn Dougherty to author.
Adela St. Johns to author.
Ruth Waterbury to author.
Terry Ramsaye to author.
John Lodge to author.
Phyllis Haver to author.
Lee Remick to author.
Mary Pickford to author.
No Bed of Roses.
Jesse Lasky to author.
Jesse Lasky Jr. to author.
Peter Lawford: The Man Who Kept the Secrets.
Adela Rogers St. Johns to author.
Tony Perkins to author.
Helen Ferguson to author.
Delight Evans to author.
JFK: Reckless Youth.

Numerous magazine and newspaper articles on subjects of this chapter.

21. Maria and Her Body Boy

Kennedys: The Next Generation.
The Kennedys: The Third Generation.
Arnold Schwarzenegger: A Portrait.
Numerous articles on Schwarzenegger and Shriver.

22. The Trials of John-John

Gregory Speck to author.
The Kennedys: The Third Generation.
Kennedys: The Next Generation.
George magazine.
A Woman Named Jackie.
Prince Charming.
Author's personal memories.

Bibliography

Andersen, Christopher. *Madonna Unauthorized*. New York, NY: Bantam-Doubleday-Dell. 1991.

Bly, Nellie. *The Kennedy Men: Three Generations of Sex, Scandal, and Secrets*. New York, NY: Kensington Books. 1996.

Brown, Peter Harry and Patte B. Barham. *Marilyn: The Last Take*. New York, NY: Dutton. 1992.

Burke, Richard E. and William and Marilyn Hoffer. *The Senator: My Ten Years with Ted Kennedy*. New York, NY: St. Martin's Press. 1992.

Burns, James MacGregor. *John Kennedy: A Political Profile*. New York, NY: Harcourt Brace. 1960.

Butler, George. *Arnold Schwarzenegger: A Portrait*. New York, NY: Simon and Schuster. 1990.

Chellis, Marcia. *The Joan Kennedy Story: Living with the Kennedys*. New York, NY: Simon and Schuster. 1960.

Collier, Peter and David Horowitz. *The Kennedys: An American Drama*. New York, NY: Summit. 1984.

Crivello, Kirk. *Fallen Angels: The Lives and Untimely Deaths of 14 Hollywood Beauties*. Secaucus, NJ: Citadel Press. 1988.

Davis, John H. *The Kennedys: Dynasty and Disaster*. New York, NY: Sure Sellers. 1991.

David, Lester. *Good Ted/Bad Ted: The Two Faces of Edward M. Kennedy*. Secaucus, NJ: Birch Lane Press. 1993.

Dinneen, Joseph F. *The Kennedy Family*. Boston, MA: Little Brown. 1959.

Fontaine, Joan. *No Bed of Roses*. New York, NY: William Morrow. 1978.

Gibson, Barbara and Ted Schwarz. *The Kennedys: The Third Generation*. New York, NY: Thunder's Mouth Press. 1993.

———. *Rose Kennedy: A Life of Faith, Family, and Tragedy*. Secaucus, NJ: Birch Lane Press. 1995.

Goodwin, Doris Kearns. *The Fitzgeralds and The Kennedys: An American Saga*. New York, NY: Simon and Schuster. 1987.

Hamilton, Nigel. *JFK: Reckless Youth*. New York, NY: Random House. 1992.

Heymann, C. David. *A Woman Named Jackie*. New York, NY: Birch Lane Press. 1994.

Higham, Charles and Roy Moseley. *Cary Grant: The Lonely Heart*. New York, NY: Harcourt Brace Jovanovich. 1989.

Higham, Charles. *Marlene: The Life of Marlene Dietrich*. New York, NY: W.W. Norton. 1977.

———. *Rose: The Life and Times of Rose Fitzgerald Kennedy*. New York, NY: Pocket Books. 1995.

Kelley, Kitty. *His Way: The Unauthorized Biography of FrankSinatra*. New York, NY: Bantam. 1986.

Kessler, Ronald. *The Sins of the Father: Joseph P. Kennedy and the Dynasty He Founded*. New York, NY: Warner Books. 1996.

King, Norman. *Madonna: The Book*. New York, NY: William Morrow. 1991.

Lawford, Patricia Seaton. *The Peter Lawford Story*. New York, NY: Carroll and Graf. 1988.

Lasky, Victor. *JFK: The Man and the Myth*. New Rochelle, NY: Arlington House. 1966.

Leigh, Wendy. *Prince Charming: The John F. Kennedy Jr. Story*. New York, NY: Dutton. 1993.

Marion, Frances. *Off With Their Heads: A Serio-Comic Tale of Hollywood*. New York, NY: MacMillan. 1972.

Martin, Ralph G. *A Hero for Our Times: An Intimate Story of the Kennedy Years*. New York, NY: MacMillan. 1983.

———. *Seeds of Destruction: Joe Kennedy and His Sons*. New York, NY: Putnam. 1995.

Mills, Judie. *John F. Kennedy*. New York, NY: Franklin Watts. 1988.

O'Connor, Patrick. *Dietrich: Style and Substance*. New York, NY: Dutton. 1992.

Oppenheimer, Jerry. *The Other Mrs. Kennedy: Ethel Skakel Kennedy*. New York, NY: St. Martin's Press. 1994.

Paris, Barry. *Garbo*. New York, NY: Alfred A. Knopf. 1995.

———. *Louise Brooks*. New York, NY: Alfred A. Knopf. 1989.

Quirk, Lawrence J. *Robert Francis Kennedy*. Los Angeles, CA: Holloway House. 1968.

———. *The Films of Gloria Swanson*. Secaucus, NJ: Citadel Press. 1984.

———. *The Films of William Powell*. Secaucus, NJ: Citadel Press. 1986.

———. *Photoplay Anthology*. New York, NY: Dover. 1971.

———. *Fasten Your Seat Belts: The Passionate Life of Bette Davis*. New York, NY: William Morrow. 1990.

———. *Norma: The Story of Norma Shearer*. New York, NY: St. Martin's Press. 1988.

———. *The Films of Paul Newman*. Secaucus, NJ: Citadel Press. 1971.

———. *The Films of Warren Beatty*. Secaucus, NJ: CitadelPress. 1979.

Reeves, Richard. *President Kennedy: Profile of Power*. New York, NY: Simon and Schuster. 1993.

Reeves, Thomas C. *A Question of Character: A Life of John F. Kennedy*. New York, NY: The Free Press-MacMillan. 1991.

Schlesinger, Arthur M. *Robert Kennedy and His Times*. New York, NY: Ballantine Books. 1978.

Schoell, William. *The Films of Al Pacino*. Secaucus, NJ: Citadel Press. 1995.

Sherrill, Robert. *The Last Kennedy*. New York, NY: The Dial Press. 1976.

Shevey, Sandra. *The Marilyn Scandal*. New York, NY: William Morrow. 1987.

Slevin, Jonathan and Maureen Spagnolo. *Kennedys: The Next Generation*. Bethesda, MD: National Press Books. 1990.

Spada, James. *Peter Lawford: The Man Who Kept the Secrets*. New York, NY: Bantam. 1991.

Speck, Gregory. *Hollywood Royalty*. New York, NY: Birch Lane Press. 1992.

Spoto, Donald. *Blue Angel: The Life of Marlene Dietrich*. New York, NY: Doubleday. 1992.

————. *Marilyn Monroe*. New York, NY: HarperCollins. 1993.

Stack, Robert and Mark Evans. *Straight Shooting*. New York, NY: MacMillan. 1980.

Swanson, Gloria. *Swanson on Swanson*. New York, NY: Random House. 1980.

Tierney, Gene. *Self-Portrait*. New York, NY: Wyden Books. 1979.

Wayne, Jane Ellen. *Marilyn's Men*. New York, NY: St. Martin's Press. 1992.

Whalen, Richard J. *The Founding Father: The Story of Joseph P. Kennedy*. New York, NY: New American Library. 1964.

PERIODICALS

Photoplay, Quirk's Reviews, Films in Review, George, New York, Vanity Fair, TV-Radio-Movie Guide, Cosmopolitan, Screen Stars, Movie World, The New York Times, New York Post, NY Daily News, Variety, People, Life, Ladies Home Journal, New Yorker, Gentleman's Quarterly, McCall's, Redbook, Time, Newsweek.

Index

A

Actor's Studio, 211, 260
Advise and Consent, 160
Agee, James, 199
Albee, Edward, 41
Aldrich Family, The, 66
Alexander, Susan, 122
All My Children, 191, 195
All Quiet on the Western Front, 126
All the President's Men, 277
Allison, May: career of, 25–26;
    Dietrich, Marlene, counseling,
    123; and Garbo, Greta, 70, 71;
    and Quirk, James, 1, 25–26, 29;
    as widow, 46–48
Allyson, June, 164, 177, 318–20
American males, thwarted creativity of,
    255
American Mercury, 24
Andrews, Dana, 152
Angel, 126
anger, 217
Arsenio Hall Show, 325
As You Desire Me, 71
Asher, Jerry: on Kennedy, Jacqueline,
    213; on Lawford, Peter, 187,
    319; on Mansfield, Jayne, 267,
    268; on Monroe, Marilyn, 212,
    215; on Remick, Lee, 307–8,
    309
Ayres, Lew, 110

B

Bacharach, Burt, 311
Back Street, 65, 150
Ball, Lucille, 112

Bara, Theda, 25
Barlow, Billy. *See* Connery, William P.,
    Jr.
Barrowman, John, 281, 311
Barrymore, Lionel, 306
Beatty, Warren, 271–72, 276–77, 344
Beery, Wallace, 50
Benchley, Robert, 16
Bennett, Barbara, 68
Bennett, Constance (Connie): and
    Kennedy, Joe, affair, 44, 69; and
    Marquis de la Falaise, 58; and
    Swanson, Gloria, 67–68, 69
Bennett, Joan, 68–69
Berman, Pandro, 112
Bessette, Carolyn, 349
Bessie, Alvah, 279
Best Foot Forward, 320
Best Man, The, 273
Bethlehem Steel Yard, 19
Beulah, 183
Billings, Fred, 136
Billings, Kirk Le Moyne (Lem)
    appearance of, 134
    drug use of, 339
    heart problems of, 140
    homosexuality of, 133–34
    Kennedys: considering book on,
        137; loyalty to, 137; treatment
        by, 133–34, 136
    Kennedy, Jack: accounts of, 126–27,
        132, 138, 150, 213; relationship
        with, 133–38, 141
    on Kennedy, Jacqueline, payoff, 212
    and Lawford, Chris, 193–94
    on Marilyn-JFK involvement, 213

pedigree of, 135
on *PT-109*, 273
rumors about, 140
on Tierney, Gene and JFK, 153, 158
White House room for, 138
Biograph, 293, 295, 299, 301
Bisset, Jacqueline, 274
Blue Angel, The, 121, 124
Bogart, Humphrey, 157
Bohemian Grove, 45
Boles, John, 65
Boston: banks, 10; East, xiii, 9, 15; Irish immigrants in, 9–10; North End, xiii, 11, 15; politics of, 4, 5, 11–12
Boston Advertiser, 14
Boston College Law School, 194
Boston Record-American, xi
Boston University, xii
Bouvier, Jacqueline. *See* Kennedy, Jacqueline
Bouvier, Lee. *See* Radziwill, Princess Lee
box-office-poison stars, 126
Bramble Bush, The, 311
Brando, Marlon, 210
Brat Pack, 201
Brent, Evelyn, 26, 37, 306
Brokaw, Tom, 328
Bronxville, 26
Brookline, 18
Brown Daily Herald, 341
Browne, Jackson, 347
Browning, Elizabeth Barrett, 122
Bryn Mawr, 112
Buckingham Hotel (New York), 29
Bus Stop, 211, 218
Bush, George, 333
Byrnes, Ed, 272
Byron, Walter, 123, 300–1

C

Cacoyannis, Michael, 149
Camille, 294
Cape Cod, 27
Capote, Truman, 148–50
Carroll, Nancy: career of, 64, 65, 66; and Kennedy, Joe, affair, 27,

63–65, 66, 123; on Kennedy, Rose, 66–67; on Moore, Eddie, 67; on Quirk, James, 65–66
Cassini, Oleg, 6, 152, 154
Castro, Fidel, 200
Catholic conventions, 15–16
Catholic schools, 9
CBS, 281
CBS Morning News, 328
censorship, 21, 24, 51, 124
Central Park West, 281–82, 311
Chaplin, Charlie, 24, 295
Chappaquiddick, xv, 255
Chappaquiddick (film treatment), 281
Charlie, 273
Chatterton, Ruth, 64
Chicago, 23
Chicken a la King, 67
Choate, 133, 134
Cimber, Matt, 262
Citizen Kane, 122
Clark, Ramsey, 194, 197
Cleveland society, 48
Clift, Montgomery, 201, 219
Cody, Lew, 296
Colbert, Claudette, 114
Colleran, Bill, 307, 308–9
Collins, Stephen, 275
Colman, Ronald, 131
Columbia, 168
Columbia Trust Company, 10, 17, 19
Colvin, Edwin, 22–23
Communist threat, 104, 107
Conan the Barbarian, 332
Conan the Destroyer, 332
Connery, Bridget Clancy, 11
Connery, Lawrence J., xii, 5
Connery, Patrick, 11
Connery, William P., Jr., xii, 5, 11, 118, 120
Connery, William P., Sr., xii, 5, 119
Constant Nymph, The, 317
Cooper, Gary, 121
Cooper, Jackie, 177
Corman, Roger, 270
Cosmopolitan, 2, 45
Costello, Frank, 20
Council of Physical Fitness, 333
Coward, Noel, 126, 188

Crawford, Cindy, 343
Crawford, Joan: helping others, 75–76;
    and Kennedys, 72–73; and
    Monroe, Marilyn, 216, 218
Crews, Laura Hope, 55, 294–95
Crosby, Bing, 200
"Cuban nuisance", 200
Cukor, George: on Kennedy, Joe, 112;
    and Lawford, Peter, 181, 182,
    187–88; on Monroe, Marilyn,
    210, 211, 216; *Something's Got to
    Give*, 204–5
Cummins, Peggy, 311–13
Curley, James Michael, 18
Currier, Guy, 16, 19
Cutting Edge with Maria Shriver, 321

D

Dandridge, Dorothy, 183–84
Davies, Marion: career of, 122; as
    mistress of Hearst, William
    Randolph, 30, 116; and
    Kennedy, Joe, 116–17
Davis, Bette, 59, 169, 217, 218
Davis, John H., 16–17
De Mille, Cecil B., 50, 305
De Niro, Robert, 343
Dead Ringer, 169
Dear Phoebe, 168
dearos, 11. *See also* Boston, politics of
Death of a President, The, 286
Depend Undergarments, 318
Depression, Great, 103–4
Derr, E.B., 19, 40, 43
Destry Rides Again, 129, 130, 132
Devane, William, 282
Devil's Holiday, The, 64
Devil's Own, The, 317
Dickinson, Angie, 281, 309–11
Dickinson, Gene, 311
Dietrich, Marlene: career of, 121, 124,
    126, 128–29; and Kennedy, Jack,
    127, 132; and Kennedy, Joe, 121,
    122–32; in *Scarlet Empress*, 297;
    WWII, during, 130–31
DiMaggio, Joe: and Monroe, Marilyn,
    208, 220–21; and Monroe,
    Marilyn, funeral, 203–4, 216;
    and Sinatra, Frank, 203–4

Dougherty, Kathryn ("Kay Dee"): on
    Long, Ray, 28; as *Photoplay*
    owner, 46–47; on Quirk-Allison
    marriage, 29; and Quirk, James,
    working with, 23
Douglas, Melvyn, 59
Downey, Morton, 68
Dozier, Bill, 318
Dragonwyck, 151
Drake, Tom: on Gardner, Ava, 186; and
    Lawford, Peter, affair with,
    180–81; on Lawford, Peter, 184,
    188
Drayne, Richard, 289
Du Barry, Madame, 266
Dunne, Dominick, 280
Dunne, Irene, 65
Durante, Jimmy, 199
Durbin, Deanna, 145

E

Eagle's Talons, The, 96
East Boston. *See* Boston: East
Easter Parade, 183
Eastman, Robert M., 22
Edward, Prince of Wales, 33
Eighteenth Amendment. *See*
    Prohibition
Ellis, Robert, 25
Enemy Within, The: 270–71
Enwright, Fred, 13
Etheridge, Eric, 344
Ettinger, Margaret, 30, 315
Evans, Delight, 203, 312, 313
Executive Action, 276
Exhibitors Herald, 23
Exner, Judith Campbell, 139, 200

F

Face in the Crowd, A, 307
Fairbanks, Douglas, Jr., 72
Fairbanks, Douglas, Sr., 49, 299
Famous Players-Lasky, 305
fan magazine: Allison, May, in, 25;
    Dietrich, Marlene, in, 131;
    Kennedy, Jackie, in, 286–90,
    292; Lawford, Peter, in, 185
Farmer, Michael, 59
Father Takes a Wife, 60

Fay, Red, 310, 314
FBO. *See* Film Booking Office
Ferguson, Helen, 212, 220–21, 305–6
Film Booking Office (FBO): mergers
    and deals concerning, 41, 43;
    purchase of, 33; stars at, 304;
    Westerns, 96, 302
First Love, 145
First National, 42, 301
Fitzgeralds: Lodges, animosity toward,
    297
Fitzgerald, John F. ("Honey Fitz"): dis-
    honesty and graft of, 13; as
    "higher-class Irish," 15, 16; and
    JFK campaign, 4–5; Kennedy,
    Patrick, relationship with,
    12–13; as "movie magnate," 33;
    political career of, xii, 11–12, 18,
    19; Quirk, James, helping,
    12–13; and Swanson-Kennedy
    affair, 56; womanizing of, 14, 18;
    youth of, xiii
Fitzgerald, Josie, 14, 18
Five Easy Pieces, 271
Flag Room, 146–48
Fonda, Jane, 324
Fonda, Peter, 272
Fontaine, Joan, 113, 316–18
Fool There Was, A, 25
Ford, Barbara, 180
Fore River Shipyard, 19, 104
Fox Films, 303
Franciscus, James, 274–75
Free Soul, A, 306
From Here to Eternity, 201
Front Page, 6

G

Gabin, Jean, 126
Gable, Clark, 72, 204, 209, 222
Garbo, Greta: and Kennedy, Joe,
    69–72; Oscar nomination, 64; in
    Photoplay, 66
Gardner, Ava, 185–86, 202
Gardner, Hy, 287
Gargan, Ed, 44
Garland, Judy, 177, 180, 183
Garner, John Nance, 104
Garrison, Jim, 277
Gay Illiterate, 75

Gentlemen Prefer Blondes, 211
George, 343–44; contents, 271, 344;
    Monroes review in, 283; on
    Murphy Brown, 346
Giancana, Sam, 20, 200
Gibson, Barbara, 325–26, 341–42,
    347–48
Gilbert, John, 71
Gilda, 185
Gish, Lillian, 25
Gloria Productions, 42
Goldwyn, Samuel, 59, 305
Gone with the Wind, 294
Goodbye Again, 209
Goulding, Edmund (Eddie), 55, 69,
    295
Gowens, Kip, 307
Grady, Billy, 189
Grahame, Gloria, 199
Grand Hotel, 70
Grange, Red, 34, 40–41
Granger, Farley, 148, 149–50, 180
Grant, Cary, 317
Grayson, Kathryn, 199
Great Romantic Films, The, 255
Greed, 53–54
Greek Tycoon, The, 274–75
Greenwich Village parties, 47
Griffith, D.W., 293, 299
Griffith, Melanie, 350
Guthman, Ed, 288

H

Haag, Christina, 340, 342
Hachett Filipacchi Magazines, 344
Hagood, Wesley, 310
Haines, Billy, 182
Halliwell, Leslie, 273, 276
Hamilton, Nigel, 312
Hardin, Ty, 273
Hargitay, Mickey, 261, 262
Harty, Chris, 340–41
Harvard, 9, 15, 135, 154
Harvard Business School seminar on
    movies, 35
Hatfield, Hurd, 167, 187
Haver, Phyllis, 37–38, 298–99
Havilland, Olivia de, 317
Hawks, Howard, 311
Hayden Stone and Company, 19

Hays Office, 65, 124. *See also* censorship
Hays, Will, 21, 24
Hayward, Leland, 111
Hayworth, Rita, 185
Hearst, William Randolph: estate of, 117; and FDR nomination, 104; magazines of, 29; and Marion, Frances, 77; mistress of, 30, 116, 122; movies of, 116; newspapers of, 6, 116, 117; prissiness of, 121–22
Heffron, Richard, 274
Heiress, The, 61
Henderson, Daniel, 24
Henie, Sonja, 314–16
Hepburn, Katharine, 109, 111–12, 297
Hepburn, Tom, 112
Hertz, John, 21
Heymann, C. David, 275
Hill, George William, 100–1
Hitchcock, Alfred, 180
Hitler, Adolph, 126
Holliday, Judy, 168
Hollywood aristocracy, 39
Hollywood Ice Review Extravaganzas, 315
Hollywood Royalty, 221–22
Hollywood Stars, The, 286
homosexuality, 167
Honey Fitz. *See* Fitzgerald, John F.
Hoover, Herbert, 103
Hoover, J. Edgar, 182
Hopkins, Miriam, 29, 46–48, 306
Hopper, Hedda, 100, 117, 308
horse operas, 40
Horsemen, 40, 44
Hotel Bellevue, xiii
House Labor Committee, 5, 118
Howard, Sidney, 43, 56
Howe, Louis Henry, 105
Howey, Walter, 6, 20–21, 117, 118
Hudson Riverkeeper Fund, 191
Hurst, Fannie, 65
Huston, John, 208
Hyde, Johnny, 279

I

I Blow My Horn, 305
I'm for Roosevelt, 108, 269

Iceland, 315
Immortals, The, 280
In the Boom Boom Room, 340
Indiscreet, 58
Intimate Visit to the Homes of Film Magnates, An, 36
Ireland: ambassadorship post, 105, 326
Irish-Americans: Dietrich, Marlene, on, 127, 131
Irish Arts Theater, 340
Irish curse, 119
Irish immigrants, xiii, 9, 10, 11
Irish Protection Squad, 20
It Happened in Brooklyn, 199
It Should Happen to You, 168
It's a Pleasure, 315

J

Jacqueline Bouvier Kennedy, 275
James, Henry, 314
Jannings, Emil, 121, 124
Jerome, Stephen, 256
Jesse L. Lasky Feature Play Company, 305
JFK, 277–78
Johnson, Julian, 23
Johnson, Lyndon, 271
Johnson, Van, 177, 187
Jones, Jennifer, 179
Judas of Wall Street, 107

K

Kalem Studios, 293
KAO. *See* Keith-Albee-Orpheum
Kane, Bob, xvi, 51, 153
Kazan, Elia, 307
Keith-Albee-Orpheum (KAO), 41, 42
Kennedy, Bobby. *See* Kennedy, Robert F.
Kennedy, Bobby, Jr. *See* Kennedy, Robert, Jr.
Kennedy, Bridget Murphy, 11
Kennedy, Caroline. *See* Schlossberg, Caroline Kennedy
Kennedy, David: creativity of, 347; death of, 193; drug use of, 255, 339; and Lawford, Chris, 195
Kennedy, Edward Moore (Ted): birth, 18, 141; Chappaquiddick, 255, 281; as father, 256; and

Hollywood ladies, 256; and
Lawford, Chris, 193
Kennedy, Ethel, 338
Kennedy, Eunice, 18, 137, 193, 194
Kennedy family: and Billings, Lem,
136; and fan magazine coverage
of Jackie, 288–92; good in,
256–57; Hollywood obsession
of, xvi; and homosexuality, 134;
image of, 337–38; and Lawford,
Peter, 169–70, 189; and media,
xv, 7; media manipulations, 269,
280; pressures of, 193; as publicity seeking, 285, 290, 291, 292;
as soap opera, xiv–xv, 285; television show about, 282–83;
thwarted creativity in, 255, 291;
as vulgar, 150
Kennedy, Jacqueline:
fan magazine coverage, 286–90, 292
father-in-law, 138–39, 212
gay men as confidants, 139
Kennedy family approval, 159
Kennedy, Jack, relationship with,
138–39
Lawford, Peter, 338
Monroe, Marilyn, 213, 214
movies about, 274–75
opinions on: Beatty, Warren, 271;
Dickinson, Angie, 139; Exner,
Judith Campbell, 139; father-in-
law, 38; Hannah, Daryl, 348;
homosexuality, 140; Kennedy,
Rosemary, 139; Mansfield,
Jayne, 139; Monroe, Marilyn,
139; Tierney, Gene, 139
Sinatra, Frank, 205, 338
son: controlling life of, 339; hopes
for, 140; hostility toward acting
of, 337–38, 340, 345
womanizing, attitude toward,
138–39, 212
Kennedy, Jean. See Smith, Jean
Kennedy
Kennedy, Joan, 212, 256
Kennedy, Joe:
Allison, May, 46–47
ambassador to Great Britain, 126,
127, 130

ambitions, xiv
anti-Semitism, latent, 36
banking and finance, 16–17, 19,
20–21. See also Kennedy, Joe:
Hollywood, wheeler-dealings in
Bennett, Constance, affair with, 68,
69
big business: contempt for, 108;
support for, 118–19
Billings, Lem, feelings about,
134–35
bootlegging, 19–20, 40, 119–20. See
also Kennedy, Joe: liquor interests
booze, opinion on, 31–32
Brent, Evelyn, affair with, 26, 37,
306
Carroll, Nancy, affair with, 63–65,
66
Catholism, 38, 56
Connery family, dislike for, 118–20
Crawford, Joan, 72
Davies, Marion, relationship with,
116–17
Dietrich, Marlene, relationship
with, 121, 122–32, 297
disregard for conventions, 55
ego, 53, 60
failure, reaction to, 55, 57
father-in-law, 33–34
FDR: campaign, 103–4; government post with, 104–8. See also
Kennedy, Joe: ambassador to
Great Britain
Film Booking Office (FBO), 33–34,
40–41, 96
films. See producing
financial genius, 21
Fontaine, Joan, 316
fortune, 103, 108
Garbo, Greta, pursuit of, 69–72
Gloria Productions, 42, 43
goody-goodies, opinion on, 285
Harvard, 15, 16
Haver, Phyllis, affair with, 38, 298
health, 44. See also Kennedy, Joe:
ulcers
Hearst, William Randolph, relationship with, 116–18

help for others, 20–21, 75
Henie, Sonja, 316
Hepburn, Katharine, 109, 111–12
Hollywood: actresses in, 37–38; family obsession with, xvi; reputation in, 34, 40; wheeler-dealings in, 39–43
homosexuality, views on, 134–35, 192
Horsemen, 40
hypocrisy, 36, 38, 53, 124
I'm for Roosevelt, 108
Kennedy, Jacqueline, paying off, 138–39, 212
Kennedy, John: fears about, 134–35; jealous of, 130; relationship with, 44, 155–56
Kennedy, Rose: courting, 17; dating, 15; marriage to, 18; meeting, 13; relationship with, 27–28, 44. *See also* Kennedy, Rose
Kennedy, Rosemary, 57, 119
ladies' man image, 64
Lasky, Jesse, relationship with, 304
Lawford, Peter, investigation of, 169, 182
liquor business, 106, 108. *See also* Kennedy, Joe: bootlegging
liquor business, curse of, 119–20
Lodges, hatred for, 297
Long, Ray, 32
media manipulation, 269–70
miserliness, 39
money: as priority, 16; as power, 108, 109
Monroe, Marilyn, payoff, 213
Moore, Eddie, friendship with, 141–43. *See also* Moore, Eddie
mother, relationship with, 9–10, 14–16
movies: bigwigs of, 35–36, 39; future of, 36; interests in, 21; and working class, views on, 32
Nazi appeasement policies, 127, 130–32
"pants-pressers," 32, 125
Paramount, 114–15
poor and underprivileged, views on, 17

producing: Dietrich, Marlene, film, 128; at FBO, 34–35, 40, 96; Swanson, Gloria, films, 54–55, 295; talent for, 53
prostitution, 45, 63, 113
public image, 1
publicity seeking, 7, 125, 132
Quirk, James (Jimmy): advice from, 31, 33, 34–35, 304; envy for, 1, 2, 25, 26, 28, 29; views on, 22, 30, 32
RKO, 109
Rogers, Ginger, 109–11
Roosevelt, Eleanor, 105–6
salaries and fees, 41, 109, 114, 117
Securities and Exchange Commission chairman, 106–8, 118
self-confidence, 15
self-made man, 9
Sinatra, Frank, 201
stocks, kiting, 20–21. *See also* Securities and Exchange Commission
stroke, 76, 222
studio consultant, 109, 114–15
Swanson, Gloria: affair, 3, 28, 52, 55–57; encounters after affair, 59–60; films together, 53–55; "friendly" parting, 64; jealousy over, 300, 301–2; meeting, 51; preventing her pictures, 60; reaction to her comeback, 60–61; unloading, 43
Thomson, Fred: death of, 101–2; friendship with, 76–77, 95–98, 141
trust funds, children's, 44
ulcers, 27, 33, 38
upward climber, xiv, 111
West Fifty-Eighth Street establishment, 2
West, Mae, 115
women: appeal to, 73; attitude toward, 155, 318; reputation with, 306; taste in, 115, 116
WWI, during, 19
Yankee aristocracy: dislike for, 135, 297; opinion of, 32; snubs by, 15;
Kennedy, Joe, Jr.: birth of, 18; as bully,

136; death of, 7–8, 131; on
   Grange, Red, 40–41; as teenager,
   xii
Kennedy, Joe, III, 255–56
Kennedy, John F. (Jack)
   Allyson, June, 318–20
   assasination fictionalization, 276–78
   back problems, 138, 211, 313
   Billings, Lem, relationship with,
     133–38
   birth, 18
   books, 151, 269
   campaigns: for Congress, 4–8, 151;
     for Senate, 297
   Catholicism, 154
   cavalier attitude, 312–13, 314
   charisma and charm, 145, 154, 219
   common touch, 157
   Crawford, Joan, 72–73
   Cummins, Peggy, 311–12
   Dickinson, Angie, 309–10
   Dietrich, Marlene, 126–27, 132
   father: heir to power of, 7, 131–32;
     influence of, 3–4; relationship
     with, 44, 155–56; womanizing,
     reaction to, 316
   Fontaine, Joan, 316
   Grange, Red, 40–41
   health, 7, 8. *See also* Kennedy, John
     F.: back problems
   Henie, Sonja, affair with, 314–16
   Hollywood: as escape, 312, 313; in
     1940s, xvi, 6, 73, 146–48; sexual
     dynamism in, 319; starlets of,
     150
   Kennedy, Joe, Jr., relationship with,
     7, 136
   Lawford, Peter, treatment of, 170
   Mansfield, Jayne, affair with,
     262–67
   Monroe, Marilyn: affair with, xvi,
     208, 210–15; mistreatment of
     220; movies about, 279–80
   Nixon, Richard, 278
   oral sex, 133, 263
   political campaigns, 4–8, 151, 297
   PT-109: incident, 7; movie, opinion
     of, 271–72, 273
   Quirk family, xii
   Quirk, Jimmy, opinion on, 5

   sexual preferences, 211
   Stack, Robert, friendship with,
     146–48
   Sullavan, Margaret, meeting, 150
   sympathy, 153–54
   threatened manhood, 213
   Tierney, Gene: affair with, 6, 151,
     152–60; on JFK death, 161
   Williams, Tennesse, 150
   womanizing, 138, 145, 159
Kennedy, John F., Jr. (John-John)
   actor, 337, 340–43, 346
   George: 343–44, 345; in magazine,
     271, 277
   girlfriend, 349
   Hollywood involvements: Griffith,
     Melanie, 350; Hannah, Daryl,
     347–48; , 347–50; Madonna,
     348–49; Roberts, Julia, 349–50
   legal career, 342
   mother: resentment of, 345; run-
     ning life, 339–40
   relationships, 140
   television depiction, 281
Kennedy, Kathleen, xii, 18, 134, 169
Kennedy, Mary Hickey, 9–10, 14, 16
Kennedy men: aping each other,
   255–56; macho attitudes toward
   women, 255
Kennedy, Patricia. See Lawford,
   Patricia Kennedy
Kennedy, Patrick ("PJ") (Joe's father),
   9, 10–11, 12–13, 256
Kennedy, Robert F. (Bobby): as attorney general, 200, 307–8; birth,
   18; as child, xii; and fan magazine coverage of Jackie, 288; and
   Kennedy, Jack, 220, 307; and
   Monroe, Marilyn, xvi, 208, 214,
   220; and Monroe, Marilyn, fic-
   tional account of, 280; movie
   about, 270–71; and Newman,
   Paul, 270; presidential campaign,
   291; and Remick, Lee, affair,
   307–8; senate campaign, 271
Kennedy, Robert, Jr. (Bobby): and
   Billings, Lem, 137, 140, 194;
   drug use of, 137, 193, 339
Kennedy, Rose Fitzgerald
   Carroll, Nancy, 66–67

daughter Rosemary, 119
disappointment, 15
fan magazine coverage of Jackie, 292
father's womanizing, 18, 27–28
in Hollywood, 96
Kennedy, Joe: affairs, attitude toward, 27, 55–56; dating, 15; courtship, 17; marriage, 18; meeting, 13; relationship, 44, 98, 119, 255
Lawford, Peter, opinion of, 169
liquor business, 120
marriage, view on, 28
Quirk, James, 14, 28
social polish, 16
Kennedy, Rosemary, 18, 57, 119–20, 153, 161
Kennedy, Teddy, Jr., 256–57
Kennedys: Dynasty and Disaster, The, 17
Kerwin, Lance, 274
Kirkland, Jack, 63, 123
Kismet, 131
Kogan, Lisa, 283
Korda, Michael, 280

L
La Hiff, Billy, 64
Lancaster, Burt, 276
Lansky, Meyer, 20
Lasky, Jesse L., 21, 304–5
Last Action Hero, 333
Latin School, 14, 135
Laura (original), 152
Laura (remake), 148–50, 345
Lawford, Christopher Kennedy: as actor, 195, 197; as also-ran, xvi; and Billings, Lem, 137; childhood of, 192; as counselor, 194–95; drug problem of, 137, 172, 192–93, 339; and father, 166, 171–72, 194; future of, 197; getting act together, 194; and Kennedy family, 192, 193; as unfulfilled, 191–92
Lawford, Lady May, 164, 181, 189–90
Lawford, Patricia Kennedy: birth, 18; divorce, 171, 193; husband's affairs, 308–9; and Marilyn-JFK involvement, 213–14; marriage,

xvi, 169–70, 309; Very Special Arts, 191
Lawford, Patricia Seaton, 172, 195, 256
Lawford, Peter
Allyson, June, 319
bisexuality, 164, 167, 184, 190
career, 163–65, 167–69
children, 166, 171–72, 192, 194, 195
Cukor, George, 187–88
Dandridge, Dorothy, affair with, 183–84
death, 172
decline, 168–69, 171–72; reasons for, 173–74, 178
Drake, Tom, affair with, 180–81
drugs and alcohol, 171
England, longing for, 174
Gardner, Ava, affair with, 185–86
Garland, Judy, 183
Hayworth, Rita, 185
hero, search for, 175–77
homosexual relationships, 164, 196
image, 165
Kennedy, Edward, 256
Kennedy, Jacqueline, sympathy of, 338
Kennedy, Jack: hero worship of, 188; Marilyn-JFK, go-between for, xvi, 188–89, 262–63, 266, 310; opinion of, 263; relationship with, 170
Kennedy, Joe, investigation by, 169
Kennedy, Patricia: marriage, xvi, 169, 309; divorce, 171
Kennedy, Robert: go-between for affair of, 307; and *Robert Francis Kennedy*, 170, 291–92
Mansfield-JFK affair, 263–64, 267
Marilyn-JFK affair, 171, 213–14
marriages, xvi, 169, 171, 309
MGM, opinion of, 183
narcissism, 188
oral sex, 188
outsider, 175
parents: mother's jealousy, 189–90; public school, views on, 175; son's devotion, 165–66
Picture of Dorian Gray, 167, 187
Robert Francis Kennedy, 170, 291–92
sex life, 179, 184, 187, 196

Sinatra, Frank, 165, 199, 200–2
    stud image, 164, 184, 186
    thoughtfulness, 165
    vixenish side, 263
    Walker, Robert, affair with, 179–80
Lawford, Robin, 195
Lawford, Sir Sidney, 164
Lawford, Sydney, 195
Lawford, Victoria, 195–96
Le Baron, William, 115
Le Moyne, Doctor Francis, 135
Leave Her to Heaven, 151–52
Lee, Howard, 157, 160, 162
Leeds, Andrea, 112
Left Hand of God, The, 157
Legion of Decency, 114. *See also* Hays,
    Will: censorship
Let's Make Love, 209
Letter from an Unknown Woman, 317
Lieber, Perry, 222
Little Women, 297
Lockwood, Harold, 25
Lodge, Henry Cabot, 296, 297
Lodge, Henry Cabot, Jr., 296, 297
Lodge, John, 296–97
Lomasney, Martin, 12
Long Goodbye, The, 332
Long, Ray, 2, 28, 29, 32, 45, 46
Longet, Claudine, 308
Lord Jeff, 164
Los Angeles, 264
Lovelight, 95
Loves of Sunya, The, 49
Loy, Myrna, 21
Luciano crime syndicate, 20
Lynn, Massachussetts, xii, xiii, 5

M
MacArthur, Charlie, 6
MacLean, Barbara Barondess, 219–20,
    221, 222, 255, 256
MacLean, Douglas, 219
MacMurray, Fred, 114
Madame X, 68
Madonna, 348–49, 344
Mafia, 20
Main Street, 322
Malone, Dorothy, 146
Mamoulian, Rouben, 72

Man of Honor, A, 20
Manchester, William, 286, 290
Mannix, Eddie, 71, 72, 113
Mansfield, Jayne, 259–68
Manski, Al, 257
Mantle, Burns, 24
Marilyn and Me, 279
Marilyn: The Untold Story, 279
Marion, Frances: career of, 77, 95–96,
    101; and Kennedy, Joe, 75–76,
    95–96, 98, 141; marriages of,
    77–78, 97, 100–1; and Thomson,
    Fred, 77–78, 97, 99–100
marquess of Hartington, 169
Marquis de la Falaise (Henri), 51, 58,
    68, 69
Martin, Dean: and Monroe, Marilyn,
    204–5, 210; on Sinatra and
    DiMaggio, 203; on Sinatra and
    Kennedys, 202
Martinson, Leslie, 273
Masterton, John, 343–44
Matter of Degree, A, 342
Maugham, Somerset, 49
Mayer, Louis B.: and Kennedy, Joe, 60,
    71; and Lawford, Peter, 167,
    169, 181–82
McAdoo, William G., 104
McClure's, 29
McGovern, George, 321
McSweeney, Myles, 6–7
Media Industry Newsletter, 343
Meet Me in St. Louis, 180
Mencken, H. L., 24
Merry Widow, The, 53
Metro-Goldwyn-Mayer (MGM):
    female stars at, 167; gay actors
    at, 182; and Hearst, William
    Randolph, 122; Lawford, Peter,
    at, 163; in 1940s, 183; publicity
    department of, 131, 176–77;
    Schary, Dore, regime, 168;
    Shearer, Norma, at, 113;
    Swanson, Gloria, at, 60
Miller, Arthur, 208–9, 211, 219
Miller, David, 276
Miller, Marilyn, 302
Million and One Nights, A, 24
Minnelli, Vincente, 183

Misfits, 204, 208–9
Mitchum, Robert, 218
Mix, Tom, 34, 38–39 302–3
Mommie Dearest, 75
Monroe, Marilyn
  abortion, 215
  at Actor's Studio, 211, 260
  as actress, 208, 216
  and Crawford, Joan, 216–17
  death of, 171, 215, 222
  and DiMaggio, Joe, 203, 220–21
  as egomaniac, 217
  funeral of, 203, 216
  with Hollywood leading men, 210
  and Kennedy, Jacqueline, 139, 213
  and Kennedy, Jack, xvi, 208, 210–15
  and Kennedy, Robert, xvi, 208
  and Kennedys, movies about,
    279–80
  and Martin, Dean, 204–5, 210
  and Miller, Arthur, 208–9, 211, 219
  in *Misfits*, 209
  and obsession with famous men,
    208
  and opinions on: Kennedy, Jack,
    219; Mansfield, Jayne, 266;
    Mitchum, Robert, 218; Rogers,
    Ginger, 218; Russell, Jane, 218
  and oral sex, 211, 221
  publicists for, 211–12
  as self-pitying and self-dramatizing,
    207
  and Sinatra, Frank, 203–4
  as victim, 207, 212, 220, 221
Monroes, The, 282–83
Montand, Yves, 209
Moore, Colleen, 6
Moore, Eddie: on Billings, Lem, 134;
    and Carroll, Nancy, 65; devotion
    of, 40, 67, 141–42; dirty work of,
    142; Kennedy named for, 44,
    141; as Kennedy pimp, 37, 63,
    110; as loyal friend, 76–77
Moore, Mary, 77, 141, 142
Moore, Owen, 299–300
Morath, Inge, 209
Morgan, Michele, 159
Morocco, 121
Motion Picture Country Home, 294

Movie and TV Guide, 276
Movie and Video Guide, 273
movie soaps, 68
Movie World, 287
movies: crossing class and culture lines,
    32; Harvard Business School
    seminar, 35; industry in 1920s,
    21; radio threat, 32; violence in,
    323
Mulhern, Mary, 302
Murphy Brown, 346
Murray, Don, 211
Murray, Mae, 53
Music in the Air, 60
My Son John, 180

N
Nazi appeasement policies, 127,
    130–32
Neilan, Marshall (Mickey): on Allison,
    May, 46; on Brent, Evelyn, 37;
    career of, 293–94, 307; Haver,
    Phyllis, affair with, 298;
    Kennedy, Joe, dislike for, 294,
    296; on Kennedy, Joe, and Eddie
    Moore, 40; on Kennedy, Joe, and
    Fred Thomson, 76; on Quirk,
    James, 24; as womanizer, 28
New Hercules in New York, 332
New York American, 117
Newman, Paul, 270
Nicholson, Jack, 270–71
1920s era, 20, 21
Nixon (film), 278
Nixon, Richard M., 160, 278, 297
No Bed of Roses, 316
Normand, Mabel, 295–96
North End. *See* Boston, North End
North, Elizabeth (Quirk, Mrs. James),
    1, 46
Novarro, Ramon, 182

O
O'Brien, Hugh, 10
O'Connell, Cardinal William, 15, 18,
    56
O'Leary, Ted, 40
Oceans 11, 311
Old Colony Realty, 16–17

Old Orchard Beach, 13
Olivier, Sir Laurence, 60, 211, 219, 260, 317
Olsson, Jeannie, 191, 194
Onassis, Aristotle, 292, 345
Onassis, Jacqueline Kennedy. *See* Kennedy, Jacqueline
One in a Million, 315
Osborne, Carl Norton, 47–48
Oscars, 24, 64
Otash, Fred, 265

P

Pagnol, Marcel, 128
Pakula, Alan J., 276–77
Palm Beach, 27
Palmer, Vera Jayne. *See* Mansfield, Jayne
"pants-pressers," 39, 42
Parallax View, The, 276
Paramount: Dietrich, Marlene, at, 123, 124, 125; financial problems of, 114; precursor of, 305; Swanson, Gloria, at, 49, 50, 61
Parkins, Barbara, 274
Parsons, Louella, 24, 75–76, 116, 121
Pasternak, Joe, 129
Pathé, 41, 42, 67
Peace Corps, 321, 327
Perfect Understanding, 60
Perkins, Tony, 209, 317, 318
Perry, Kathryn, 299
Photoplay Gold Medal, 24
Photoplay Magazine Awards, 216
Photoplay: Allison, May, in, 25–26; Dietrich, Marlene, article, 131; on Greed, 54; independence of, 24; Kennedy, Jacqueline, coverage, 288; Kennedy, Joe, in, 125; Kennedy, Rose, on, 28; Kennedys in, 5, 36, 288; Meneken, H. L., in, 24; Normand, Mabel, in, 296; as prestigious magazine, 22–24; and Quirk, James, xii, 1, 45; Quirk, Lawrence, dreams of editing, 287, 289; St. Johns, Adela Rogers, at, 306; star build-up in, 65–66; stock of, 46; Swanson, Gloria, in, 57

Pickford, Jack, 301–2
Pickford, Lottie, 301
Pickford, Mary: family, 301; husbands, 299; leading men, 95, 293 Pickford-Lasky Productions, 305; United Artists, 49
Pickford-Lasky Productions, 305
Picture of Dorian Gray, The, 164, 167
Plant, Phil, 68
Playboy of the Western World, 340–41
Plymouth plantation, 135
PM Magazine, 328
Police Woman, 311
Poor Old Bill, 164
Popular Mechanics, 22
Poster, Randy, 342
Powell, Dick, 319
Powell, William, 120
Power, Tyrone, 152, 157–58
Preminger, Otto, 160
presidential campaign: 1932, 103; 1936, 108
Prince and the Showgirl, The, 211, 219
Private Hargrove pictures, 179
Profiles in Courage, 269
Prohibition, 19–20, 106
Protestant aristocracy. *See* Yankee aristocracy
Prowse, Juliet, 210
PT-109 (movie), 7, 131, 151, 270, 271–73
Pumping Iron, 329

Q

Queen Christina, 71
Queen Kelly, 39, 42, 54, 123–24, 300–1
Quigley, Martin, 23
Quinn, Anthony, 274–75
Quirk, James R. (Jimmy)
    Allison, May, 25–26, 29
    bachelor life, 1–2
    career, 14, 22–24
    Catholic conventions, defying, 2
    death, 45–46
    Fitzgeralds, xii, 12–13
    hard times, 45
    Hearst, William Randolph, relationship with, 29–30
    Kennedy, Joe: movie advice to, xvi, 57, 123; opinion of, 15, 34–35;

relationship with, xii; and
Swanson, Gloria, affair, 49, 56
Kennedy, Rose, 14, 56
marriages, 1–2
Moore, Eddie, opinion of, 142
Photoplay: running, 22–25, 45, 46;
writing in, 54, 57, 296
sayings, 24–25
Swanson, Gloria: and Kennedy, Joe,
affair, 49, 56; opinion of, 50, 57
Von Stroheim, Erich, opinion of,
53–54
West Fifty-Eighth Street establish-
ment, 2, 45
womanizing, 28
Quirk, Joanna Carr, 11
Quirk, Lawrence: Billings, Lem, 133,
136, 137; career, xi–xii, 286, 290;
family's immigration, 11;
Fitzgerald, John, relationship
with, 4; Kennedy, Jacqueline,
policy on, 286, 291; Kennedy,
Robert, campaign, 291–92;
Kennedys, meeting, xii, 5–6;
Lawford, Peter, friendship, 163,
165–66, 168; Mansfield, Jayne,
interview, 259–61; protesting
exploitation of Jackie in fan
magazines, 287–90
Quirk, Martin, 11, 14, 28
Quirk, Mary Haven, 11
Quirk, Mary Reddy, 11–12
Quirk, William, 11
Quirk's Reviews, 276

R

radio threat to movies, 32
Radio-Keith-Orpheum (RKO), 43, 60,
109
Radziwill, Princess Lee (Lee Bouvier)
148–49, 345
Raimu, 128
Rain, 49
Ramsaye, Terry, 24, 36, 125
Randall, Carl, 175–76
Rat Pack: and Kennedy, Jacqueline,
338; Lawford, Peter, in, 165,
168, 173; and Monroe, Marilyn,
210; and Sinatra, Frank, 201
Razor's Edge, The, 157

RCA Photophone, 41, 43
Reagan, Ronald, 348
Rebecca, 317
Reid, Jim, 214, 268
Remarque, Erich Maria, 126
Remick, Lee, 307–9
Republic, xii, 5, 12
Rio Bravo, 311
Riverdale, 26
RKO, 43, 60, 109
Robert Francis Kennedy (book), 137, 170,
291–92
Robert Francis Kennedy Tennis
Tournament, 330
Roberts, Julia, 349–50
Robertson, Cliff, 272–73
Roger, Earl, 306
Rogers, Ginger, 109–11, 218
Roosevelt, Eleanor, 105–6
Roosevelt, Franklin D., 19, 59, 103–4,
106
Roosevelt, Jimmy, 106
Rose Elizabeth, 3
Ross, Herbert, 148, 345
Rubens, Alma, 45
Russell, Jane, 218
Russell, William, 306
Ryan, Elizabeth "Toodles," 14, 18, 27
Ryan, Robert, 276

S

Sadie Thompson, 49, 51, 53
Salinger, Pierre, 271
San Francisco Examiner, 77, 117
San Simeon, 116
Sarnoff, David, 41, 43, 109
Scarlet Empress, The, 297
Schary, Dore, 168
Schenck, Joseph, 32, 58, 59, 60
Schiffrin, Lalo, 275
Schlossberg, Caroline Kennedy,
256–57, 341
Schoell, William, 334
Schwab, Charles, 19
Schwarzenegger, Arnold: career of,
331–34; in *Jayne Mansfield Story,
The*, 261–62; and Kennedy fami-
ly, 325, 331; marriage of, xvi,
321–26; marriage, future of,
334–35; profit motive of, 324;

public image of, 327; Republican politics of, 323, 325, 333; Shriver, Maria, meeting, 329–30; and Waldheim, Kurt, 333; violence in movies of, 323
Screen Stars, 287
Season in Purgatory, A, 280
Secretary of Treasury, 105
Securities and Exchange Commission (SEC), 106–8
Self-Portrait, 161–62
Selznick, David O., 179
Sennett, Mack, 295, 298
Seven Sinners, 132
Seventh Massachusetts District, 5
Sex Symbol, The, 279
Shearer, Norma, 64, 113, 122
Shriver, Eunice, 321, 322, 326-27
Shriver, Maria: on career and motherhood, 322, 334; career of, 321, 328–29; family's influence on, 327; and Kennedy family, 330–31; marriage of, xvi, 321–26; marriage, future of, 334–35; mother's influence on, 321, 322; as privileged, 324–25, 328–29; Schwarzenegger, Arnold, meeting, 329–30; strict upbringing of, 322, 325; womanizing, attitude toward, 330
Shriver, R. Sargent, 321, 326, 327–28
Sieber, Rudy, 123, 126
Signoret, Simone, 209
silent screen, 32
Silver Cord, The, 294
Silver King, 95–96, 99, 302
Sinatra, Frank: and Dickinson-JFK affair, 309–10; and DiMaggio, Joe, 203–4; gays, tolerance of, 201; helping others, 75–76; and Kennedys, 200, 205; and Lawford, Peter, 165, 168, 173, 199, 200–2; and Monroe, Marilyn, 203–4, 210; Rat Pack of, 201
Sinatra, Nancy, 203
Since You Went Away, 179
Sins of Rachel Cade, The, 311
Skakel, Thomas, 280
Slatzer, Bob, 279
Smart Set, 29

Smith, Jaclyn, 275
Smith, Jean Kennedy, 193, 289, 326
Smith, Stephen, 136, 139, 141, 289, 326
Smith, William Kennedy, xv
Somborn, Herbert, 50
Something's Got to Give, 204–5, 210, 215
Sommer, Josef, 275
Song of Bernadette, The, 179
Spada, James, 318–19
Spalding, Betty, 312
Spaulding, Chuck, 318–19
Special Olympics, 321, 328
Speck, Gregory, 221–22, 349
Splendor in the Grass, 271
Squaw Man, The, 305
St. Johns, Adela Rogers: on Byron, Walter, 300; on Davies, Marion, 122; and Dietrich, Marlene, 131; on Kennedy and Dietrich, 124; on Kennedy, Joe, 38; at *Photoplay*, 24, 306; Quirk-Allison courtship, helping, 26; on Swanson-Kennedy affair, 52
St. Johns, Ike, 26
Stack, Robert: career of, 145–46; and Kennedy, Jack, 132, 146–48; in *Laura*, 148–49; marriage of, 306; on Monroe, Marilyn, 221–22
Starr, Darren, 281
Sternberg, Josef Von, 122–23, 126, 128–29
Stevens, Connie, 279
Stevens, George, 110, 113
Stewart, Jimmy, 129, 130
stock market crash, 43
Stone, Galen, 19, 20, 21
Stone, Oliver, 277–78
Story of the Films, The, 35
Straight Shooting, 146
Strait, Raymond, 262, 263, 264, 266, 309–10
Strangers on a Train, 180
Strauss, Peter, 274
Strickling, Howard, 72, 131
Stroheim, Erich Von. *See* Von Stroheim, Erich
Strong, Arnold. *See* Schwarzenegger, Arnold
Suffolk University, xi, 5